"It's Our World Too"

"It's Our World Too"

Socially Responsive Learners in Middle School Language Arts

Beverly Busching
University of South Carolina

Betty Ann Slesinger
Lady's Island Middle School
Beaufort, South Carolina

National Council of Teachers of English
1111 W. Kenyon Road, Urbana, Illinois 61801-1096

Staff Editor: Bonny Graham

Interior Design: Doug Burnett

Cover Design: Jenny Jensen Greenleaf

NCTE Stock Number: 38330-3050

Library of Congress Cataloging-in-Publication Data

Busching, Beverly A., 1937–
    "It's our world too" : socially responsive learners in middle school language arts / Beverly Busching, Betty Ann Slesinger.
        p. cm.
Includes bibliographical references (p.   ).
    ISBN 0-8141-3833-0 (pbk.)
    1. Language arts (Middle school)—United States—Curricula. 2. Citizenship—Study and teaching (Middle school)—United States. 3. Active learning—United States. I. Slesinger, Betty Ann. II. Title.
    LB1631 .B794 2002
    428' .0071'2—dc21

                                                              2002005821

For Dixie Goswami
who started everything

and

the students
who helped us see it

Into the Darkness

You can douse the fire, Yet the flames still burn.
Blow the candle, Yet the light still shines.

Surrender to the music, Yet the melody lingers.
Lock the memory, Still it roams free.

Extinguish the passion, Yet it remains eternal.
Squelch the anger, But the pain dominates all.

Close your eyes, And the world still turns.
You can hide in the dark, But the shot can still be heard.

The blood can still be smelled, The fire can still be smelled.
The fire can still be seen, The emotion can still be felt.

Within the darkness, Where reality rushes,
Violent pangs of remorse. Search the solitude of the night

Into the depth of the dark,
Into the darkness.

Rina

Contents

Introduction

This book grew out of a sense of unease. The two of us, a middle school teacher and a language arts professor, have worked together for many years to bring active learning into our classrooms. We worked to bring a stronger sense of author's craft into Betty's writing program, building inquiry units around novels and text sets, and we introduced these ideas and our teacher-researcher stance into Beverly's teacher education classes. Yet each of us carried an unspoken underlying sense of regret that we had not done more. We regretted that we had to leave an important part of ourselves behind when we taught. We opposed our country's involvement in repressive military actions and its unjust economic policies, but even the liberal, whole language middle school classroom seemed far removed from those concerns.

Betty was discouraged by cynical and irresponsible student behavior at school. She remembers confronting a boy in her class about some missing work: "You just lied to me about that," she said. "Yeah, so what?" was his response. She worried about the boy's future and the society in which his attitude is common, one in which so many youth feel alienated due to a culture that focuses on power, privilege, and material wealth.

So when we found ourselves in the National Council of Teachers of English (NCTE) Elementary Section meeting in November 1993 listening to Carole Edelsky's rousing speech about critical literacy and the needs of our democracy, we were primed to hear her message. She challenged us to reexamine and restructure our language arts curriculum. The activities and classroom experiences described in this book constitute our response to that challenge.

Yevgeny Yevtushenko's searing indictment in the poem "Lies" of silent adults who do not share their knowledge about injustice with the younger generation seems to be spoken directly to us: "Telling lies to the young is wrong" (p. 3). The young already sense much of what is wrong with the world, and adults need to openly discuss these wrongs with them. Many of us today believe that promoting this kind of openness is the right thing to do, but much work has to be done before it will be clear *how* to do it. We need the kind of vision that Maxine Greene (1995) calls social imagination: "looking beyond the boundary where the backyard ends or the road narrows . . . [to] where we might reach if we tried" (p. 26).

Our collaborative teacher inquiry keeps pulling us forward and helping us through the days when we are tired and overwhelmed. Betty remembers one such time:

It was summer and I had several hours on a Sunday afternoon to spread out the stacks of student papers I had collected over the World War II project a few months before. As I began rereading, the voices of the students touched me. So many students had left a personal statement; so many had articulated universal needs and values. I had already read all of these papers to grade them, but not with the same deliberation I gave them that afternoon. Why, I wondered, hadn't I valued the kids and their work as I did that afternoon?

We like the interaction of—and sometimes conflict in—our differing roles. Betty, the insider, has the emic perspective (Cochran-Smith & Lytle, 1993) on the meanings being constructed in the daily life of the classroom. She makes most of the discoveries of our partnership as she tests ideas through her holistic experience of teaching and learning. As the outsider, Beverly brings a broader view of what's going on and can sometimes see through the distracting details of the everyday. Together we watch our theories at work in the real context of Betty's school.

A problem for the teacher-insider is the constant flood of new experiences that erase the "aha's" of yesterday. Too much has happened since then. The outsider performs the important role of holding the critical moments in mind while the insider is moving into new experiences. Emotional support is also important. Betty is often overwhelmed with classroom negatives, and Beverly helps her see the value in what *was* accomplished.

How to Read This Book

We have planned this book to be as useful as possible to teachers as they build their own critical literacy programs. It is not a book of alternative activities, although activities are described. Instead, it provides a picture of how students can be engaged in social justice issues and the competencies of democratic citizenship *throughout an entire year.* We have come to believe that no one activity, or even a single unit, can be effective in and of itself. Democratic values can be influential only when they are embedded in many different texts, activities, and critical perspectives throughout the year.

Readers may want first to turn to Chapters 2 and 5, which tell the story of how student inquiry unfolded in two extended historical units. In these chapters, readers can gain a sense of how literature, research, discussion, interviews, writing, reflection, and presentations work together in a dynamic sequence of activities to engage students in issues of social importance.

Another way to enter into this book is to start with Chapter 1, which presents the model that helped us implement a curriculum for democratic citizenship in the middle school, a model that we call "immersion in cycles of social inquiry." Also presented in the first chapter is the conceptual framework for the critical literacy program described in the remaining chapters.

The other chapters look more closely at each important dimension of this socially conscious inquiry. Chapter 3 examines classroom life as classroom power shifts toward a more democratic model: relationships, collaborative stance, and shared assessment. Chapter 4 focuses on the processes of inquiry—journals, literature logs, interviews, expert studies, and the like—and ways to strengthen students' capacities as questioners and investigators.

Chapter 6 looks more closely at the texts and how integration of fiction and nonfiction supports student learning about social issues. Speaking out is the focus of Chapter 7. The writing curriculum is reexamined through the lens of democratic citizenship, revealing new perspectives on authentic communication. Chapter 8 focuses on taking learning and concerns beyond the classroom and out into the school as a whole and into the community.

Acknowledgments

Each year we have found more and more colleagues who are eager to explore ways to make the language arts curriculum responsive to the needs of democratic citizenship. Our long-term South Carolina colleagues Heidi Mills, Phyllis Whitin, and Katie Wood Ray have made an enormous difference in our work. We are privileged to work with so many committed teachers and writers who have pushed our work forward.

We especially value the inspiration of Dixie Goswami, who made us care about activating silenced voices. Many years ago her message about the importance of teacher research started us on our enduring research partnership, and she has been a constant presence stimulating us to search for new ideas. Dixie showed us how students can write for authentic purposes in the community, and she generously included us in many grant-funded meetings, bringing us together with like-minded teachers, historians, researchers, artists, and technology buffs. Her enthusiasm and belief in us have been immeasurably important.

Many grants have supported our work through the years: Rockefeller Foundation REACH grants, Dewitt-Wallace Breadloaf Rural Teacher grants,

National Endowment for the Arts TEACH seminars, the National Writing Project and our local Midlands Writing Project, and the University of South Carolina. None of the work Betty has done would have been possible without the openness, latitude, and trust that her administrators afforded experienced teachers at her school. Her seventh-grade team members were tolerant of the noisy confusion in their area and joined in several projects in important ways.

Our greatest appreciation, of course, is for the students and their amazing outpouring of caring, questioning, and protesting. Everyone whose work is included here generously gave permission, but names have been changed to protect their privacy. They, however, will be able to find themselves.

Teaching issues of society and citizenship is for us a small protest against what we find offensive and unfair in our culture. We hope for the day when schools will find ways to break the conspiracy of silence and create schools that reconnect students with the large, troubling, and interesting world we live in.

1 The Curricular Stance: Active Learning into Active Citizenship

Teaching for social justice is teaching for the sake of arousing the kinds of vivid, reflective, experiential responses that might move students to come together in serious efforts to understand what social justice actually means and what it might demand.

> Maxine Greene, *Teaching for Social Justice* (Ayers, Hunt, & Quinn)

CHAPTER OVERVIEW

In this chapter, we share our explorations of a curriculum for democratic citizenship, what we have come to call a "socially conscious language arts curriculum." We explain how we restructured an active reading and writing classroom in order to use active literacy to address the complex issues of a democratic society. Betty wanted her seventh-grade students to see the actions of citizens as they supported democracy's strengths or caused democracy to disintegrate. She wanted them to investigate how the forces of society create justice and injustice. The curriculum-planning model that helped Betty organize activities for socially conscious student inquiry is presented, with descriptions of the predictable phases that occurred during extended units of work. We give an overview of the major units of study during one year. (Readers can see this curriculum framework in action in the stories of two different historical units in Chapters 2 and 5.) This chapter also provides an introduction to the more detailed examinations of inquiry, classroom atmosphere, literacy instruction, literature choices, and student activism that are provided in later chapters.

A Story of Student and Teacher Discoveries

The fifth-period literature class was reading and discussing a *Read* magazine docudrama that featured a family of immigrants on the ocean liner

Titanic. In the middle of the dramatic action, when the third-class passengers realize that no lifeboats have been reserved for them, Carrie suddenly burst out: "Mrs. Slesinger, what I want to know is, would we have been third class?"

A moment of quiet surprise followed Carrie's penetrating question. Betty was as startled as the students were, and as they turned to her, she stammered, "I'm not sure, but . . . but we certainly wouldn't have been first class, would we?"

Now the literature discussion turned personal and passionate. The possibility that they might have been caught on the sinking ship without a lifeboat brought a flurry of noisy protests. "No way! Hey, they can't do that!" Some students were horrified that the steerage passengers were kept below until it was too late, but others defended the impulse to survive that drove the first-class passengers to exercise the privilege of economic power. "Who's to say who should go first? I would've got my family in a boat!"

Carrie's question had hit a nerve. The kids realized it and Betty realized it. They weren't sure how to talk about it or what to do with the issue, and neither was she. They wanted to pin the blame for the disaster on some one person—the captain, the company, or the builder of the great ship. The exchange was a burst of strong but naive concern, and Betty's reactions were tentative at best. But it was a critical point in the intellectual life of the class that year.

Compassionate concern about others' welfare had been aroused, but what was the next step? Certainly the students' responses were "vivid" and "experiential," as Maxine Greene calls for, but could they become more reflective? How could they go beyond spontaneous outrage to a more informed understanding of the social forces that created injustice on the *Titanic?* Could their aroused interest become a serious effort "to understand what social justice actually means"?

Betty knew she needed to extend the students' engagement with this issue, so she planned a "public hearing" on the topic of "Who was to blame for this accident?" Staging such a hearing could validate the students' passion yet expose them to multiple viewpoints that might reveal the complexities of the situation. Speakers would have to present evidence for their opinions, reinforcing the idea that in a democracy opinion depends on information as well as compassion.

The hearing was a lively exchange that exposed everyone to the points of view of the responsible parties. Betty was fortunate to have copies of a firsthand account by the captain of the rescue ship *Carpathian* and of other factual analyses. Students did their own research out of class.

Here is a persuasive, surprisingly well-researched statement written by Allen in "officialese" in preparation for his oral presentation:

> The Colonial After-Life insurance inspector hereby fines the engineers of the ocean liner the Titanic for a flaw that cost the lives of over 1500 innocent people. We blame the accused with the suffering of the survivors and ask for damages to the families of victims of the disaster. This blame was approved by the Colonial After-Life insurance company.
>
> The metal used in the hull of the Titanic was not as pressure-resistant as possible because it had nothing to keep it from shattering and eventually sinking. If the engineer had used a sulfur/steel alloy in the hull's watertight compartments the Titanic's hull-compartments would have bent and stretched under water pressure, but it wouldn't shatter. Therefore, theoretically, the ship would have been more unsinkable.

As the students listened to statements about the responsibilities of the manufacturers, the inspectors, the captain, the ship owner, the radio operator (who was asleep), and the captain of the *Carpathian,* many of them moved beyond their initial focus on blaming a single person who had done wrong. Their final discussion was more than just a passionate outburst. When Al complained, "I still think that the captain was to blame because he was in charge," other students were quick to mention the captain's lack of crucial data about the ship and other contributing factors. As they talked, students were weighing the different kinds of responsibilities involved in the accident and making connections between individual acts and the surrounding circumstances. Their opinions, brought into a public arena, were challenged or supported and thus refined, a small moment of the kind of informed dialogue that we value for a democratic society. And Betty, as a teacher who has to meet external requirements, was relieved that this foray into social justice issues fulfilled the grade-level objectives in the area of public speaking.

A Way to Talk about Social Class

Carrie's penetrating question about social class had further consequences for the curriculum that year—it provided the students with a metaphor that allowed them to begin to address the confusing and complex issues of economic privilege. Later in the year, when they sensed a social inequity more complex than their ability to verbalize it (for example, in Dickens's *A Christmas Carol*), a student might say, "Hey, this sounds like Third Class to me!" and other students would know what he meant.

Yes, it was a shortcut, and yes, it did simplify the complexities that create inequity, but young students need some way to begin to verbalize

their unfocused feelings about their society. We came to see these generalized statements as a place to start. Students need ways to enter into the
complex issues of social justice. The connections between unjust acts and
the unspoken issues of social class and economics are difficult even for
adults to understand. Although children absorb some of the principles of
our democracy in their daily experiences, classroom inquiry into these
complex forces can be overwhelming. Even though they readily recognize
individual instances of injustice in their reading, the problem of how to
initiate inquiry into the social forces behind these instances is not easy to
solve.

The Challenges of Welcoming Democracy into a Middle School

Isolation. Schools have done very little to help students use their energy
to address the problems or the possibilities that exist in society. At the same
time that we complain about the idleness and lack of responsibility of our
youth, we operate school environments that prevent them from developing habits of concern and social responsibility. Shut in behind school walls,
students have little exposure to what goes on outside and little opportunity to participate in the collaborative social action that sustains a democracy. Cumbersome procedures and extra costs virtually prevent teachers
from taking students out of the school. And the curriculum itself gives students little exposure to the current issues in society and rarely acknowl-
edges the unjust forces that buffet the lives of many citizens, including those
of many students. For some students, an unsettling dichotomy grows between what the school says life is and what they see happening around
them and to them. This pretense may be a contributing factor to the negative behaviors adults observe, the alienation and withdrawal and the dis-
tractive social whirlwind of adolescence.

If an issue or activity hints of controversy, schools shy away. The
dilemma of schools is much like the world's governments. They profess
more idealism than actually exists in the policies that direct the operation
of their systems. Those few teachers who may be interested in social education find little support or training. Faced with unspoken pressures and
even overt directives from administrators, teachers feel constrained to stay
with noncontroversial subjects. In the tense and authoritarian atmosphere
created by bureaucratic priorities and test results, schools turn their backs
on social issues.

It is an unusual school in the United States today that addresses problems of economics and class, or the more difficult problems of race, economics, and class. Despite conflict resolution and peacemaking programs,

rarely are the very real social problems within schools named and discussed in classrooms. As teachers we are concerned when prejudice breaks out in ugly conflicts at school, but we shrink from letting students research the contexts that support this prejudice. We are left to deal again and again with the fallout of conflict—the fights, the vandalism, and the vicious gossip. We try to find ways to stop the fighting and we punish students, but we do not help students understand how intolerance emerges in the social relationships of the school, or how economic and social systems nurture intolerance in our larger society.

Restructuring a Language Arts Curriculum

Inspired by the growing national conversation about democratic values, the two of us, a seventh-grade language arts teacher and a college language arts professor, decided to confront a daunting question: If a democracy needs committed and informed citizens, shouldn't our classrooms be preparing students for these active roles? And if so, what would this classroom look like?

Rethinking Our Beliefs

Confronting these questions led us to challenge Betty's constructivist and humanities-based curriculum—a curriculum we valued and had worked together to create. Her focus on lifelong habits of literacy brought a valuable depth and authenticity to the language arts curriculum. We had been pleased to watch the students actively engaged in drafting, conferring, and publishing their writing, and we had begun making steps toward restructuring the literature program into topics rather than genres.

But now we wanted to ask harder questions. Could we call this active engagement with literacy authentic when it rarely touched the world outside the school? How valuable was inquiry that ignored the realities students lived in? What were we doing to help students be critical thinkers about their society? Were students actually collaborators in decisions that affected their lives in school? Betty recalls:

> Like most teachers, I believed that I was already running a democratic classroom. I was overt in my acceptance and praise of diverse cultures. The mantra of justice is engrained in teachers like me. I used multicultural texts. At every turn I tried to model fairness and kindness to each child and hoped for it back. I tried to provide attention and opportunities equally for all. I aimed for objectivity when I mediated altercations. But when I began to think about what a democracy means, especially what it means when each person has a say in decisions affecting their lives, I saw many more possibilities.

When her students seemed to focus only on the surface activities of their lives in their "authentic authorship," Betty realized how dissatisfied she was. Yes, they wrote for real audiences, but usually only for their peers. Yes, they made choices about topics, as authors in the real world do, but how superficial and limited these topics were. She wanted to expand their inquiry to the wider world and have writing and discussion emerge from that inquiry. "I wanted my students to find their own opportunities to question, investigate, learn, and connect," she remembers. "I wanted their work to be generative, each part taking them deeper into their inquiry."

The NCTE Committee on Teaching about Genocide and Intolerance was helpful in expanding our view of the possibilities of engagement with social issues. The committee (Robertson, 1999, p.13) offers this challenge:

> The aim of the English studies/language arts classroom is to invite informed dialogue and reflection on language and literature so that students and teachers examine the ways persons and groups build respect for differences or contribute to the forces of hate.

> [T]eaching about acceptance and value for others sensitizes students to events of intolerance and genocide. Reading, discussing, and writing about texts that deal with intolerance and genocide help students learn about human deeds of violence throughout history, and illumine parallels existing in human behaviors that make hatred and suffering possible today.

From Habits of Literacy to Habits of Literate Citizenship

We needed to find a perspective on democracy and its values that would help us guide our work. Although we agreed with Carole Edelsky (1994) that we would have to "re-theorize language education" (p. 254), our direction was still uncertain. We were not proposing a study of the governance system of democracy; we wanted to create a socially conscious English language arts program, not a civics program. Betty would approach these issues through the literature, the writing, and the speaking and listening that were her responsibility to teach. We looked for a way to think about democracy as it exists in the lives of people and their stories.

We found that we had to look at the way people lived together to find a guiding definition of democracy. Democracy can be viewed as a social system in which all participants can—have the opportunity to—influence the decisions that affect their lives. Greene elaborates:

> Justice . . . is incarnated in human action in spaces where people live together. Most of us would agree that there should be an equitable, a fair distribution of goods and services . . . , and, surely, people

> ought not to be used for others' benefit, certainly not without being consulted. Indeed, one of the requirements in a just society ought to be that everyone affected by a decision ought to have a part in making the decision. (Ayers, Hunt, & Quinn, 1998, pp. xxviii–xxix)

At the core of a vision of democracy are the values of justice, equity, and citizen responsibility. In a true democracy, the core values of justice and equity are embodied in daily life. "Who gets what" would be determined through a political process involving participation among equals (Ayers, Hunt, & Quinn, 1998) rather than by a system such as we have now in which all might *be able to participate,* but a few benefit from privileges that are denied to others.

Edelsky (1999) makes it clear that in order for students to envision these core values of democracy they must give attention to those forces that threaten democracy and "undermine the nature of the existing political system in the United States" (p. 9). The systems of domination that create the unequal social conditions we have now can be invisible if not consciously examined. Edelsky (1996) highlights Ira Shor's important insight: "If we do not teach in opposition to the existing inequality of races, classes, and sexes, then we are teaching to support it. If we don't teach critically against domination in society, then we allow dominant forces a free hand in school and out" (p. 3). As we began to think about the task of addressing issues with students, Edelsky's (1994) three dimensions of engagement defined some of the kinds of activities that would be important:

1. Critique: a critical discussion of taken-for-granted issues and institutionalized decisions
2. Hope: learning from others who have successfully challenged undemocratic and unjust systems
3. Action: doing something to further a just society

The core value of citizen responsibility had significant implications for the content of the curriculum but even more implications for how the classroom would be run. We had a strong sense that democracy is built and maintained by its local citizens, so we wanted the students to have more opportunities to work together to make decisions in their own classroom. We began to see how the two faces of democratic education—"studying democracy" and "doing democracy"—would influence and strengthen each other. We also wanted students to know adults who question, who work to benefit others, and who strengthen democratic values. We would need to highlight these people in literature, in the news, and as citizens in the local community.

The Citizenship Potential of Twelve-Year-Olds

One might suppose that middle schoolers would prove poor subjects for engagement in selfless social concerns. Seventh graders tend to be at the same time obsessed with themselves and uneasy with themselves. They are often erratic and emotionally volatile in their changing social relationships. They are prone to hiding their own individuality from their peers, and they can be quick to ridicule others. Their developmental insecurities can sometimes intensify an intolerant stance toward people that they have absorbed uncritically from the culture around them. Our students were all of these things, yet, given the chance, they proved to be interested in the study of issues and values of a democratic society. They liked that it was "real," they told us.

Our students were suburban, and few of them had experienced the massive frustrations and crises common to inner-city families. Their economic backgrounds ranged from working class to professional, for the most part, though many families had lived through tragedies and disruptions (and these touching stories entered Betty's classroom through family inquiry projects). Our student population engaged with the realities of injustice primarily through life stories of others. These stories created in students empathy for other people and also allowed them to reflect on their own experiences of hurt, ranging from social isolation to child abuse. In other communities, where families live injustice daily, the students' own lives would be a more central focus of their work (see Bernabei, 1996; Bigelow, Christensen, Karp, Miner, & Peterson, 1994; Edelsky, 1999). All groups of students have to shape their own particular journeys of inquiry through their own questions and concerns. There is no scope and sequence chart for this work.

Looking out at the world, the students tended to seesaw between knowing the score and believing in rosy stereotypes. They recognized some of the unfairness that exists "out there," but the glittering world of television had made its impression on their life views. Poised at a time of growing awareness yet without having taken on responsibilities in society, they clung to the security of believing that opportunities exist for anyone. They expressed deeply empathetic feelings about individual life tragedies, but they wanted to think that everyone has a chance to succeed. Positive energy is one of middle schoolers' pleasurable traits, but when a positive outlook on life is carried uncritically into adulthood, it produces citizens who, for instance, view homeless people as nuisances and who are heedless of the ways in which their own material benefits may have negative consequences for others. We aimed for a more critical and informed energy.

Taking a Proactive Stance

As teachers we do not have to accept passively whatever mix of apprecia-tion or intolerance students bring to our classrooms. Although it is not easy, the daily routines of instruction and the content of the curriculum can be restructured to move students toward greater understanding and empa-thy for others. Maxine Greene (1995) states this vision of ethical growth as a kind of critical social imagination:

> I am reaching toward an idea of imagination that brings an ethical concern to the fore, a concern that . . . has to do with the commu-nity that ought to be in the making, . . . visions of what should be and what might be in our deficient society, on the streets where we live, in our schools. (p. 5)

The students were far from realizing such a far-reaching vision, but we could see that certain texts caught their imagination through the high drama of real life struggles, and some students did reach toward a vision of a different life. Betty shared her own compassion for others and worked to make the classroom a safe place for explorations of social difference and conflict (Meier, 1995). She encouraged students to speak up from and for their emerging convictions and made some progress (though not as much as she would have liked) to break through the school walls to the community outside.

Rethinking Reader Response and Literature Choices

Literature was the starting place for student exploration of society. A broad definition of the term "literature" (and in fact "texts" may be a better term) includes not only high-quality fiction, poetry, drama, and nonfiction, but also magazines, newspapers, speeches, documents, interviews, and other texts that bring to students the lives of other people and the conditions that affect these lives.

We knew that the current level of exposure of students to social is-sues in our school was not enough. Betty overheard students reacting to current and historical events with trite sound bites, applying sitcom views of life to the struggles of citizens. Published research on social studies in-struction confirmed Betty's experience. Studies find that students tend to make limited representations and broad, vague inferences as they attempt to make sense of history. Supplying improved texts or providing back-ground information before reading standard texts is not sufficient to make history come alive for students. After reviewing this research, McKeown and Beck (1994) call for "more powerful enhancements of learning" (pp. 20–24) that provide compelling narratives of history and extended oppor-tunities to inquire, reflect, and construct understandings.

It was not our intent to "teach" democratic values through teacher presentations. Our intention was—and has continued to be—to expose students to as fine an array of diverse, authentic, and humane voices as we could find and to support student responses to those voices. Betty's role was to collect more socially conscious literature and to push the students to probe more deeply into an issue, not to teach them the ideas we were committed to. We believed we could depend on the texts and the voices of our democracy to do that job.

Laura Apol (1998, p.33) provides insight about our profession's over-emphasis on the processes of literature response, noting that we have been so intent on creating meaningful connections between students' lives and the literature they read that we have unwittingly fallen into the trap of thinking that the reader's response is the *end* of the reading process rather than the *means* to cultural understandings. Too much attention has been paid to how readers act on texts to the exclusion of how texts act on readers.

Applebee (1993) similarly cautions against too much emphasis on the students' response but points out that the response can be a starting point for cultural conversations. Students can then examine the social contexts of the texts and how the author is socially situated. Readers can look *at* the text and also *beyond* the text, constructing interpretations as a means of entering into larger cultural conversations. Conversations about the cultural implications of students' reading can create a place for their emerging thoughts, a place safe from teacher correction and peer criticism.

Betty's greatest asset was the wealth of new young adult literature that brings to the classroom a richness of voices not previously available to students. Voices of the disenfranchised—from the fields, the ghettos, and the welfare hotels—spoke to the students through firsthand accounts and well-structured fiction.

The Competencies of Democratic Citizenship

What are the competencies that enable citizens to work together, to protest wrongs, to rethink and rebuild their democracy when needed? As Maxine Greene points out, "More is required than indignant or empathetic responses to what may be discovered in the world around, once people's eyes are opened." (p. xxx). We were pleased to discover that many of the competencies laid out in our new state language arts standards were also competencies of citizenship—investigation, critical judgment, collaboration and negotiation, and a public voice. Our new, socially conscious curriculum could be built on the core seventh-grade requirements. It could make use of, but extend beyond, the standard literature anthology and personal writing topics into texts and topics that were more issues oriented.

David Bloome (1993) agrees that there is a close connection between democracy and literacy. But teaching students how to read and write does not necessarily help them learn how to use reading and writing for democracy. Bloome asks teachers to consider the question, "What are the genres of writing needed for participation in a democracy?" Given this consideration, nonfiction and persuasive genres would be more prominent, and the oral communication of investigation, negotiation, and persuasion would not only be more prominent but also more authentically linked to social purposes. As we continued to think about this issue, we added to our vision other essentials of democratic citizenship such as respect for diverse points of view, initiative, experience with a democratic environment, and the confidence to put into practice new ideas.

Classroom Life

William Ayers helped us look carefully at the life of the classroom. Studying democracy, he believes, inevitably integrates itself with doing democracy. He points out that to learn about social justice, students must live in an environment that is abundant with opportunities to practice social justice (Ayers, Hunt, & Quinn, 1998, p. xxv). Although students in Betty's classroom often had choices in writing topics, choices in personal literature responses, and choices about whether to work by themselves or in a group, we knew that their classroom life was far from embodying responsible citizenship and shared decision making. And certainly it was very far from the vision of a just society in which those affected by a decision have a part in making that decision. Schools are quite unjust societies when viewed through such a lens, but established conventions cannot be changed overnight. The slow steps Betty took toward changing the classroom into a more democratic community are described in Chapter 3.

Researching the Emerging Curriculum

We knew it was important to study what happened as Betty opened up the curriculum for students' questions about society, and we knew we would have to find ways to fit the research into our already full schedules. Neither of us had released time to do research. Beverly came to visit Betty's classes from time to time, and we talked through curriculum plans and student work on a regular basis, usually each week. Sometimes during the several years of this work, we systematically examined classroom data, and at other times Betty saved evidence of student inquiry for later review— photocopies of journal entries and other written work, audiotapes of discussions, notes on interviews. We kept our separate journals. Periodically, we went through these data to see what we thought was happening. One year we tracked how student questions changed during a unit of study and how they led to new learning or projects (Busching & Slesinger, 1995).

We formulated questions to guide our study. At the beginning, these were our questions:

> How would the integration of factual and fictional texts change how the students read literature?
>
> What questions would they raise, and in what contexts?
>
> Would the curriculum activate biased attitudes, or would students move to a larger human sense of the world? (We especially worried that the World War II unit would create prejudice toward Germans.)
>
> How would parents react to their children discussing controversial issues in the classroom?

When Betty began making changes in the curriculum, she was still teaching five classes of either reading or language arts each day. Some, but not all, of the students were in both reading and language arts. She was able to accomplish more, especially to expand student decision making, when she taught fewer students in a block schedule the next year. Student work from several different years is included in this book.

As we reflected on the students' work during the first year, we made many of the major discoveries that still guide our work. Perhaps the most important discovery was that students need opportunities to return again and again to a topic in order to go beyond their initial, generalized emotional reactions to a level of (somewhat) informed analysis. Integrating factual texts with fiction is a powerful stimulus for the kind of active inquiry that leads students to rethink a topic more analytically. The curriculum model used in planning experiences to encourage students to engage with and rethink social issues is described in the following section.

Units of Study: A Model of Immersion in Socially Conscious Inquiry

Our approach to planning a unit for student engagement with social issues was not to create a predetermined sequence of teacher-created thinking activities. Rather than stimulating students' thinking, this teacher package approach too often interferes with students' ability to think for themselves. Nevertheless, some kind of planned curriculum structure is necessary in order to manage a middle school program that integrates language arts objectives with student initiative in a full day of classes.

Instead, we used a model of topic immersion through inquiry—a plan for sustained student engagement in a variety of reading, writing, listening, viewing, and talking activities that immersed them in the topic from a variety of perspectives over a long stretch of time (Short & Burke, 1991). We started with broad topics rather than teacher-created themes. A topic such as World War II offers multiple themes that raise questions about individual courage, despair, and suffering, and about patriotism, social control, and international relations. In this model, a *topic* is not a *theme*. When compelling literature is forced into theme units, the predetermined theme may close off the potential wealth of diverse connections as students engage their life experiences and beliefs with the text. Thus, the value of literature may be diminished when a theme is predetermined (Christenbury, 1994).

The two extended units of inquiry described in detail in Chapters 2 and 5 were both organized around topics from historical periods of social upheaval. These long units (and others during the year), along with many opportunities to return again and again to important issues, provided opportunities for the slow accumulation of awareness and understanding during the entire year. We have come to believe that unless we provide students with repeated opportunities to dig at complex issues, we will not discover students' potential to understand how society works. No one lesson, or even one unit, is sufficient.

Betty worked hard to prepare each unit but did not create a day-by-day plan. Using a rich collection of texts, other resources, and activities allowed for teacher flexibility as the unit unfolded. Betty could respond to student needs as they appeared. The grade-level language arts objectives were reviewed for appropriate tie-ins. The "launch," the initial activity, was carefully planned in advance to capture students' imagination. Although the unit was ongoing, Betty's daily and weekly planning became an interplay between prepared ideas and fluid responses to emerging student needs, interests, and suggestions. Betty built on her understanding of where students were, thinking through what the next step should be. In this way, a unit was neither preplanned nor unplanned.

Phases of Learning in a Unit of Socially Conscious Inquiry

The unit model offered in Figure 1.1 is based on multiple opportunities for the development of student understanding as students cycle back into a topic again and again through different perspectives, different materials, and different sign systems. We have been strongly influenced by the work of Short, Harste, and Burke (1996). Students benefit from certain types

Figure 1.1. A model of immersion in social issues through inquiry in units of study. Adapted from the inquiry model in Short, Harste, and Burke (1996).

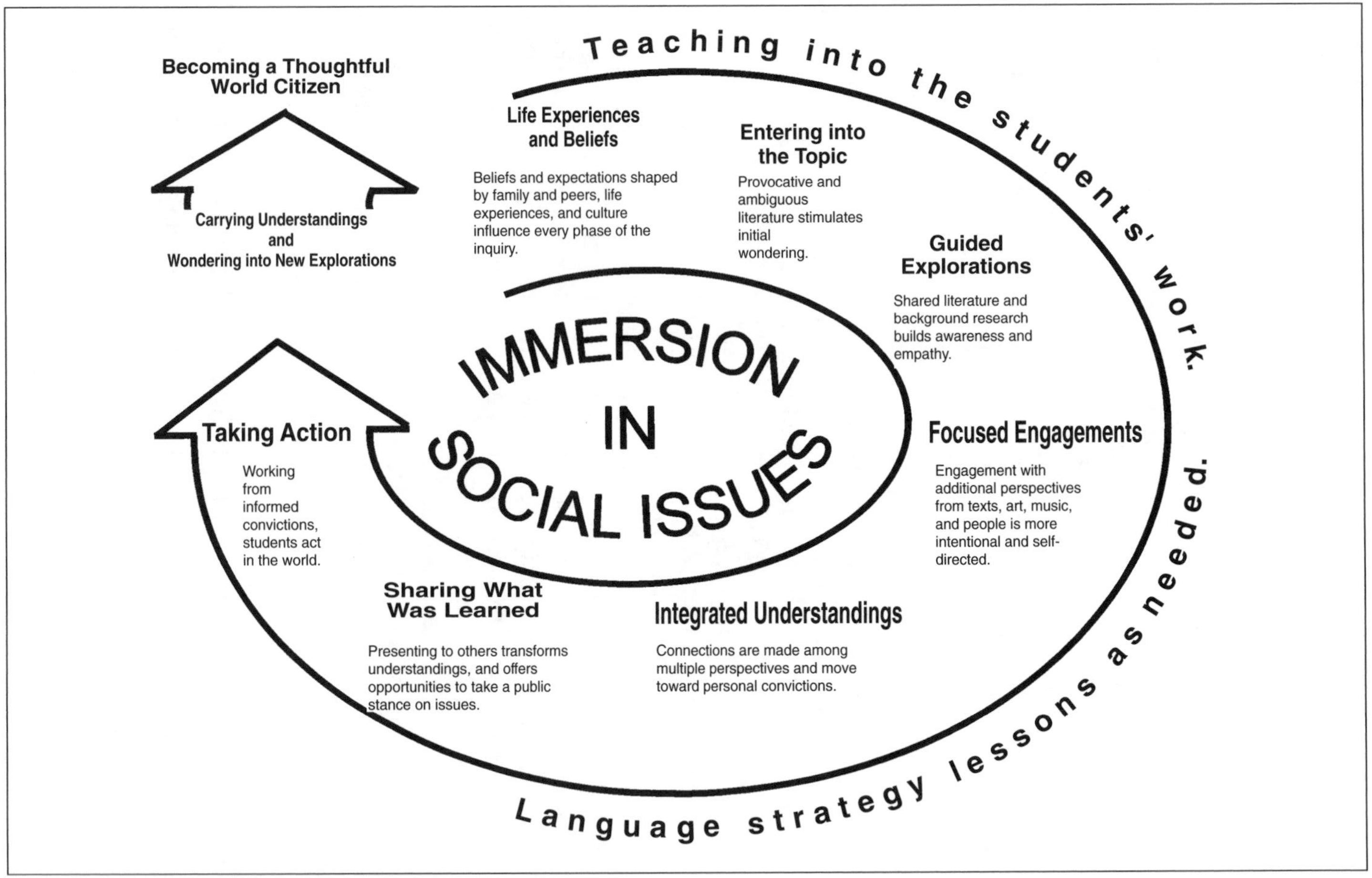

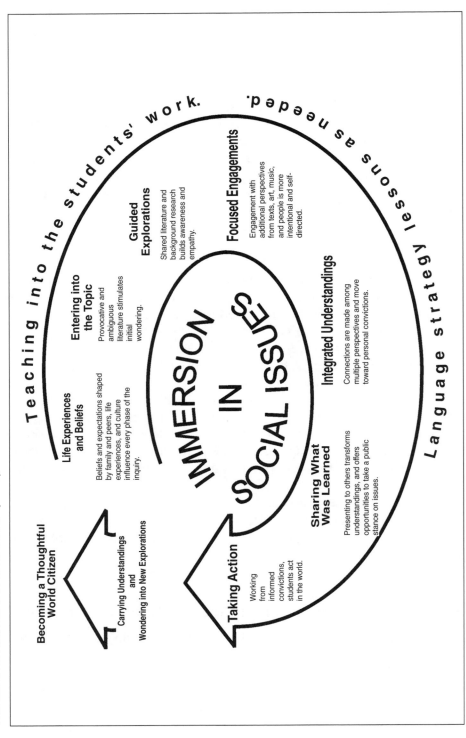

of activities as they enter into a topic and from other kinds of assignments and activities as they stay with the topic over a long stretch of time. To some extent, this is a sequential model of teacher planning, as it reflects predictable patterns of learning, but it is also recursive in that students cycle back to earlier modes of thinking as they move forward toward deeper understandings. The dimensions of the model are described in the following list.

> *Life experiences and beliefs.* All phases of the students' inquiry are shaped by their individual perspectives. They enter the inquiry with certain beliefs, expectations, and attitudes that have been shaped by their life experiences, by their family and peer interactions, and certainly by their experiences as a member of a culture. But this inquiry is not just a matter of prior knowledge; it is a matter of interaction between the texts and the background brought to it. Not only do students' experiences with people influence their interpretations of characters in literature, but also their encounters with characters in literature influence their interpretations of real people and how any encounter with people is played out (Apol, 1998). At each phase of inquiry, there is the potential for reinforcement of these beliefs and also potential for change, renegotiation, and transformation.

> *Entering the topic and guided explorations.* Curiosity is aroused by new experiences that challenge or stretch current views of the world. A compelling but puzzling short text or video raises questions and pulls students into the study of the topic, which is usually a historical era or contemporary issue. Once students care about the lives of the people involved and raise their own questions, they are launched into exploring the topic. The students' questions lead to a teacher-guided informational search. The enthusiasm and curiosity of the most assertive students feed the less involved as students begin to gather pieces of background information. Each student's small piece of research is shared with the rest of the class in an authentically purposeful manner.

> Teacher-selected whole class readings or the beginning chapters of a core novel bring more stories of the period into the classroom, as fact and fiction work together to weave an empathetic understanding of the people whose lives are part of history. In this phase, a foundation of shared experiences is laid for later, more broadly conceptual and individual thinking. Students build from the "known" in their inquiry, but now what is known is greatly expanded through student inquiry. When heartfelt questions about society are raised,

students will continue to find answers in many places. In this phase, the teacher is active in providing instruction in active reading, genre study, and inquiry processes.

Focused engagements. Now, as a community of inquirers with a shared base of understanding and literary experiences, the students expand their views of the world and perhaps venture into new cultural territories. Students begin to create their own journeys of inquiry through self-selected novels in literature study groups. Teachers plan an array of book choices, making sure that the voices of marginalized peoples are heard through firsthand accounts and interviews.

Poetry, short stories, videos, and music provide opportunities to view the topic through multiple literacies. What can be learned by looking at pictures of the bombed remains of Dresden? How does World War II look through the eyes of Picasso? How do the photographs of bombed European cities or English airfields look different after students have seen through Picasso's eyes? Students stretch their interpretations as they respond to poetry, art, and music.

Visiting experts bring different systems of knowledge and investigation, such as history, anthropology, or family counseling, to bear on the subject. Social studies classes might support the students' inquiry with lessons on geographical and historical background, current events, or civics. Literature response journals and writer's notebooks, class discussions, and quickwrites create spaces for dialogue (Jennings, O'Keefe, & Shamlin, 1999). Informal sharing introduces more perspectives into the classroom and allows students to test their assumptions and opinions in the arena of their peers. New questions arise that probe more deeply into issues. Contrasts and anomalies among the different sources of information stimulate new levels of insight.

Integrated understandings. Students make connections between the separate pieces and layers of information, images, stories, and feelings they have gathered. Creating poetry, visuals, charts, and scenarios; holding debates; prioritizing sessions; and other activities that require the integration of perspectives assist this process. Students analyze, challenge, and integrate their understandings. Many students are working from strong convictions and raise critical questions about the past and the future.

Sharing what was learned. Students have the opportunity to share their understandings and convictions with public audiences, in and out of the school. The process of creating finished reports, plays, stories, essays, bound books, and speeches adds further layers of understanding and integrated thinking. Students create strong bonds with each other as they share the results of their extensive work. Making their compassionate feelings about society public is a more emotional process than merely giving a factual report. Choices in the mode of communication give ownership and authority to the students.

Taking action in the world. Students' concern about issues may stimulate the desire to act on their concern. When students have strong convictions about injustice, opportunities to take some kind of action may prevent them from becoming cynical or apathetic. Students can write or speak to those in authority, or find ways to contribute their own efforts. With adult support, students can experience the satisfaction of making productive contributions to society. Service learning projects, student-initiated projects that arise spontaneously from their concerns, and letters to the editor are all valuable ways for students to take action. Students may interact with local adults in a variety of ways so they can better understand and appreciate how groups of citizens work together for social good.

Carrying understandings and wondering into new units of study. Each inquiry unit during the year adds its own layer of questions, concerns, and understandings and leads students into the next encounter, which they approach with more appreciative eyes. Exposure to issues surrounding the Great Depression in the United States helps students see the implications of economic deprivation in Germany before World War II. Teachers can relax when students do not "get it" when they know that the issues of justice and injustice will be revisited throughout the year.

Becoming a thoughtful world citizen. Of course, we have not had a chance to watch the students as adult citizens, but we have learned that some of them were vocal in a protest against a banned rock group in high school, and others are still engaged in social issues work. The thoughtful comments they made at the end of seventh grade about themselves and about the world they would like to see gave us hope for their future. Clay, after hearing a Holocaust survivor at the state museum, wrote, "[This] story made me realize that I don't have it hard, because a lot of problems have been coming up in our family and I felt like I had it hard." Addy wrote that it "hurts to think that there were cruel enough people to torture another human being the way that they did. Seeing that the United States didn't respond either makes me feel ashamed." Bert wrote about becoming the kind of citizen who might work to avoid devastating social crises: "We can learn from our mistakes or we can learn from history. We learned about the practice of senseless prejudice and changes that have slowly come. We learned about hard times that people pulled through. We learned from the lessons of history."

Parents and the Socially Conscious Curriculum

We were anxious about initiating a curriculum that invited students to take a critical stance toward their society given the conservative atmosphere of our southern city. Conservative opposition to concepts labeled "inquiry" and "whole language" was widespread. Conservative takeovers of school districts and a push for a phonics-based state curriculum were prominent forces at that time. School administrators warned teachers about controversial books and activities that appeared to oppose local religious values.

But the political opposition that we feared did not materialize. No parent complained about the controversial topics or critical perspectives, although some complained about the "too much work" that an inquiry curriculum requires of students. We found that some parents shared our sense of regret that public school avoids social realities, and Betty received very welcome reassurance from these parents, who thanked her for what she was doing.

Why, in the thick of conservative pressures, was this curriculum unchallenged? We can guess at several reasons. At the beginning of the year, the students explored their own family origins in an autobiographical study and wrote about the people and activities of their family at home and at church. These projects were presented in an evening celebration, and parents saw their own family values—expressed in religion, acts of courage and togetherness, humorous and happy times—being valued by the school. Betty also invited parents that she knew would have concerns to preview controversial books, and she honored their reactions by making many choices available to students. She communicated frequently through informal newsletters and was available for conferences.

Furthermore, critical perspectives entered the classroom through students' responses to literature, their research, and their interpretations of the media. Betty did not "teach" her critical stance. She emphasized to students the importance of respecting one another's beliefs and then encouraged them to share with each other freely. The more conservative students heard critical, or controversial, stances through the voices of other students rather than through the single voice of the teacher.

Competencies of citizenship, such as the responsibility to have an informed voice and to care for and collaborate with others, were valued by us and parents alike. This emphasis was another possible reason why parents tolerated this curriculum. As they saw their children growing more responsible, perhaps they overlooked aspects of the curriculum that made them uneasy.

When we started, we didn't realize that within students' families are enormous resources for strengthening democratic values. Relatives who lived through World War II, for example, had reflective thoughts about the costs of war and the damage to people of military conflict. Leah wrote about her grandmother as part of her portfolio at the end of the year: "The most important thing I think she ever said was, 'I think the government should govern not rule, that money should not be power, and that all people should have a chance.' . . . I think that should be in one of those famous quote books." So do we.

Inquiry into Issues throughout the Year

The students' cumulative exposure to social issues during successive inquiry units throughout the year gave them time to grow into the essential roles of active citizens—being able to question, assess, and critique; being able to gather knowledge competently; being able to make informed judgments; being able to speak out in a voice of commitment; being able to work for change (Busching & Slesinger, 1999). Students brought an increasingly stronger information base and a more focused sense of direction to the later units. They also, appropriately, took more and more control of their learning tasks. The major inquiry units during one year were:

> Memoir and autobiography genre study: Many Cultures, Many Voices
> (combined with Growing into Me autobiography project)
>
> Media Watch
> (combined with connections to nonprofit organizations)
>
> Novel study of *Roll of Thunder, Hear My Cry* (Taylor)
> (combined with Depression: Then and Now unit)
>
> Novel study of *When the Stars Begin to Fall* (Collier)
> (combined with environmental issues and activities)
>
> Multigenre study of World War II

Of course, inquiry into social issues was not the only focus of the curriculum. Middle school is a busy, complicated place with diverse demands and requirements. Literature offers a scope too broad to be limited to social issues units. The students also read a multitude of stories and plays, did a poetry genre study and a unit on mysteries, told scary legends and tales at Halloween, practiced for standardized tests, and worked on standard vocabulary exercises.

Betty was excited when she found students extending insights from their social inquiry to other work. One year at Christmas time, students in the advanced class reading an excerpt of Charles Dickens's *A Christmas Carol* in their literature book noticed the social context as much as the personal messages of the story. Andrew wrote in his opinion essay, "During the time of Charles Dickens people were not doing very good in terms of being wealthy and often had poor living space. It was almost like the depression time of London. Most kids were working [in] factories to get their families and themselves by." Keith came back from eighth grade one day in the spring to borrow Betty's materials on child labor for a persuasive speech he had been assigned. He still was concerned that children today were made to work against their will, and he heard from friends that Betty had "some new stuff."

Ending Thoughts

As we sat in Beverly's living room one evening thinking about this chapter, news came on the radio of a new outbreak of hostility in Israel. As we listened, Betty remembered Heather's interview of her great uncle Harold. Heather learned that the European war was in all the newspapers, on the radio, and in adult conversations when Germany was invading European countries. When Harold was in high school and the United States entered the conflict, the war came home to Americans. Frightened and confused, the boys knew they would have to face this terrible unknown. Harold and his best friend talked together privately about their fears. He remembered that his friend said, "If I go, I'll never come back." But even though students faced immediate involvement and possible death in the war, there was no discussion of it in his school. Heather closed her interview with the statement that wars are not necessary but that they will continue until we do something about it. She asked of us that we *do* talk about war in schools and that we find new ways to get along with people of other nations.

Just as the kids were changing because of their inquiry, we were changing because of our inquiry. That evening, because of Heather and the other students, we listened to the radio not just to learn about a faraway event. It seemed close to home, and we wondered how we could bring the issues into the classroom.

Students do not know the cost to their ancestors of the freedoms the students now enjoy unless we teach them. They will not care enough to preserve the rights and freedoms they have today unless they engage with the society in which they reside. Although the law says there can be no discrimination, it insidiously permeates our lives every day. Many young people naively believe these civil rights issues have been settled. As adults we do not need to perpetuate half-truths about the issues of equity in our country. Adults who don't choose to acknowledge the underlying animosity and unfairness that are part of their daily lives prevent students from developing a concerned and caring stance. The many families who are faced with personal and economic hardships might find unexpected resources by inviting their children to understand those concerns. We wish that more adults could have an experience like ours, a chance to see the worth and potential in young people. It might change their image of teens and encourage communities to offer teens significant roles in our society.

Additional Readings for Teachers

Social Issues and Education

Allen, J. (Ed.). (1999). *Class actions: Teaching for social justice in elementary and middle school.* New York: Teachers College Press.

Comber, B., & Simpson, A. (Eds.). (2001). *Negotiating critical literacies in classrooms.* Mahwah, NJ: Erlbaum.

Freire, P. (1998). *Pedagogy of freedom: Ethics, democracy, and civic courage.* Lanham, MD: Rowman & Littlefield.

Nieto, S. (1999). *The light in their eyes: Creating multicultural learning communities.* New York: Teachers College Press.

Nieto, S. (2002). *Language, culture, and teaching: Critical perspectives for a new century.* Mahwah, NJ: Erlbaum.

Noya, G. C., Geismar, K., & Nicoleau, G. (Eds.). (1995). *Shifting histories: Transforming education for social change.* Cambridge, MA: Harvard Educational Review.

Routman, R. (1996). *Literacy at the crossroads.* Portsmouth, NH: Heinemann.

Teaching Social Inquiry

Bigelow, B., Christensen, L., Karp, S., Miner, B., & Peterson, P. (Eds.). (1994). *Rethinking our classrooms: Teaching for equity and justice.* Milwaukee, WI: Rethinking Schools.

Christensen, L. (2000). *Reading, writing, and rising up: Teaching about social justice and the power of the written word.* Milwaukee, WI: Rethinking Schools.

Danks, C., & Rabinsky, L. B. (Eds.). (1999). *Teaching for a tolerant world: Grades 9–12*. National Council of Teachers of English.

Edinger, M., & Fins, S. (1998). *Far away and long ago: Young historians in the classroom*. York, ME: Stenhouse.

Gamberg, R., Kwak, W., Hutchings, M., & Altheim, J. (1988). *Learning and loving it: Theme studies in the classroom*. Portsmouth, NH: Heinemann.

Harvey, S. (1998). *Nonfiction matters: Reading, writing, and research in grades 3–8*. Portland, ME: Stenhouse.

Makler, A., & Hubbard, R. S. (Eds.). (2000). *Teaching for justice in the social studies classroom: Millions of intricate moves*. Portsmouth, NH: Heinemann.

Short, K., & Burke, C. (1991). *Creating curriculum: Teachers and students as community of learners*. Portsmouth, NH: Heinemann.

Totten, S., & Pedersen, J. (1997). *Social issues and service at the middle level*. Boston: Allyn and Bacon.

Centers and Web Sites

Center for Teaching for Social Justice
This center at the University of California, Santa Barbara School of Education is dedicated to providing resources for the teaching of social justice in K–12 educational settings.
http://www.education.ucsb.edu/socialjustice

Rethinking Schools
A cooperative of teachers dedicated to discussing issues and providing resources for equity and justice in schools. Publishes the journal *Rethinking Schools* and other useful materials.
http://www.rethinkingschools.org

Social Issues Units by Fellows of the Yale-New Haven Teachers Institute 1978–2001.
Writing from the critical perspective of constitutional rights, teachers have posted units for students on a wide variety of topics.
http://www.yale.edu/ynhti/curriculum/units/

Southern Poverty Law Center
Publishes *Teaching Tolerance,* a free magazine for teachers, and produces videos and teaching materials on historical and current incidents and issues of racial violence and hatred. The Web site is planned as an online community for resources and sharing of ideas.
http://www.teachingtolerance.org

Materials for Teachers

Checklist for Social Inquiry Unit Planning

Does your unit plan:

___ address themes and issues related to enduring human values?

___ provide a framework to meet requirements in existing, required curricula?

___ provide opportunities for students to become active learners?

___ create opportunities to work with peers and share learning?

___ promote questioning?

___ require student research and information gathering?

___ offer connections between school and life, including local issues, so that students may become active in the school and community?

___ create a rich and deep context for learning through diverse and trustworthy resources?

2 The World War II and Holocaust Inquiry Unit

I must love the questions . . . like locked rooms full of treasure.

Alice Walker, "Reassurance"
In Search of My Mother's Gardens

Why did people follow a man like Hitler?
What is it like to live in constant fear of being caught?
What if the D-Day invasion hadn't worked?
What happened to people who helped Jews?
Why do people hate?

Students in third-period literature class

CHAPTER OVERVIEW

This chapter follows students as they inquire into the World War II era. Their inquiry begins with the Entering into the Topic phase of the immersion model and continues into deeper and more connected thinking in the later phases of their immersion in the topic, finally ending with Sharing What Was Learned and Taking Action. One phase of inquiry leads into the next, as the classroom tone, inquiry processes, literature, and writing and speaking all work together in a dynamic flow of discovery and collaboration. The story of the students' explorations as presented here is taken primarily from the experiences of the students in Betty's classes the first year she let student inquiry be at the center of the curriculum, although she continued to teach this unit for several years. We wanted to recapture the processes of our early explorations, showing how the students led us to discoveries about how to support their inquiry in a busy middle school curriculum. Readers will see how Betty moved from her prepared plans in the first two phases of the unit into less charted teaching territory by watching for clues to the next teaching steps.

The students were not new inquirers. They entered this unit in the spring with considerable experience as authors, journal keepers, literature responders, discussion participants, raisers of questions, and researchers. Most students felt a certain amount of confidence in researching ideas and in finding their own perspective for a poem or an essay, and all were used to doing part of their work in collaborative groups. Some students still sat passively too much of the time and others still struggled as writers; one of the classes was a heterogeneous language arts extension class. Students had already inquired into the adversity people face in life, stretched their awareness of diversity, and analyzed the influence of the public media earlier in the year.

Entering the Topic

Betty gathered the students in close for a read-aloud. Some of them scooted their desks together, and others sat on the floor in front of her. Robert Innocenti's *Rose Blanche* is a poignant tale of a young girl whose village is invaded by German soldiers. The text tells a simple story of one child's experience, but the illustrations vividly depict the subtle details of Nazi oppression and deprivation. One day Rose sees a young schoolmate apprehended and taken away in a truck by the soldiers. Upset and curious, she follows the truck's route out of town. Farther away from home than she's ever wandered, Rose finds a starkly fenced prison camp full of thin, ragged children. Throughout the winter, she saves and steals bits of food to give to the young prisoners. During a visit on a dark and foggy day, she is caught in the midst of a sudden military skirmish. The last page shows a single rose caught on the barbed wire fence of the prison camp.

Instead of responding to the immediate outcry and the flurry of raised hands, Betty made a spontaneous decision to ask the students to write their questions in their literature response journals. As she reread the book, she gave students additional time to study the illustrations. A concentrated hush fell over the group as they listened, looked, and wrote. The resulting number of questions was large, at least thirty-three different questions in a single class period. It was evident that the students were hooked. But when we looked over the journals, Betty was disappointed in the "low level" of the questions. They were mainly basic fact-seeking questions such as "Where are the trucks going?"; "Why were the soldiers there?"; "What were the children doing inside that barbed wire fence?" Few students seemed able to interpret the text thoughtfully and inferentially. Had the students really concentrated on the story? Why weren't they able to infer "better" interpretations of the story?

How fortunate that our research project drove us to photocopy and reflect together on the entire group of questions from several classes. We soon realized that the students *had* invested themselves in the story; they simply had very little background knowledge about the period.

Students had concentrated intensely on the pictures, which they found puzzling but powerful. When we talked with the students, we saw how emotionally captivated many of them were by the power of the illustrations. Students agreed with Tom's reaction: "They [the pictures] are like watching a TV show, one that's to be continued. You are in suspense so you'll watch the next episode." Renee's comment revealed how intensely she had concentrated on interpreting changes in the illustrations: "The pictures were wonderful! I liked the way the sky always fit the story." Chantelle showed that even though she couldn't interpret the ending, as a reader she did not back away from the challenge of trying to puzzle it out: she liked the ending of Rose Blanche because "it keeps you guessing and lets your imagination run wild with all the different endings you can think of. It turns a children's book more into a book I would read."

We had assumed that the detailed illustrations would provide an informational introduction to the period, but we hadn't realized how much interpretation was needed to understand the pictures. What to adult readers was a clear and searing chronicle of invasion, betrayal, and death was to the seventh graders a confusing barrage of ominous images. Students were horrified by the obvious oppression but couldn't think coherently about it.

They needed to know the basic facts before they could interpret the context (what Nazis were, what the countries of Europe were, who the Jews were, what concentration camps were). Their "knowledge" was based primarily on movies, GI Joe play, video games, and adult talk during patriotic parades. We were pleasantly surprised to see how eager they were to get information. This was a pivotal moment in the development of our curricular vision. From this incident grew our understanding that compelling literature about culture and society offers a richer reading experience when surrounded by an informational context, and that students are eager to gather background facts once they care about a character. Fact and fiction can interact in powerful ways.

Guided Explorations

Student Questions Lead the Way

The ambiguity of *Rose Blanche* was just what we needed to launch the unit. This text offered a brief, concrete introduction to the themes that were ultimately our goal and provided a compelling shared experience that brought the class together as a learning community. It hinted at events and suggested the milieu of the Nazi era. By implying the realities of persecution and suffering rather than stating them, this book fostered many questions, and this empathetic wondering set the stage for the next phase of the unit. Now that the students cared about a character's life, they were motivated to fill in the blanks in their background understanding.

Gathering Facts: Students as Resources for Peers

Betty provided a clear structure for the students' first informational search of the unit. She created sets of three factual topics for each student to research, drawing from their *Rose Blanche* questions and from her knowledge of basic facts about World War II. To encourage even the most reluctant students, she made a large classroom research center with booklets, articles, and nonfiction books from the school and public libraries. Students used these resources, the school library, and online resources at home to research their assigned key facts and terms. A World War II fact wall, with the journalistic "Five Ws," provided an organizer for the growing display of factual information brought in by students. The students were surrounded by the factual context of their reading, such as:

> 1913—The Nazi Party is formed.
>
> 1933, January—Adolf Hitler elected chancellor of Germany.
>
> 1933, April 1—Official boycott of all Jewish shops begins.
>
> Krystalnicht—Destruction of Jewish stores, synagogues, and homes.
>
> Chancellor—The prime minister of Germany has lots of power, even more than our president.

Mitch, a committed student who loved the accuracy of factual research, volunteered to use the Timeline computer program to compile a timeline display from his classmates' information. Soon this timeline snaked around the walls and became an important class resource.

Shared Literature

Excerpts from the diary of Anne Frank were reprinted in the seventh-grade literature anthology. An assortment of articles and multiple copies of the play version of the diary were available, so a text set revolving around Anne and her family was an early focus for whole class engagements led by Betty. Anne's comparable age made her an especially empathetic heroine for middle school readers (and her use of the journal format advanced Betty's instruction in journal keeping). As they read, students made entries in their literature response journals that showed their engagement with the topic and its issues and their concern for the Frank family. Also apparent was their lack of knowledge about the stark facts of oppression inherent in the dilemmas the Jews faced. Clark wrote:

> I would have at least tried to escape. I think the Jews also should have tried to protect themselves. If I would know I was about to be sent to a death camp, I would have tried to stop the Nazis. I think the Jews were a little weak and should have stood up if they knew they were going to die anyway.

Gerrick had a general statement of caring and wonder: "To think of all the pain the Nazis inflicted on the Jews, it made you wonder how cruel people can really be and if this could ever happen to us." Many questions in their journals still focused on fact gathering, such as:

> Is Anne still alive?
>
> What was life like in the attic?
>
> Who found Anne's diary?
>
> Where were the Franks sent?
>
> What happened in the camp?

Although students were thinking about both the factual and the emotional, they were not yet integrating the two. Nevertheless, in this phase of Guided Explorations they were gathering a foundation of information that would help them come to deeper understanding later. They were making empathetic ties and taking in impressions and bits of information; more interpretive thought would be constructed later. Figure 2.1 shows a summary of the inquiry activities in each phase of immersion in the topic of World War II.

Focused Engagements

In this phase of the unit, students added layers of new information and insights as they cycled back into the issues of World War II through new stories, poetry, art, and informational articles. Some of their work was done

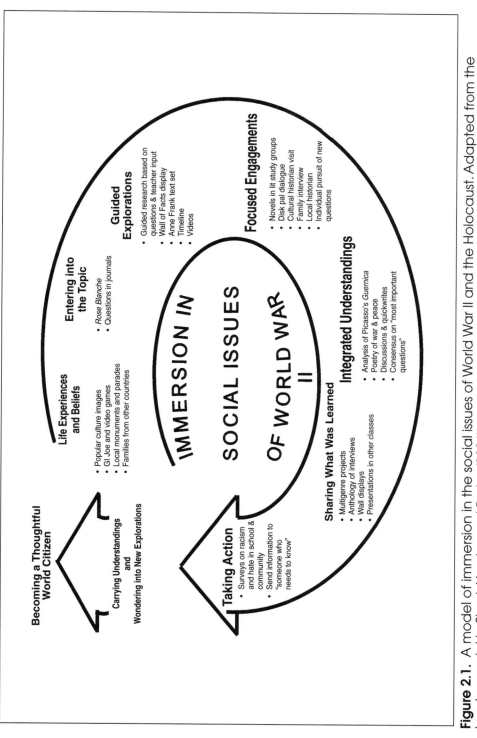

Becoming a Thoughtful World Citizen

Carrying Understandings and Wondering into New Explorations

Entering into the Topic
- *Rose Blanche*
- Questions in journals

Guided Explorations
- Guided research based on questions & teacher input
- Wall of Facts display
- Anne Frank text set
- Timeline
- Videos

Focused Engagements
- Novels in lit study groups
- Disk pal dialogue
- Cultural historian visit
- Family interview
- Local historian
- Individual pursuit of new questions

Life Experiences and Beliefs
- Popular culture images
- GI Joe and video games
- Local monuments and parades
- Families from other countries

IMMERSION IN SOCIAL ISSUES OF WORLD WAR II

Integrated Understandings
- Analysis of Picasso's *Guernica*
- Poetry of war & peace
- Discussions & quickwrites
- Consensus on "most important questions"

Sharing What Was Learned
- Multigenre projects
- Anthology of interviews
- Wall displays
- Presentations in other classes

Taking Action
- Surveys on racism and hate in school & community
- Send information to "someone who needs to know"

Figure 2.1. A model of immersion in the social issues of World War II and the Holocaust. Adapted from the inquiry model in Short, Harste, and Burke (1996).

in groups and some was done individually, at home and at school. Their inquiry was more intentional now because students had begun to develop individual interests and questions, building on the information and stories previously encountered.

Literature Study Groups

From ten titles available in multiple copies, students selected a historical novel. They set a schedule for reading and met in groups every few days to share journal responses on their novel. The response journal entries (with separate sections for Facts, Personal Response, Questions, and Author Strategies) were helpful in making small group conversations richer and more focused. Kate's entry shows her strong feelings and the basic, yet limited understandings she is constructing at this early point in the inquiry.

Facts (Information)

In the 1930's and 1940's Hitler created the Holocaust.

Thousands of Jews were murdered in concentration camps.

Many of them hid from the Nazis.

One of the families that did were the Franks.

Personal Response

I feel that the Nazis were terrible people.

They were brain-washed by Hitler.

The characters in "The Diary" were very brave.

They dealt with their problems without going crazy (though Anne was getting pretty close).

I feel very lucky that I don't have to go through what the Franks did.

Questions

What I have been wondering is since the Nazis were so horrible to the Jews, why didn't they fight back?

Author Strategies

The journal was like being there.

While some students were quickly drawn to larger issues of humanity, others tended to focus on small, concrete elements. For example, Derrick's all-male group loved their book, Harry Mazur's *The Last Mission,* and had lively talk about airborne warfare. Derrick's early journal entries reflect his concrete level of thinking as he began the book.

Facts

They flew in a B-17, and its top speed was 170 mph.

It was so cold that ice formed on his mask.

A piece of flak can tear a man to pieces.

Personal Feelings

The experienced fighters teased the rookies.

They like to curse in the Air Force.

The first mission is usually the hardest.

Questions

Is it safe for someone so young to be flying that much?

How long will his luck last?

Author Strategies

The author described things, like the plane.

He took that and made you actually see the plane.

He made you feel like you were really there.

To help some students respond more analytically to their reading without dampening their obviously sincere and spontaneous responses, Betty offered a series of coaching minilessons, sharing thoughtful interpretive samples from student journals and other kinds of reading response strategies, as described in Chapter 6. She encouraged students to share their facts and insights in whole class sessions.

Disk Pal Dialogue

To create more dialogue around the novels in a busy schedule, Betty assigned a disk to each novel, and students took the disks to the computer room to respond to one another across classes. The sincerity and immediacy of their disk talk showed the influence of "talking" to a real audience of their peers. When Derrick began reading *The Last Mission,* he read this message from Carl: "I think the *Last Mission* gets more and more exciting the farther along you are. I have only read a little more than half the book, but there has already been a lot of action."

Derrick had yet to read much of the novel, so he wrote back saying, "It has not a very good beginning; it's pretty boring but from all the other people that are reading this book they tell me that it is a very good book so I hope you enjoy it." This is a more candid remark than Betty would receive in traditional book reporting, yet the honesty was coupled with a greater interest in reading. Marginal students who often gave up on their books now seemed to persist because they wanted to get answers to their questions and stay in the conversation with their peers. Students offered each other encouragement: "Don't worry if you don't get it at the beginning; keep reading, it's worth it in the end." The enthusiasm of the other boys kept Derrick reading until he was caught up in the dramatic trials of the hero.

Allison was also honest in her rating of Johanna Reiss's *The Upstairs Room*. She said, "[O]n a scale from one to ten my rating would be a 4. It is a 'sort-a of, a kind-a of' good book. I'm not very interested in it, [but] I have a lot of questions about the book. What kind of sickness does Annie's mother have? How far is the old house from the new?"

Because we were consciously trying to build more active questioning habits, we were pleased to see that students asked each other questions. Their questions gave Betty clues about what intrigued or puzzled them as they read: "So, what do you think will happen to Misha? Does he make it back to the orphanage?" (Christa Laird, *Shadow of the Wall*). "When Hannah is teleported into a new location, I would like to know what happened to her?" (Jane Yolen, *The Devil's Arithmetic*).

Classroom as Reference Library

The classroom walls became a reference book constructed by the students, and a reference center grew steadily in one corner of the room. Barbara Rogasky's stunning book *Smoke and Ashes* was a central feature of this display. As the novels they read opened up new informational questions, the classroom gave students immediate access to research resources. Beverly remembers seeing a crowd of rowdy boys one morning clustered in a corner of the room, jostling and pushing one another. She was astonished to find that their excitement was over a historical map showing the boundaries of Poland during the war. "Hey, look at this! Poland! Lemme see! Lemme see!" as they pushed in to see the map that depicted this mysterious country from their novels.

Betty began posting students' unanswered questions on the wall and encouraging students to share with others when they found new information that shed light on one of these questions. In this way, all the students could benefit from the more assertive inquirers, and even if their reading ability was limited, they could gain a wide range of knowledge about the period. Looking at some of the questions from this phase of the unit, one can see how the accumulating background knowledge supported more probing questions:

> Why did Germany go to war again so soon after World War I?
>
> Why didn't the Jews fight back?
>
> Who helped the Jews, and what happened to them?
>
> What were the strategies, plans, and hopes for D-Day?

In one discussion of journal entries from different books, a student asked how Nazis got started. He was not asking about the economic and political conditions in Germany but trying to figure out why he was reading about so many different kinds of oppression. In one book, people were taken off to concentration camps, and in another people were harassed on the street. And what about the time when Jews could walk around and go to school even if they had to wear yellow stars? It was confusing. Betty talked a bit about the subtle ways in which the oppressive regime gradually began limiting people's lives and how people did not think to oppose it at that time. It was only a short discussion, but a few students were quite taken with the fact that they knew families of mixed race—families that would have been at risk in Germany. (Now the Holocaust Museum Web site is available for students to see a chronological list of the race laws that trace the slow accumulation of oppression.)

Students began bringing additional resources to class—videos and books, pictures, newspaper articles, a World War II helmet, a ration book. (Betty needed to screen these materials just as she had screened the resources she gathered herself. A video brought by a student from the public library contained horrific images of concentration camps with little interpretation, so while Betty let some friends of the student watch it at recess, she did not share it with the whole class or invite others to view it.) Students could reach for information when they needed it just by glancing around the room.

Betty also made the time to teach the language arts skills her curriculum mandated and that the students needed for their work. Each class period usually began with a relevant minilesson on topics such as organizing reports, writing dates correctly, or writing leads for reports. Also, one day a week was usually spent on separate vocabulary study, reading skills, or other language arts requirements not easily integrated into the inquiry unit.

Personalizing History: Guest Historian

An article featuring World War II bombing practice over the tiny islands in a huge local lake made a serendipitous appearance in our local newspaper. Suddenly, bombings were not such a far-away event, and students began to see that the war was part of life in their own community. Betty invited a local historian to help students understand how the war affected our part of the world, and Mr. Moore had them enthralled as he described the bombing practice over the lake—for example, the "bombs" were often actually bags of flour. He painted a broader picture of local involvement, explaining that German POWs worked on local farms when men were away at war, and that children collected tin foil and other scrap metal. A few students who had read Bette Greene's *Summer of My German Soldier* now commented on the similarity between events and fears featured in this novel and the conditions in their own area described by Mr. Moore. They were connecting literature to life and also motivating classmates to read a new book.

Mr. Moore provided an important demonstration of the processes of inquiry in his academic discipline as he modeled for students how historians think—what questions they ask and how information is collected and used in a professional context. Afterwards, as one of her repeated strategies to draw all the students into an active level of engagement, Betty asked students to list facts about World War II they had learned, and also what they had learned about the professional use of data and ideas. Then she compiled their ideas into a rather impressive overview of historical research, which included:

> You can gather information from firsthand accounts such as letters and interviews.
>
> You can get information on the country from papers at the National Archives.
>
> The state has archives in Columbia where you can get information on South Carolina.
>
> Newspapers often give researchers ideas for topics and places to find information.

Students entered their facts and research insights on the computer. Cleaned up a little by Betty, the resulting documents were printed out and distributed to everyone.

Personalizing History: Family Interviews

Now that the students were thinking about local involvement in the war effort, Betty introduced the idea of family interviews: how were the students' relatives involved in the war? To provide a demonstration of the kinds of stories students might gather, Betty told them what she had learned by talking to her father. He was sorely disappointed at being rejected by the army because of a slight disability from childhood polio. She told about how guilty he felt, knowing that his brothers and good friends were all at war when he could not go. He tried to do his part by writing letters to servicemen every week, getting his Red Cross certification, and serving as an air raid warden in the neighborhood.

The students got on the phone and sent inquiry letters to relatives who had lived through the war (with a series of coaching lessons for these seventh-grade language arts competencies). As they brought the very different experiences and points of view of their relatives back to the class, students became more aware of the diversity of war experiences. Their stories became part of the text set on the war.

Jill began her interview of her grandfather thinking that his World War II experiences would be "interesting," but then she learned what an ordeal a prison was and how complicated the issues and alliances of war are. She reported to the class that her grandfather was captured by German soldiers and had to wear wooden shoes so he couldn't get away. Since they didn't get much food, the prisoners killed small animals. Her grandfather told her that one reason he wasn't tortured or killed was because the German soldiers knew that he was German himself.

John was one of the boys who seemed to buy into war stereotypes of bravery and glory. His uncle, however, revealed to him some realities about the psychological and ethical pressures of war and how his own beliefs had changed:

> Uncle Mason was a sergeant and a commander responsible for many tanks. He organized the group to cross France and go into Germany. He carried a New Testament from his wife with a front cover that was bullet proof. . . . Upon returning to the States, he found it very hard to readjust. He was very tense and nervous. His youth was gone. Uncle Mason was drafted but he states that if he were called again, he doesn't feel that he would go to war.

These interviews are prime examples of the power of social learning. They opened up previously hidden lives of the students' relatives and led to family conversations quite different from the silences that trouble so many parents. Several parents made a point of telling Betty how grateful they were for the opportunity to interact with their children in this positive way. Students were amazed at the war experiences and the views of their relatives. As students wrote up their interviews with the help of response groups and shared them in presentations, they created an entire text set of war experiences and viewpoints. In some cases, their family stories had more complexities than the novels they had read.

Visual Images

Visual images had a strong impact on the students' imaginations. Students came back again and again to the pictures in *Smoke and Ashes,* but the videos made an even stronger impression. *Miracle at Moreaux* (a story of a convent that hid Jewish children), with its perilous escape scenes, evoked a strong response, and the riveting documentary *Never Forget* (the report of a Jewish man, Merle Mermelstein, who is harassed by an organization trying to erase the Holocaust from history) deepened their personal convictions about justice. Students revealed the impact of these films in their notebook responses, such as the following:

> Mr. Mermelstein's problems and case showed me how one man could take a stand and make a difference. It was also a good example of how people's hate can create such a controversy. If it wasn't for Mr. Mermelstein, we may not be learning about the Holocaust today.
>
> Derrick

> They showed us that in many wars that people fight but don't believe in what they were fighting for. I think they just fought for their country because they lived there. Most time you think all Germans were Nazis but that isn't true. The stories also told us that people will go through any thing to be free.
>
> Clark

> I like these stories because they showed the struggles and hard times of the Jews of this time. I wish everyone could understand that prejudice is wrong and killing could be stopped if the world would just care.
>
> Nathan

> I learned differences and similarities of Christian and Jews. When the Jews are taken in by Christians it showed that the human spirit is a powerful thing.
>
> Tamara

Poetry

At this phase of inquiry, the strong feelings and understandings the students had accumulated helped them appreciate the strong feelings that poets have expressed about their war-devastated lives and their yearning for peace. Students could empathize with the powerful images poets used to express the horrors and fears, the courage and hope, of lives ravaged by war. Collections of wartime poetry that are especially appropriate for middle schoolers are Marjorie Agosin's *Dear Anne Frank: Poems* and Laura Robb's *Music and Drum: Voices of War and Peace, Hope and Dreams*.

Coming to Integrated Understanding

Students were beginning to grasp the enormity of the effects of the war. Kelsey said, "An awful lot of people know a lot about World War II and the Holocaust. The more sources you use, the more different information you get." Students began to see the truly global nature of this war, which reached to such far-flung places as Burma, Africa, Venezuela, Denmark, Russia, and the Pacific Rim, and came home to Texas, Oklahoma, and South

Carolina. They were surprised to discover that all parts of the world were touched by rationing, blackouts, espionage, prison camps, and the draft, even if everyone didn't experience air raids, invasion, and occupation. Renee noted, "[People] see the Holocaust and the war in many different ways. I began to realize the hurt of war for everyone."

A multitude of concepts and words such as Star of David, Seder, genocide, D-Day, and the ironic Bergen Belsen motto, *Work will make you free,* were now part of the class conversation. We could see in questions such as "Why did Hitler hate the Jews so much and go after them?" and "How could Nazis threaten people so horribly?" that their compassion for the victims of war and racism was more intense. Students began tying together a personal web of understanding, and questions moved into larger dilemmas. This insightful question, for example, led to a new area of investigation for one student: "Were the Nazis mainly after the Jews? Why not Christians or blacks or the Indians or anyone else?"

Integration through Visual Arts

Influenced by Phyllis Whitin, a fellow middle school teacher who was interested in using visual symbols to stimulate higher levels of thinking (Whitin, 1996), Betty decided to introduce students to Picasso's painting *Guernica* as representative of art that was created to express strong feelings of outrage. Students could bring their accumulated understanding to bear as they worked to interpret the painting. Students' initial response to the images of screaming and disemboweled horses and mutilated mothers and babies was shock that "such an ugly picture" could be valuable and could have come from an artist who was famous. Their first questions were as literal as "Why is a bull in it?"

But as the class questioned and talked and looked some more, they began to speculate about why Picasso chose some of the symbols he did. Doug saw the eye as a symbol of "people closing their eyes on one another." Kerry said, "Symbols that are clearly shown would lead you to the thought that the Holocaust was yet to come. . . . The swastika and Star of David now will never be forgotten." Several students felt the constraints of the room depicted in the picture and thought about its symbolism: "I feel it looks like people are trapped in a room where monsters are devouring them. This fits in well with the Holocaust because . . . people were also trapped and killed by monsters (Nazis)."

Students empathized with the horror and disgust that Picasso must have felt about war. They understood that "not only were the Jews affected by war, that everyone is affected and when one is killed there is an equal amount of pain shared by their family and friends." One boy thought the painting showed Picasso's confused feelings, and it made him feel "uncertain" about the future. Others were relieved to find what they agreed might be a lightbulb that was the artist's sign of hope.

Now students had more insight into the emotional impact of symbols such as the yellow star and the swastika. They paid more attention to how degrading it must have been to wear a yellow star. The somber photos in *Smoke and Ashes* and the articles about and poignant snapshots of the last days of Anne Frank were more important to them now.

Sharing What Was Learned

Students began preparing for their final projects, which would express what they had come to know and feel about World War II and the Holocaust. As students began thinking about their projects, Betty saw that many of them needed help in focusing on important issues. Warren and Richard had abandoned their earlier insightful questions and were working on a list of major battles. Monica couldn't find a topic on which to focus her essay. Other students pulled out earlier work but were uncertain what to do with it.

Finding Most Important Questions

Betty initiated a session in which the class reviewed questions from their journals and the walls of the room. "What are our most important questions?" she asked, and then led a consensus session that yielded the seven most important ones. Interestingly, important questions suggested by students tended to be the ones that remained unanswered, such as "How could adults go along with this kind of awful stuff the Nazis were doing and let it get so out of control?" The students also chose, for example, "Why did Hitler hate the Jews?" and "Who helped the Jews?"

Students then used these questions to help focus their final projects. The prioritizing process focused attention on larger issues and concerns, while at the same time allowing the students' questioning to remain at the center of their work. It also provided a common vocabulary for the students as they began to work on their final projects.

Final Projects

Students were encouraged to share what they had learned through multitext and multigenre projects as a way of supporting a wide range of feelings and understandings. Students made their choices from poetry, short stories, play scripts, visuals, cartoon strips, essays, book reports, and mapmaking, each worth a different amount of points that contributed to their grade (see the guide for the World War II inquiry unit in Materials for Teachers at the end of the chapter). In heterogeneously grouped classes such as these, it is important to offer all students a chance to succeed at their level of ability and involvement. Students went back to their journal entries and other earlier written work to find ideas. Some projects were revisions of earlier work, and others were newly written pieces.

As the students worked on these projects, new questions came up. At this point, the unit was winding down, so some interesting questions were never pursued (although some of them may have been beyond a seventh-grade class anyway). Some boys who were reviewing battles found lists of enormous, overwhelming amounts of equipment, and they asked, "How was there enough money to fight a war?" A fascinating question came from a girl who remembered the 150,000 World War I vets who marched on the White House; she had also been doing some background reading on the Vietnam War for the novel she'd chosen, *Park's Quest* by Katherine Paterson. She wondered if the Vietnam vets had ever marched on Washington. We hoped, of course, that these questions would continue to emerge long after students had left the seventh grade and that they would continue to research issues that interested them.

The classroom began to fill up with colorful maps, and groups were hard at work editing their stories, plays, and reports. Students reaped the benefits of the extended immersion in facts and fiction. We felt that some of the students' fictional work truly moved into the world of literary imagination, with convincing characters worthy of the reader's empathy, set against contextual details of European cities, concentration camp life, or battlefields.

Student Stories

Grayson's long, complicated, and beautiful story "The Necklace" opens in the dockside community of Hamburg; through the actions of a family and their neighbors, readers learn about curfews, the Hitler Youth movement, food rationing, and other political conditions (and European food preferences) of the late 1930s. Drawing from novels she had read—Lois Lowry's *Number the Stars,* Johanna Reiss's *The Upstairs Room,* and Jane Yolen's *The Devil's Arithmetic*—Grayson wove an original story of courage and deprivation. At the end, nothing of the family is left for the granddaughter but a pearl necklace.

Clark's story surprised Betty in its recognition of the impact of war on innocent citizens. He writes about Robert, a young man who joins the U.S. army when German submarines attack his South Carolina coastal community. When Robert becomes a soldier, he discovers that war is more than defending one's country. Robert expresses his growing concern about his role as a soldier through a letter he writes to his family: "I realize that we are too busy killing to recognize that we are killing families, women, children. When we bomb a country we bomb more civilians than solders. We have ruined everything."

Edward couldn't get over the fact that Nazi values could still live in today's world and wanted his short story to show how a boy could be drawn gradually into more and more inhumane actions. His realistic dialogue and detailed context draw readers with compelling verisimilitude into the early stages of a group of modern German boys' fascination with the trappings of power when they discover a "golden swastika." Edward depicts Kurt and his friends in their transformation into thrill-seeking neo-Nazis. This story stunned us with its depth of conviction and insight into how acts of hate can happen. Only a personal quest would lead a seventh grader to exert such effort over many days to pull off such a story.

Poetry

The students' poetry was especially passionate. Brenda's poem takes us into the inner being of a young Jewish girl who faces up to her situation in a concentration camp, and it ends with a moving plea:

> . . .
> You think I'm different since I'm a Jew.
> But I have a heart and a mind just like you,
> and I don't want this to happen again.

In her searing poem "We Are," Candy takes on the roles of both insider and outsider. She is able to juxtapose the confusion and fears of designated victims against the cold determination of ruthlessly intentional oppressors.

We Are

We are people who hurt others.
We wonder what it's like for them, then focus on our jobs.
We hear their cries to stop and help, but who cares?
We want to kill more and more.
We are people who hurt others.

We pretend they are dogs sometimes if it gets hard to do.
We feel they are less than us because they are Jews.
We touch them—never.
We worry that we won't succeed in killing them off.
We dream about a Jewless world.

We pretend we're not Jews.
We feel the hate surround us.

Figure 2.2. The last frame of Tamara's cartoon about how people justified inaction in the face of Nazi oppression.

> We run so we can breathe.
> We touch our stars and pray.
> We worry we will be caught.
> We hope we can get through—alive.
> We are the innocent.

> We don't understand why they do this.
> We say we will survive.
> We dream about our freedom.
> We try to get through with our sanity.
> We want to get away.
> We are the innocent.

Essays and Editorial Comments

Tamara showed her convictions in an eight-frame cartoon based on the cartoon book by Art Spiegelman, *Maus I: A Survivor's Story* (see Figure 2.2). In explaining her strip, she said:

> The point of the cartoon was to show that probably a lot of people living in Germany and Poland didn't like the killing [of Jews] but didn't say anything about it. If they had all of got together and tried to stop Hitler I bet they would have succeeded. So the moral is that you always need to stand up for what you believe is right.

Tamara also wrote about the need for citizens to stand up for their beliefs in times of crisis in an editorial about learning from history. Her editorial, quoted in Chapter 7, ends: "Next time a Hitler is running to be a leader, silence him by banding together and speaking what you feel is right in your heart."

Just as the students' fiction was rich with informative social realities of the World War II era, their essays were rich with supportive information as students wrote about the "most important questions" of the war. Eva begins with some of her background knowledge and then addresses her question:

> Ghetto uprisings occurred in Karakow, Bialystock, Vilna, Kaunas, Minsk, and Slutsk, as well as in Warsaw (April to May 1943). Warsaw, the capital and principal city of Poland, was the site of a massive rebellion. Yet, the Jews were suppressed and about 56,000 of them were killed in the process. By the time the war ended the remaining Jews involved in this uprising had been exterminated. The US army finally succeeded in ending the holocaust and the persecution of the Jews, but it began the war with Germany for political reasons.
>
> . . . [W]hen I look back on the question "Who helped the Jews?" I feel much remorse for the Jews because they were not helped by anyone except themselves. [Note: Other students disagreed with this conclusion.] The involvement of the United States was not directly related to what they were going through as a people. I think it was very brave for the Jews to stand up for themselves, although they were defeated during their uprisings. This fact created my respect for them.

Some of the essays pushed the critical stance even further. Mitch, initially consumed with battles and dates, in his final paper generated a complex premise that addressed the moral obligation of governments in the face of genocide: "The US was just as responsible for the Holocaust as Germany because they stood by and let it happen."

Such a change from encyclopedia reports! Students were inquirers, not paraphrasers. Their projects had personal voice, authority, substance, and style. The long immersion in the topic and the students' persistent efforts to bring coherence to multiple perspectives had led to moral convictions and the confidence to express them to others.

Taking Action

While the students were at work on their final projects, a journal entry made earlier by Allison about Anne Frank came to light. She wrote: "She [Anne] was the victim of racism and I am, too, because I hear and see it almost every day." Other students agreed. It was evident that students needed to make some kind of concrete response to these unresolved concerns. So Betty created an additional phase of the unit called "Hate and Its Causes," which featured gathering and sharing information in the school and local neighborhoods. This was a good opportunity for students to bring their convictions home and to engage in the kind of data gathering that is needed for informed citizen action in a democracy.

In order to choose a focus for their project, the students, working in groups, brainstormed ways in which their own lives were problematic because of racism and expressions of hatred. Betty taught them about the process of developing a survey and provided guiding questions. "What do we want to know?" helped students create questions for questionnaires and surveys. "Who do we want to ask?" led them to a target audience. After revising and editing, they sent out their surveys to teachers and conducted interviews at lunchtime or at home. When the information came back, they worked hard on ways to present the information, including visual displays.

A few of the groups took a different approach. One group surveyed intolerance on the Internet and presented their information to the class in an evening news format. Another group used their survey information to create a children's picture book that they shared in the Salvation Army's day care (a service learning project for the unit).

Sarah's group found that students agreed that intolerance was widespread in the school and that there were even kids they would describe as "hating others." Students gave these reasons for negative attitudes, in order of frequency:

1. skin color and appearance
2. their families taught hate
3. people's actions
4. other reasons: meanness, differences, and hating back

This group was discouraged that no one had suggestions for positive antidotes to violence, but another group found students who had these suggestions:

- Be kind to all people and set an example for others.
- Show people who hate the positive qualities in those they hate.
- Give people who hate the facts to help them understand others.
- Stop hating others yourself.

Renee and Anna surveyed the one hundred-plus school staff members about their feelings and beliefs about hate. Only forty questionnaires were returned, but all participants answered "yes" to the question, "Do you believe there is a lot of hate in the world today?" The questionnaires stimulated conversations among teachers and staff in our school, and some of them stopped students in the hall to talk about it. Students derived satisfaction at having their work taken seriously and felt good about adults being concerned about the same things they were concerned about. But Betty was discouraged that no adults wanted to take these projects further. Nothing seemed to change in the school.

In subsequent years, the survey project was expanded to send information collected by the students to audiences beyond Betty's classroom, as described in Chapter 8. But even in this first year, the students had at least taken a critical stance with regard to issues in their own lives and had a more informed basis for their concerns. Conversations about injustice and the war had actually taken place in hallways usually filled with talk about the upcoming basketball game or trip to the mall. At least their concern had not been silenced because it was time to move on to the next topic in the curriculum. An important step had been taken, even though it was far from fulfilling our vision of what a democratic school should be.

Carrying Understandings and Wondering into New Explorations

At the end of the year, after being involved in several units that addressed justice issues, students were asked to connect their classroom learning to the world. Some students felt strongly about the need to continue to care about justice. Andrea was hopeful that the foundation laid in studying the war might carry over and encourage our students to work for a better future: "I feel if people look back, they can prevent World War Three." Excerpts from Laura's final essay point to a similar commitment but a more hard-edged view of people's ability to change:

> [A]s I watched the movies and read the stories, I finally began to realize the reality of the world. Some people are just filled with hate and [are] in need of a conscience. . . . Hate was alive in WWII and it is alive today. I have always thought that your religion or skin color makes you no better or worse than any other person, but I have realized that a large percent of the world doesn't feel that way. History does repeat itself, and it also stays with us and lives inside of people every day and can only stop if they really want it to.

Additional Literature for Students

World War II Fiction

Avi. (1992). *Who was that masked man anyway?* New York: HarperTrophy.

Avi. (2001). *Don't you know there's a war on?* New York: HarperCollins.

Bunting, E. (1998). *So far from the sea*. New York: Scholastic.

Burch, R. (1974). *Homefront heroes*. New York: Puffin.

Butterworth, E. (1982). *As the waltz was ending*. New York: Scholastic.

Choi, S. N. (1991). *Year of impossible goodbyes*. New York: Dell.

Garner, E. R. (1999). *Eleanor's story: An American girl in Hitler's Germany*. Atlanta, GA: Peachtree.

Greene, B. (1973). *Summer of my German soldier*. New York: Scholastic.

Hahn, M. (1991). *Stepping on the cracks*. New York: Avon.

Hesse, K. (1992). *Letters from Rifka*. New York: Scholastic.

Houtzig, E. (1987). *The endless steppe: Growing up in Siberia*. New York: HarperCollins.

Kaplan, W. (1998). *One more border*. Toronto: Douglas & McIntyre.

Lobel, A. (2000). *No pretty pictures: A child of war*. New York: Avon.

Magorian, M. (1981). *Good night, Mr. Tom*. New York: HarperCollins.

Matas, C. (1993). *Daniel's story*. New York: Scholastic.

Matas, C. (1999). *Greater than angels: The true story of one family's escape from war-torn Europe*. New York: Aladdin.

Matas, C. (1999). *In my enemy's house*. New York: Aladdin.

Mazer, N. F. (1999). *Good night, Maman*. New York: HarperCollins.

Morpurgo, M. (1997). *Waiting for Anya*. New York: Puffin.

Napoli, D. J. (1999). *Stones in water*. New York: Scholastic.

Nolan, H. (1994). *If I should die before I wake*. San Diego: Harcourt Brace.

Orlev, U. (1991). *The man from the other side*. New York: Puffin.

Polacco, P. (2000). *The butterfly*. New York: Philomel.

Propp, V. (1999). *When the soldiers were gone*. New York: Puffin.

Ransom, C. (1993). *So young to die: The story of Hannah Senesh*. New York: Scholastic.

Salisbury, G. (2001). *Under the blood-red sun*. New York: Dell.

Schur, M. (1997). *Sacred shadows*. New York: Dial.

Uchida, Y. (1971). *Journey to Topaz: A story of the Japanese-American evacuation*. New York: Scribner.

Van Steenwyk, E. (1998). *A traitor among us*. Grand Rapids, MI: Eerdmans.

Yolen, J. (1990) *The devil's arithmetic*. New York: Puffin.

Related War Fiction

Antle, N. (1998). *Lost in the war*. New York: Dial.

Buss, F. (1991). *Journey of the sparrows*. New York: Dell.

Hesse, K. (1994). *Phoenix rising*. New York: Puffin.

Mead, A. (1999). *Soldier mom*. New York: Dell.

Myers, W. D. (1988). *Fallen angels*. New York: Scholastic.

Nelson, T. (1989). *And one for all*. New York: Dell.

Paterson, K. (1990). *Park's quest*. New York: Puffin.

Reeder, C. (1999). *Shades of gray*. New York: Aladdin.

Whelan, G. (2000). *Goodbye Vietnam*. New York: Dell.

World War II Nonfiction, Biography, and Autobiography

Anflick, C. (1999). *Resistance: Teen partisans and resisters who fought Nazi tyranny*. New York: Rosen.

Atkinson, L. (1985). *In the kindling flame: The story of Hannah Senesh*. New York: Beach Tree.

Bachrach, S. D. (2000). *Nazi Olympics: Berlin 1936*. Boston: Little, Brown.

Bitton-Jackson, L. (1999). *My bridges of hope: Searching for life and love after Auschwitz*. New York: Aladdin.

Boas, J. (1996). *We are witnesses: Five diaries of teenagers who died in the Holocaust*. New York: Scholastic.

Borden, L. (1999). *The little ships: The heroic rescue at Dunkirk in World War II*. London: Pavilion.

Colman, P. (1995). *Rosie the riveter: Women working on the home front in WWII*. New York: Crown.

Denenberg, B. (1999). *The Journal of Ben Uchida, citizen 13559, Mirror Lake Internment Camp*. New York: Scholastic.

Fry, V. (1968). *Assignment: rescue: An autobiography*. New York: Scholastic.

Giddens, S. (1999). *Escape: Teens who escaped the Holocaust to freedom*. New York: Rosen.

Grossman, M. (2000). *My secret camera: Life in the Lodz ghetto*. San Diego: Guliver.

Kuhn, B. (1999). *Angels of mercy: The army nurses of World War II*. New York: Atheneum.

Levine, E. (2001). *Darkness over Denmark: The Danish resistance and the rescue of the Jews*. New York: Scholastic.

Library of Congress. (1999). *I'll be home for Christmas: The Library of Congress revisits the spirit of Christmas during World War II*. New York: Delacorte.

Lindwer, W. (1991). *The last seven months of Anne Frank*. New York: Anchor Books.

Meltzer, M. (1976). *Never to forget: The Jews of the Holocaust*. New York: HarperCollins.

Opdyke, I. G., & Armstrong, J. (2001). *In my hands: Memories of a Holocaust rescuer.* New York: Anchor.

Rol, R. van der, & Verhoeven, R. (1993). *Anne Frank beyond the diary: A photographic rememberance.* New York: Puffin.

Stalcup, A. (1998). *On the home front: Growing up in wartime England.* North Haven, CT: Linnet.

Ungerer, T. (1998). *Tomi: A childhood under the Nazis.* Boulder, CO: Publishers Group West.

Zyskind, S. (1989). *Struggle.* Minneapolis, MN: Lerner.

Poetry

Harrison, M., & Stuart-Clark, C. (1989). *Peace and war.* Oxford: Oxford University Press.

World War II Media

Cohen, R., Magnusson, T. (Producers), & Kragh-Jacobsen, S. (Director). *The island on Bird Street* [Video]. (1996). Third Row Center Films: Lantern Lane International.

Garcia, J. (Producer), & Tait, D. (Director). (1991). *Never forget: An orientation to the Holocaust* [Video]. New York: Modern Educational Video Network.

Garner, J. (1999). *We interrupt this broadcast: Relive the events that stopped our lives* [CD]. Naperville, IL: Sourcebooks.

Platt, J. (Producer), & Shapiro, P. (Director). (1990). *Miracle at Moreaux* [Video]. Chicago: Public Media Video.

World War II Web Sites

America from the Great Depression to World War II: Photographs from the FSA-OWI, 1935–1945
http://lcweb2.loc.gov/ammem/fsowhome.html

American Memory: Historical Collections for the National Digital Library [Multimedia collection created for kids by the Library of Congress]
http://memory.loc.gov

America's Story from America's Library [Multimedia collection of American history from the Library of Congress]
http://www.americasstory.com/cgi-bin/page.cgi

The History Place [Surveys, timelines, and pictures on many historical events. The timeline and feature on Afro-Americans is helpful for World War II studies.]
http://www.historyplace.com

The United States Holocaust Memorial Museum
http://www.ushmm.org

Materials for Teachers

The following is a list of the various activities and projects in the lengthy World War II and Holocaust unit. A range of points was assigned to each item and printed on the sheet, although they are not provided here. The first activities were required and led by Betty in class. A place for students to check themselves off helped students and parents understand that the students were accomplishing substantive work and assisted in tracking makeup work. Teachers might want to give students only the first part until later in the unit.

The independent project choices were the end-of-the-unit alternatives provided to accommodate individual preference and the ability levels in a heterogeneously grouped class. The inquiry essay was worth approximately three times more than a computer disc pal printout and four times more than a book jacket.

World War II Inquiry Unit: A Guide for Your Work

Requirements

Notes you made about the *Diary of Anne Frank* and "Last Days of Anne Frank"

Questions on Play about Anne Frank, including content of story and literary elements

Responses to:

"Last Days of Anne Frank"

Quotes from Anne Frank's diary

Photos and paintings

Videos *Miracle at Moreaux* and *Never Forget*

Quickwrites: Explanations, summaries, and character descriptions

Double-Entry Journal on your selected novel. Minimum of 10 entries; 3–5 extra points for each extra entry. Include on each: title; author; pages read; opinions and feelings; important information about people, events, dates, places; questions; literary elements and features

Prewrite, Rough Draft, and Final Draft on "Lessons from the Holocaust"; 10 points each for prewrite, rough draft; 20 points for final draft (minimum 1 page)

Independent Project Choices

(If projects are done with partner, 10 fewer points each)

Disk Pal Dialogue. Print out at least 3 substantive comments and responses.

Additional Novel from list of choices provided. Check out of library or borrow from our room. Write a 1/2- to 1-page summary and create and answer 4 questions, one from each quarter of the novel.

Book Jacket of a World War II novel. Include author bio, inviting cover, summary, and opinion/recommendation.

Script. An original script of a scene. Adapted from a book, 50 points; original, 75 points. Presentation, extra 30 points.

Short Story. Create your own characters, plot, and setting. Keep in mind our discussions of what makes a good story. Use literature book if you wish.

Media Collection. Make a collection of newspaper articles, magazine articles, and TV features connected to World War II and the Holocaust. Consider the neo-Nazi movement, the "ethnic cleansing" in Bosnia, or events in other parts of the world.

Write a comment on each entry.

Write a conclusion with your opinion.

List *all* your sources.

Display, 10 extra points.

"Important Question" Essay. Investigate one of the "Most Important Questions" that our class asked. Give informational background and explain your opinion. You may not be able to actually find answers to these questions. Your investigation and thoughtful conclusions are what is important. Length: at least 2 pages.

Prejudice in Our School/Community Survey and Presentation. In groups, create a survey on an important question about hatred and prejudice in our lives. Follow the guidelines given in class. Add other sources if you wish, such as telephone calls to organizations. Come to consensus in your group about your conclusions. Plan a creative presentation such as a poster, a talk show, etc., that provides both specific information and conclusions.

3 Classroom Life: Evolving toward Democracy

Students must live in an environment that is abundant with opportunities to practice social justice.

William Ayers, *Teaching for Social Justice*
(Ayers, Hunt, & Quinn)

CHAPTER OVERVIEW

This chapter describes some of the strategies Betty found useful in building qualities of democracy in her classroom: community, responsibility, opportunity, and shared leadership. To set the stage, we first tell the story of Brice, one of the more resistant students in her classes. We then share our beliefs and the framework that guided Betty's work with the students. The next section offers some strategies Betty used to create a sense of belonging and mutual helpfulness among the students. The subsequent sections offer ideas to help energize students to collaborate with the teacher in contributing actively to the learning of others in the classroom. The chapter ends with a discussion of ways to include students (and parents) in the assessment of their work.

Most of these strategies were initiated at the beginning of the year, grew in small steps, and were relatively well established by the time the social inquiry units described in Chapters 2 and 5 began. Readers will notice an interaction between these activities and the activities to encourage an inquiry stance described in the next chapter. A collaborative stance and an inquiry stance go hand in hand. Likewise, all of the ways of teaching and learning described in other chapters were essential for changing the classroom atmosphere to a more active democratic model.

Pulling in Silenced Voices: The Story of Brice

A New Teacher Researcher Project

One fall, after several years of working toward a democratic classroom, Betty decided she wanted to focus on the students who remained on the fringes of her classes, resistant and weak in skills, despite her new strategies. If she believed that in a democracy all citizens should have a voice in what affects their lives, what could she do about the group of uninvolved, silent students who seemed to emerge every year? If she was critical of the way our society dismisses troublesome citizens as problems that society can do little about, shouldn't she be similarly critical of her own classroom? If she asked the questions, "Is everyone included? Who is left out?" the isolation of these students was a painfully obvious answer. She had already tried to involve these students, as had other teachers, but in the end they were as marginal in her class as inner-city families often are in our society.

Betty hoped that if she stepped back to watch, she might find new insights that would help pull in these students. As her research got underway, her early observations of one student highlighted her frustrations:

> Brice was noticeable even in the first week of school. His mature size singles him out, as does his persistent doodling and drawing when he is supposed to be working. Despite warnings and front row seating, the sketching continues. He seems to be a loner, and gets into little irritable scuffles with other boys. They don't seem to like him. Brice doesn't join in during our reflection sessions. I have little idea of how he is feeling. I'm not getting through to him. When I looked at his writer's notebook entries, they are copouts—formula writing and large artistic lettering to fill the pages. He seems very low in verbal ability. Will he develop as a writer?

Shortly after Betty wrote this reflection, artwork was returned to the team from a summer program for artistically talented students. When Betty displayed them on the chalkboard, kids swarmed around admiringly. Surprisingly, Brice had drawn two of the pictures. Betty had viewed his drawing as a diversionary tactic or a quiet form of defiance, but now she had an inkling that she needed to look at Brice with different eyes. Her appreciation of Brice's art was a first step toward finding a more positive lens for her observations.

She began talking to him about his drawings, and she asked him to sketch some things for the class bulletin boards. When she responded to his writing, Betty tried to make connections to art: "You see so many details to put in your drawings; do the same thing in your writing. You can make variations in word choice or in how you write sentences, just like all the ways you think of to vary your dinosaurs." She added visual art options to her assignments—for example, sketches, photos, and cutouts for their writer's notebooks—but Brice showed little overt interest.

When she checked interim grades, Betty was surprised to find that Brice had done better than she had realized. He had not missed an assignment since the third week of school, and his average on quizzes was a B. She had been seeing his weaknesses, not his strengths. He still seemed withdrawn and was not really involved in his writing, and he drew rather than explored issues in his journal. Betty continued to make positive social contact with him. As she continued to watch, she made some new discoveries:

> I discovered that Brice is a different student in the computer lab. He is alert and focused. He finishes his work and then helps others. He finished a polished piece that he seemed to care about and wanted to share with me. It was a tribute to his Uncle Kevin, with whom he shared many activities, including computers. I found out from this paper that Brice's father is dead, perhaps a reason for his uncertainty and withdrawal.

Supporting the Riskiness of Participation

In mid-September, Betty shared options for students' autobiographical projects. Brice surprised her by proposing a video as his medium of communication. Looking back, she remembered that he had worked on a program in the campus television studio and had viewed *Jurassic Park* nineteen times, but she did not yet see these activities as significant.

When it came time for class presentations of autobiography projects, Brice was nervous about the kids' reaction to his video. Although the video was visually sophisticated, she could understand his hesitation. He had spared none of the heartbreak his family had endured—the younger brother born with brittle bone disease who died at the age of two, his father dead five years later from leukemia.

The video revealed so much that Betty might never have learned about Brice. The samples of childhood drawings confirmed that his art was an exceptional talent and a persistent interest. His long-standing, passionate intent to become a cinematographer was now evident. Betty saw his deep knowledge base in the factual reporting of family travels, and the polished script showed his ability to write in a compelling manner when motivated. She now could appreciate the strength of his mother in keeping a cheerful and supportive atmosphere in their home. (Betty had assumed that his mother would be anxious about Brice, as she was.)

Brice's worries about his peers' reaction were needless. The class burst into spontaneous applause. The film was rich with Brice's impressive artwork, knowledge about the world, and candid revelation of his family's hardships. It had a real sense of visual style and sophisticated graphics, such as a segment showing Brice's image in a mirror as he narrated. Brice was revealed as relaxed and sure of himself in this alternative medium.

Brice's video was one of the projects that deepened the class bonding through its honesty and emotional power. As Brice became more confident, his talents began to emerge in the classroom, and he became a more conscientious student. A collage of his drawings of societal ills from his journal was later selected as the school's yearbook cover. And now that he was more active, the class had the benefit of his insights, energy, and demonstrations of alternative modes of communication. His initiative in requesting options seemed to help less assertive students ask for alternatives that supported their strengths. Betty reflected:

> What would I have missed learning about Brice—and others—if I had not been consciously testing my belief that all children can learn? It is easy, in the busyness of the day, to accept these students as exceptions to our beliefs. I came close to forbidding Brice to draw in my room.

Other Struggling Students

Her understanding of Brice helped Betty be more open to student alternatives in ways that contributed positively to the democratic atmosphere in the classroom. She watched rebellious students more carefully and tried to be more flexible in reaching them.

Darienne was especially irritating because she seemed to be deliberately unsuccessful much of the time. But when she learned that Brice was using a video for his expert project report, she became interested. Betty knew that Darienne enjoyed being one of the anchors on the schoolwide news program, but Betty never thought that Darienne could pull off making a video herself. Nevertheless, with her new insights, she encouraged Darienne to do just that. Darienne surprised everyone with an interesting interview of a cosmetologist and a video of herself performing correct skin care and makeup. She glowed when Betty asked to show the video in other classes.

Although Darienne was certainly not transformed, she had a more positive attitude for a while. At any rate, this success created a truce from the constant tension between Darienne and Betty. Perhaps part of what we can hope to achieve with struggling middle school students is to alter negative self-perceptions and attitudes of peers. Despite Betty's best efforts,

however, even in the midst of an atmosphere of enthusiasm and openness in the classroom there are always a few marginal students who cannot seem to find a place for themselves at school.

Moving toward Change

> The more we talked seriously about a democratic classroom, the
> more we were aware of passivity (students) and authority (adminis-
> trators and teachers) in schools. It was a little frightening to think
> that a classroom looks more like preparation for life in a dictator-
> ship than in a democracy. We had been thinking hard about student
> choice, but it didn't seem like enough. Now we saw that the choices
> students were permitted to make were actually very narrow in scope.
> They were, for the most part, choices about topics or about how to
> answer an open-ended question.
>
> (from our folder of reflections)

For many years, Betty had been discouraged by the negative tone of middle
school life. Teachers were caught in a negative cycle of trying to get kids
to behave by using entertaining tricks, rules and regulations, and, too often, punishments. All too frequently she had to "write up" a student for
aggressive or destructive behavior. Her teaching was too much an impersonal process of giving assignments, which most but not all students dutifully fulfilled. She wanted instead to share more of the class decision making with students.

Betty's daily responsibilities did not stop just because she wanted
time to think through new ways of working with her students. Her principal did not excuse her from meeting curriculum requirements while her
students became used to new ways of working together. What she hoped
to accomplish had to be done on the job.

Redirecting the power structure toward democratic participation was
not easy to get started. The years of undemocratic school classrooms had
done their work, and the students did not feel equal. Many students were
reluctant to give up the safety of a passive classroom stance. Changing the
teacher's habits of autocracy was also a slow process. Although the struggling students did become more willing to participate, they never did feel
as enfranchised to make contributions as the more academically able students. Genuine change took several years of hard, intentional, uncertain
work, and the result was progress toward Betty's goals rather than transformation.

A Framework for Change

We believe that participatory democracy is learned by participating in a
democracy. When adult citizens experience the challenges and forces that

shape a society, they gain in ability to be effective agents of change. As they try their wings at negotiating decisions, they gain confidence in themselves as negotiators and see the value of working out decisions with others. When citizens see that they might make a difference, they become more committed to action. Belief in self and belief in democratic processes grow together with experience.

It was the same in the middle school classroom. Each year Betty began once more the lengthy process of drawing students into making contributions to their classroom life. She kept pushing in the direction of more collaborative leadership. She overlooked student negativity when she saw progress. It was both confusing and energizing to her and to the students. But as they became familiar with the new expectations, their level of comfort nudged them to take more initiative. By the time spring rolled around, many students had grown noticeably as participants in a responsible learning community.

Betty hoped to evolve from a teacher who focused on lessons to a teacher who focused on her students' active processes of learning. She worked to become a better observer of classroom life, trying to recognize the students as individuals. She watched more. She tried to understand their actions and intentions before intervening. She began to do more coaching of students through their work rather than giving up on them. She practiced looking for their strengths and tried to see errors as mirrors onto the mind. When she had five periods a day, this level of involvement was frustrating. When she had three blocked classes a day, it was easier to focus on the students.

The following broad goals provided a framework for moving the climate toward a more democratically functioning classroom:

- **Students will value themselves and also others.** They will find worth in their own concerns, in their ways of learning, and in their own and others' academic work. They will appreciate their own family culture and those of others.

- **Students will grow as inquirers who actively engage with ideas.** The curriculum will invite real questions and concerns into school. Students will wonder, analyze, sort out, connect, and construct personally integrated understandings that lead into new areas of inquiry. They will inquire through the arts as well as verbal language. They will construct knowledge rather than accept it.

- **Students will find the classroom to be a safe place for the lively exchange of ideas.** Working from a sense of comfort and belonging in their classroom, students will have continuous opportunities to grow into new abilities and responsibilities. Similarly, they will be supported as they explore ideas, voice emerging opinions, and learn to give others the same support.

- **Students will grow as collaborators in creating their class-room.** Student decision making will grow beyond simply choosing between teacher-selected alternatives. Students will participate in developing the structures that guide their lives in school. Increased ownership of their lives will lead to taking more responsibility for their own work.

- **Students will begin to see a connection between their active roles in the classroom and roles in a democratic society.** They will begin to realize that the new roles and responsibilities exercised in their classroom are the same roles valued in the outside world. Their classroom roles will lead to the formation of their adult characteristics as citizens.

- **Student learning will lead to action.** Students will be useful to others and act on their beliefs inside and outside the classroom. They will be able to follow their emerging convictions into the activities of participating in, communicating with, and challenging the world around them.

Creating a Sense of Belonging

In the first weeks of school, Betty tried to ease the students into feeling that this classroom was their home base. She wanted them to feel a sense of belonging to a group that lived in this space. Ralph Peterson (1992) calls this sense of belonging "residency" and describes it this way:

> Teachers and students seek to ensure that members of the community . . . have confidence in themselves and others and that they feel at home. Individuals are in residence when they feel at ease in expressing what they think and how they feel, in taking risks, and in seeking out critique of their work in an effort to grow. Students in residence express self-esteem, can take the initiative in learning, are able to trust themselves and others, and perhaps most important, experience their existence as being of value to others. (p. 65)

A middle school classroom needs to be a balance of comfort and challenge. The first unit of the year offered many safe opportunities for students to express ideas through learning logs, paired sharing, draft writing, and structured poetry. Through shared reading of novels, students lived with diverse literary characters in difficult situations. They became used to talking about life troubles and strong emotions. These literature experiences created emotional bonds in the group.

Just as she had learned to help students "believe their way into writing," Betty had to learn how to help students believe their way into classroom citizenry. When students began to believe that they themselves were valuable, they were readier to see the value in others. More respectful attitudes and working relationships developed in the classroom; these were preadolescents, however, and hurtful putdowns, teasing, and cliquish rejection of peers never completely disappeared.

Self-Respect through Family Histories

For many students, bringing their family histories into the classroom in the first unit of the year made them realize that their lives were valuable. Their own lives seemed less shameful when they were mixed together with the stories they gathered from their parents and with the family fiction and autobiographies.

Students slowly established the classroom as a reflection of themselves. Betty consciously responded appreciatively to their ideas, their writing drafts, their helpfulness to others, and their risk taking. The walls of the room displayed their families, their pets, and scenes from their lives, and the students exchanged many stories of self throughout August and September.

Some students took huge risks to share troubles, tragedies, and bonds of love. Their peers were clearly surprised and sympathetic when these hardships were revealed. In their reflections on this unit, the students acknowledged that they had been drawn into caring about others, and these feelings of closeness were what was important about the unit for them:

- I learned what people have to live through, like deaths, abuse and little money.

- I learned a lot about other people and the hardships they had encountered, like Josh's mother almost lost her life, and how Brice's father and brother died.

- I learned that not everyone has the type of life that I originally thought they did.

- I learned that people have a lot of the same ideas and feelings, but express them in different ways.

- Now that I know what others have been through, I appreciate how my life has been.

- I learned that if you listen, people will open up and share their lives with you.

The students' final presentation of their autobiographies and heritage projects for parents was a memorable family history celebration (described at the beginning of Chapter 7). Their presentations were filled with feeling, and the students basked in their parents' enthusiastic appreciation. Students seemed to value themselves and their own expertise. They had become more aware of how their families and heritages made a positive contribution to society, and they had more empathy for others who were different. This base of comfort, and the appreciation of diversity, would be important later in the year when they addressed troublesome conflicts in society.

The Impulse to Care: From Literature Response to Class Interaction

Learning about the issues of society through autobiographies, novels, and magazine articles that revealed life struggles touched the hearts of the students. They talked about the bravery of Jonas in *The Giver* (Lowry) and the loneliness of Jean Fritz growing up in a foreign culture *(Homesick: My Own Story)*. They recognized that the children in Russell Freedman's *Kids at Work* "would think our lives are divine." In their literature discussions of such novels as *Missing May* (Rylant) and *Moves Make the Man* (Brooks), students expressed high ideals of tolerance and altruism. Christine said, "All people have feelings and opinions and should be respected even if you agree with them or not."

In addition to the inherent interest of the stories, the literature allowed students to express concern and compassion for others. It invited them to try on feelings they were not able to express in real life. Although students couldn't talk about not helping a friend when she was teased by other children, they could discuss why no one came to Helen's rescue in the lunchroom when she was humiliated in *When the Stars Begin to Fall* (Collier). Students didn't talk about their relatives who were in prison, but they could express their emotional conflicts as they followed the boy and his father who was a convict on the run in Walter Dean Meyers's *Somewhere in the Darkness*. During the World War II unit later in the year, Edward, considered one of the "cool" kids, wrote about a video of a group of Jewish children hidden in France: "I liked *Miracle at Moreaux* the best because I sort of got attached to the children."

Betty encouraged students to be aware of and value their contributions to one another. Jenna showed Jody (a new student) how to organize and tab her notebook. Jack explained how he had asked his mother to ask him questions to help him prepare his report on pet snakes. Betty made it part of her practice to mention student contributions: "Thanks, Kirsten for helping kids in the computer room. . . . Danielle had a good idea for our skits. . . . Has anyone used Jack's idea of getting someone to ask you questions yet?" Validating specific adaptations of work seemed to be an authentic and helpful form of praise. A ritual of beginning a work session by asking if anyone had helpful hints and ending the session by asking if anyone had used ideas from their peers encouraged student contributions.

Professionals Who Help

A visit by a family counselor, part of Betty's effort to put kids in touch with helping professionals in the community, gave the students a new level of respect for family problems. The students could talk in general about family problems rather than remaining anxiously silent. Their strong expressions of responsibility, kindness, and empathy (and answers to the question "What do middle school kids need from their families?") were published in the school counseling newsletter.

Supporting Acts of Caring

Despite progress, hurtful comments and cliquish rejection continued to pervade much of the students' interactions with one another. And the hurt was real. As Renee wrote in her journal, "the saying 'sticks and stones may break my bones, but words can never hurt me' is not true. Words hurt the most. . . . [P]eople should think more before they speak. Because the power of language is strong." Caring and respect was an agenda that continued to need attention throughout the year.

One of the topics that received a lot of attention at the beginning of the school year was the students' "acting out," disturbing behavior that sometimes even physically hurt other children. Students were asked to observe school life and then think of reasons for the disturbing behavior. Betty compiled their lists into nine reasons for acting out (need attention, cover up inabilities, get bored, don't care about others, don't plan for the future, and so forth) before they discussed such behavior. The list helped students see that concern about negative social interactions was widespread, and it focused their discussion.

To strengthen the inclination to care, whenever she saw a more positive tone beginning to emerge Betty asked students to reflect on the strategies they were using to help one another. Jason began the year as a loner but reported at the end of the first eight weeks that he liked working in groups. He seemed to take Betty's coaching seriously and enjoyed making his contribution: "I'd try and help people whenever we worked together, but I wouldn't just do their stuff."

A few students stood out for their willingness to extend their caring to other students. Addy paid special attention to Donald, a student with multiple sclerosis who used a wheelchair, frequently reminding Betty of

Donald's needs with quiet asides such as "Don't forget Donald needs to get up closer, Mrs. S." A group of rather sophisticated girls, after first holding back, invited a new, very awkward girl to eat with them at lunch. Rina, who recently had come from war-torn Macedonia, was particularly sensitive to issues of hatred and intolerance. She surprised Betty with this journal entry she wrote while she was reading World War II literature:

> [I]n a world filled with the hatred and cruelty that we all know, somehow I know that the kind of people that escalated this event are the same kind of people who will do these kind of things when they grow up, except to do it on a much larger scale.
>
> It happened near the end of the year in the sixth grade when in our science class we were told to form groups for an activity we were about to do. Everyone scattered to be with their friends as a slightly unpopular girl was left alone at her table.
>
> [The teacher] . . . asked whether anyone would like to be with her and I was shocked that no one made even the slightest gesture to get nearer to the girl. I thought it was terrible that she had to live through this uncomfortable moment. In the dead silence that followed I pictured the world and its people as dark, unfeeling creatures and I'm sure she did also. Finally I just stood up and joined her vowing to look at things from her point of view more in the future.

Rina's traumatic wartime experiences had given her a depth of understanding and maturity beyond those of other students, and the socially conscious curriculum provided an avenue for her to express her concerns and commitments.

Routines and Rituals Build Community

During the first months of the school year, a number of routines and rituals emerged to support democratic life in the classroom. Some were routines that eased the transitions into class and assignments, providing a sense of comfort during the day, and others put students in active relationships with each other. Routines that helped students have independent access to resources and information were a noticeable sign of Betty's belief in students' ability to manage their own learning as much as possible. As John Dewey (Fishman & McCarthy, 1998) noted: "School routines become, in important ways, ends, for they determine student personality and moral character. The residue from classroom activities, supposedly *mere* ends, remains long after the so-called *more important* end products have been forgotten" (p. 26).

When Beverly visited for a few days in early October, she noted that students moved around the room without teacher direction as the class got started and slowly settled when Betty moved toward the overhead projector. Some of the beginning-of-class rituals that helped students become a learning community were:

- A transparency on the overhead outlining the day's work
- Beginning the class by reviewing the outline
- Turning in learning logs in the class crate
- Picking up learning logs Betty had responded to
- Checking homework assignments posted on a chart
- Checking books in and out of the class library
- Chatting with Betty about ongoing projects
- Consulting research sources (when needed)
- Pulling chairs together for a literature circle

Betty found that other rituals helped the group work together collaboratively and let everyone know what to expect. Here are some that she found to be flexible and useful:

- Beginning a writing or reading activity/workshop with a minilesson
- Making overheads of past minilessons available in a binder
- Posting assignments for a grading period on the wall
- Making assignment handouts available in a binder
- Using student work as positive examples in minilessons
- Bringing reading annotations or literature logs to discussions
- Inviting informal reaction to activities and requirements in "exit slips"
- Complimenting students often for contributions and new ideas
- Applauding their writing and other good work
- Noticing and using student questions in teaching
- Putting hanging folders of student work in boxes
- Placing student disks in a box according to class periods
- Displaying informative and fiction books on a current topic on the chalkboard tray
- Letting students find a nook in the room to huddle together with their response partner
- Sharing individual ideas to make a class compilation (everyone feels smart!)
- Displaying quotes of the week on a wall
- Keeping extra time activities on a back table

- Having students keep a resource notebook: journal ideas, sample book reviews, business letters, government offices telephone numbers and addresses, etc.
- Putting up on walls language skill/criteria charts with student examples

Inviting Students to React and Contribute

At the beginning of the school year, Betty made a concerted effort to integrate bits and pieces of student work as she taught in order to help students believe they had a contribution to make to the learning of the entire class. She wanted them to be responsible for more than just attending to her directions and finishing their work on time. Therefore, she asked them to tell her what helped them learn, what was frustrating, and what their problems were. Students' evaluative comments were usually written on scrap paper at the end of the week. Betty then used these "exit slips" in her teaching to show that she valued the students' thinking. She picked up on students' questions and suggestions and found ways to incorporate them, and she looked for opportunities to highlight students' ideas when they happened spontaneously. Betty asked Annalee, for example, to explain how she used her Canadian grandparents to get more information for a report about Ontario. "Some of you may have resources in your family to help you," Betty concluded. She frequently gleaned ideas from students' journal entries and began the next class with this list. Put together, the students' ideas seemed impressive.

On occasion a student would provide the impetus for an important change in the curriculum. For example, Allison's journal about Anne Frank, quoted in Chapter 2, created an entirely new class assignment. Other students agreed with Allison when she said, "I'm like Anne Frank. I see racism and prejudice every day." The resulting discussion about racist graffiti and slurs led to an inquiry project about the causes and remedies of prejudice in the school. Not all student contributions will result in big changes, but cumulatively the small moments will build a more inclusive classroom.

Students as Teachers

Betty also looked for opportunities for the academically energized students to teach lessons when their learning moved ahead of the rest of the class. Annalee explained how she kept her notebook entries for her I-Search project on separate pages, one section for how she was going about her topic search and the decisions she was making, and another part for subject information and resources she was finding. She walked around the room showing the sections to make her point. Byron gave a lesson on irony using a poem on war he had found in a magazine, even preparing questions for class response (see Chapter 7).

Inquiry Approach

The active learning at the heart of the social inquiry approach (see Chapter 4) made possible the development of a democratic tone. Response groups, literature circles, cooperative group projects, research projects—the real questions and real feelings created energy and purpose in student work. Literature that brought real life struggles into the classroom, as well as writing and speaking that put students in touch with the real world, created a sense of being part of something important. As Doug commented, "I like doing projects. Your mind is asking questions, looking for information. You're learning from the people around you. It's more like what people do in life on a job. Nobody sits down at work and tells you everything."

Teria wrote in a self-assessment that she was proud of developing a public voice that tied in to real life for her. She wrote, "[The projects] teach us to be assertive to our society and express our feelings. I gave good points in my editorial on student handbook punishments [for rule infractions]. And I showed how much I love my great Grandmother." We were pleased that she liked having both a voice of protest and a voice of caring. She ended with a typical excessive seventh-grade burst of enthusiasm: "We need to be selfless to make a good community."

Changing the Power Structure toward Collaboration

In a democratically functioning group, everyone contributes ideas about how the group will work together. Betty wanted students to go beyond just involving themselves actively with their own learning. She wanted them to see themselves as sharing responsibility with her for *creating* an effective atmosphere for learning.

Betty was relieved to find that her fears about having to water down her instructional goals in order to give students more power in the classroom and input in decision making were unfounded. She tried to make her goals for learning more accessible to students and invited them to join her in making adjustments and finding better ways to achieve these goals. There was, of course, a flood of frivolous suggestions once she invited student ideas. Going out to play basketball was a popular suggestion. She was thankful that students provided enough useful ideas to encourage the more hesitant students to contribute, and she could laugh with them at some of the more outrageous suggestions. Some ideas that at first seemed off-task turned out to be valuable.

Using Students' Work in Lessons

Students' work became the heart of some minilessons through a discussion of the significant qualities of the work. With students' permission to use their names or anonymously, Betty would put on the overhead perhaps only one paragraph of a journal entry, a lead for an essay, or a collection of sentences from several students as a positive example of achievement. She stopped using student work for negative examples until very late in the year, when students were more confident. Or she asked the student to explain the thinking and process behind the work.

Here are some additional, easy-to-implement ways to incorporate student ideas into lessons:

- During lessons, encourage comments from fellow students that validate a student's product or practices.
- Invite a former student who knows the ropes to explain expectations for this class.
- Encourage students to bring in sources on a topic—guest speakers, books they like, artifacts. Students have surprising riches of special contributions they and their families can make to learning.
- Provide a bulletin board for students to add examples or ideas on a topic such as strong leads, compound sentences, or interview questions. Have sentence strips handy. Ask students to give explanations as time allows. A computer document can also be used for this purpose.
- Use a bulletin board space for students to add questions about a topic of significance to the class.
- Assign a student to be class reporter and post the report on a bulletin board or on a computer document that all students can access when needed (creating a class log).
- Assign a student to be homework reporter, and keep a large poster so parents and students can check on all the assignments for a grading period.
- When discussing criteria for a project, ask students for strategies that will help them meet these standards, and then post the list of ideas.
- Ask students to make up lists of troublesome words and then compile and photocopy the lists for everyone.

Individual Ideas Compiled for Collaborative "Texts"

Throughout the year, students responded many times with individual ideas to a question, a topic, or a classroom problem. Betty realized that using these responses could provide a collaborative basis for teaching. Everyone could contribute at least one idea. Merged, the collaborative list was rich with good ideas. This list was then discussed, posted on the wall, or distributed for use in writing, studying for tests, or completing projects.

Many times during the year, Betty used this same approach to address topics about learning such as what help students need in order to succeed, how to choose books to read, recommended good books, book report format suggestions, strategies for improving spelling, and goals for doing well this year. These sessions that used students' individual insights invited students to take control of improving their learning strategies, rather than turning into one more scolding session by the teacher.

Sometimes the compilations were of information each student had learned. When the class was working on local organizations that contributed to society, for example, each student searched the newspaper and found only a couple at most, but the total list contained more than thirty-five diverse organizations, ranging from the well-known NAACP and Red Cross to more obscure garden clubs and auxiliaries. In this way, student contributions could lead to high levels of teaching and learning.

Students also shared their comments on and recommendations of classroom library books by leaving sticky notes on the front cover or creating bookmarks to be kept in a can in the classroom library (see the collage of bookmark recommendations in Figure 3.1). Students frequently used their peers' recommendations when choosing books.

New Purposes for Displaying Work

Student work that was posted on the walls functioned as more than just a display of "good work," which is a static kind of inclusion. Betty wanted many of the displayed items to make a real contribution to learning. They could be new ideas, questions, student interpretations of criteria, demonstrations of a genre, or suggestions for good work. Students' displayed work could become resources for learning.

What was posted depended on what was needed. At the beginning of almost every unit of study, facts were needed, so the results of students' research were posted. Sometimes examples of different genres of writing were needed, and student demonstrations were displayed. Bulletin boards could invite student examples for such topics as strong leads, compound sentences, and interview questions. Having sentence strips, poster board, and markers available helped students add their examples without too much disruption to classroom activities. Then the posted examples could be discussed in instructional minilessons.

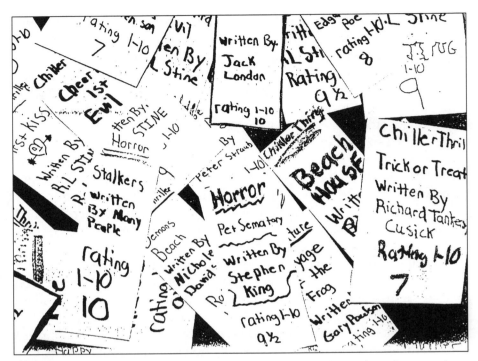

Figure 3.1. Student readers rated books they had read and passed on their opinions to potential readers through bookmark recommendations.

Using displayed work in instruction helped create a sense of belonging. Students had a respected part in the curriculum and the classroom. Feeling respected became a foundation for acting more responsibly.

Student Roles in Solving Classroom Problems

Student Conflicts

Naturally, conflicts and tensions between students were plentiful; these students were twelve-year-olds and they loved to argue and place blame. Arguments in the hallways spilled over into the room and disrupted the beginning of class. There seemed to be no end to the conflicts that upset students. A conflict resolution program had been initiated several years earlier in the school, but the procedures were not still operating. The program entailed a time-consuming, cumbersome process that was hard to sustain. Nevertheless, the program had exposed most students to the general process of talking through problems. In this seventh-grade team, teachers tried to implement a problem-solving process that involved a dialogue between two students with a teacher or sometimes with "peer jurors."

Betty used an additional strategy of requiring individual pieces of writing by the involved students, such as letters of concern or apology that helped clarify or smooth over conflicts. In all of these procedures, three questions were asked of the students:

- What could have been done differently?
- How could we have handled this better?
- What can we do now?

When students were used to considering these questions, they began to anticipate the process of addressing each one in turn. Aggressive students who struck out in anger knew they would have to contribute ideas about how they could have handled the situation better. Students whose property had been taken or damaged knew that teachers would support them in receiving some recompense by asking, "What can we do now?" The questions were posted on the wall, and though they did not solve the problems of anger, aggression, and theft in the group, they did provide a predictable structure for resolution.

Turning Complaints into Suggestions for Change

When she viewed the students as *growing into* responsibility rather than as irresponsible, Betty found that her attitude toward student complaints was more positive. She was less irritable about student whining, and she could sometimes turn complaints into occasions for asking students to take responsibility for making the classroom a more comfortable place.

When students complained about not remembering homework, Betty asked for suggestions to help them remember and followed up by posting a growing list of assignments during each grading period. Parents began to consult this list also. (Today the school Web site substitutes for such a display.) When students complained that Betty took off points for homonym problems, she set students to work creating a permanent word wall of homonyms. When they complained that other classes played more games, she asked them to share their ideas, and for several weeks, Fridays became vocabulary game day, an activity created by groups of students.

Questions and Classroom Power

The right to ask questions is one of the signs of how power is distributed in a group. Discouraging questions in the classroom is close to denying students a voice. We thought that a sense of comfort in asking questions— and even a responsibility to ask questions—was fundamental to a collaborative community, but the questioning stance was hard to develop in students.

They continued to need special invitations throughout the year to share their questions about assignments or topics they were studying, as described in Chapter 4. Asking questions seemed to require a major shift in their sense of self as students.

Once Betty began to invite questions continually in exit slips, journals, and discussions, she realized that students were holding back important questions. They did indeed seem to feel that they lacked the power to intrude on the classroom. This book is full of student questions because they are at the heart of the learning described here. As the year progressed, student questioning became more purposeful, creating energetic inquiry into social issues and a critical stance. Stronger question asking was a major force in shifting classroom control from the teacher to a more democratic, shared responsibility among all individuals in the class.

Making Room for Student Leadership

By the time spring rolled around, the more active kids were bursting with ideas for improving a lesson or project or for ways to earn extra credit. Addy, as described in the following section, almost single-handedly organized a Saturday class trip to a state park, and Kent volunteered to extend the outing by making arrangements to visit the nearby WPA-created dam. Because the teacher arrangements for earlier field trips had been shared with the class, Addy and Kent had the requisite knowledge to carry out these tasks effectively. Kirsten became the backbone of many of our philanthropic causes, and although she struggled with academic tasks, she was an excellent spokesperson on public issues, especially for improving racial equity. Developing potential leadership skills like Kirsten's can easily be crowded out of the classroom by all the pressures of curriculum and testing.

Underachieving students have been the focus of many innovations in education, and rightly so, but neither should we overlook the many obviously talented students who are waiting to blossom. Their organizational skills, initiative, and maturity are a real asset to a school. These leaders need teacher support to reach their potential, just as the less successful students do. But too often all they receive from teachers is praise for excellence on teacher assignments, the kind of praise that can operate in an undemocratic way as the "teacher's pet" syndrome.

The Story of Addy

In the first few weeks of school, Addy stood out as a capable, high-achieving student who wrote with thoughtfulness and a personal touch. She was an active reader, loved her journal, and enthusiastically conducted interviews of her family. Because of her academic ability and dependability, it was easy to assume that Addy didn't need any special accommodation. When there are so many problem students in an active classroom, it is a relief and a temptation to just accept and enjoy students like Addy. But her exit slips and other informal communications showed that Addy was extremely anxious about all the decisions she had to make as she worked.

Gaining Confidence

Betty's first move was to offer reassurance in exit slip responses and one-on-one interactions between class periods, and she used anonymous examples from Addy's work to demonstrate effective responses to assignments. Gradually, Addy seemed to relax and believe in herself. When Betty began to open her curriculum to student initiative, it became evident that, now more confident, Addy had a strong desire for leadership. She volunteered to tutor students from our team who came in for extra help after school and provided valuable assistance through her sensitive understanding of their needs.

Addy seemed to have a rare talent for understanding democratic leadership and through her actions taught others how to practice democracy. Watching her initiative, it would be easy to say that here was an independent student who needed little support. But Betty did play a crucial role in Addy's growth—she invited student leadership into the classroom, and she coached Addy along the way.

Addy's Activism Grows

It was in the spring that Addy's leadership really began to make itself felt. Our social issues curriculum and the service learning projects were taking the students out into the world beyond the school, and Addy was full of inventive ideas. In the Depression-era unit, the topic she chose to investigate was the Civilian Conservation Corps (CCC). This choice reflected Addy's commitment to helping others, as CCC was a little-known but outstanding example of citizens supported by the government to work for the good of the community. As Betty recalls:

> One Monday morning Addy greeted me with her plans for a "perfect" class field trip. While horseback riding in a state park over the weekend, she had noticed a small sign saying the park had been built by the CCC. She went straight to the park ranger to find out more. She wangled his commitment to give a historical background presentation to the class if we visited the park. She had already checked out the procedures for reserving horses to ride and had

enlisted her mother and her friends' mothers to drive the entire class to the park. She assured me that I wouldn't have to do a thing!

I popped her bubble when I reminded her that the team had already taken the permitted number of field trips. In a moment, she countered with, "We can go on a Saturday." The next morning I found a typed trip information sheet on my desk with a request to make copies for the class. After I provided the required permission form, she got the excursion together. With a picnic, trail riding, and a bit of local Depression-era history, it proved to be a lovely day for me and the students who were able to attend, about half the class.

Other Projects

On another occasion, as the class plodded dutifully through the classic text *Treasure Island* (Stevenson), Addy suggested a pirate's party as motivation for finishing the book. Betty's reservations about taking time from class for partying only brought out Addy's resourcefulness: "Don't worry. We'll only serve food they would have eaten on a sailing ship, and anyone who wants to eat will have to wear a costume of that period. I'll announce it all in class if you give me a couple of minutes." The next day Addy brought in a clever invitation with sailor jargon such as "Avast me maties!"

The class celebrated having its illustrated chapter summaries bound into a booklet that students would give to another class ready to use the novel. Wearing a motley display of bandannas, beads, vests, and cutoffs, students waved homemade pirate flags, listened to historical sea chanteys, and ate dried fruits, nuts, and beef jerky while listening to the chapter presentations. They nibbled politely at terrible, salty hardtack biscuits made by a couple of class members who had researched the recipe. Luckily there was lots of tea, not actually authentic because it was iced, but at least it wasn't Coke.

Addy obviously had fun with her projects, but they were not frivolous. Because her leadership created enjoyable activities for everyone, and because she invited her classmates to work with her, Addy had a respected niche in the team. (Another project of hers, a pet exchange, is described in Chapter 8.) As she learned more about social issues in the larger society, the focus of her anger at injustice correspondingly expanded. Betty found that Addy frequently wrote in her journal about the environment and ecology, and she wrote a long passionate letter to President Clinton about his responsibility in this area.

Learning from Addy

Addy helped us understand that middle schools have seriously underestimated the potential of student leadership. We did not realize how far students could go until Betty made room in the curriculum for activism to take flight. Students like Addy are surely present in every school but go unnoticed in the daily round of assignments given and completed. If Betty had not invited student contributions, she would never have known that Addy yearned for leadership, and the class would not have benefited from Addy's energy and ideas. Addy would not have had the opportunity to develop competence as a leader.

Only on reflection did Betty realized that her responses to Addy's ideas acted as a training program in making decisions, creating enthusiasm, carrying out details, and so forth. Addy's projects helped us see more clearly a new way in which the middle school can be preparation for democratic citizenship.

Assessment and Classroom Power

> Who gets to say what is good work is one of the most important ways we define what kind of relationship people have with each other.
>
> Jerry Harste

We wanted the assessment processes to strengthen the sense of community in the classroom, not diminish it. When Betty began asking for student feedback and suggestions in the first week of school, she was already inviting students to join her in assessment, although she did not realize it at the time. She wanted to let students know that she valued their knowledge. They understood there would be expectations for their work. They knew that testing was inevitable. The students actually wanted standards applied to their work; they just didn't want standards they couldn't meet or didn't understand. They wanted to see themselves as having some influence on their fate as learners.

Betty aimed for assessment that would help students learn rather than discourage them (see Figure 3.2). Assessment should be a process that strengthens students' belief in their ability to be successful. Spandel (2001) describes the kind of atmosphere Betty wanted to create:

> They become part of a writing community in which their opinions about the quality of writing are frequently, actively sought. It is a good feeling to have your opinion valued. It teaches you to think, and it makes you feel as if your presence in the classroom might have purpose. (p. 9)

Spandel further argues that students cannot take charge of their own process until they know the difference between a weak and a strong piece of work. For most students, the high levels of stress they experience about being graded are largely due to uncertainty. Too many students sit in fear that their piece of writing will be the one judged to be weak. The problem is often not that they are being graded; the problem is that they don't know *how* they will be graded. Students need to know, in specific and clear terms, what constitutes good work in a class.

To strengthen students' belief in themselves and to build habits of attention to criteria, Betty began the year by asking students what they already knew about good work. She asked them to jot down what makes a good interview, what makes a good report, what makes a good reading choice. As she shared with them a compiled list, she reinforced their best insights and let them know what was important to her. These lists were often posted or copied and put in students' class notebooks. They were the standards for work at the beginning of the year, and more students gave them attention because they had collaborated on their creation. Here is an example of a student reflecting with great authority on two pieces of writing during the fall, using class-derived criteria and his rather confident understanding of how to meet these criteria:

Paper #1 My Trip to Gettysburg	**Paper #2 Talking to Obie H. Brown**
I wrote quickly without details	I used more mature words
This one had many short sentences	I took time to revise and type it
The beginning and ending stunk	It got correct sentences, punctuation and spelling
I told about nothing	I told about history

But a list is only a beginning. Betty held many more sessions in which she and the students interpreted criteria. Their yearlong involvement with social issues put them in touch with many kinds of compelling authentic texts. They looked closely at weak and strong examples on the overhead and scanned their folders for passages that exemplified characteristics of a good paper. Through these sessions, students came to understand better the differences between a weak and a strong piece of writing. They began to learn what to look for. In her comments on papers, Betty would refer back to their class discussion.

Betty also needed to teach, again and again, the processes of creating a paper, an interview, or a report. The students needed to know how to *use* their knowledge about good work, or it would be useless. They needed to know how to write stronger drafts, create a better speech, or read more analytically. Betty wanted them to become confident that they knew a variety of ways to make their work better. She wanted her comments to help them see ideas to apply to their next pieces of work. The students were still capable of turning in weak writing, but in general they came to recognize when they were or weren't writing well.

Some of the things Betty wanted to accomplish with her approach to assessment included:

- Show students how to be successful by demonstrating the criteria in action.
- Continue to teach criteria through demonstrations, chats, and tips so that students can grow into a sense of good work.
- Involve students actively in interpreting criteria and identifying examples of good work (and sometimes creating criteria).
- Provide clear, immediate, and constructive feedback (both teacher and peers).
- Recognize and celebrate signs of growth.
- Build habits of monitoring the self as a learner.
- Build habits of setting personal goals for future work.
- Allow choices in how to meet standards.
- Make connections between academic criteria and real-world attainments.

"Shopping Around"

Betty wanted students to have access to high-quality examples or demonstrations of the kinds of products they were asked to create. When students were creating visuals or 3-D projects, Betty would post samples around the room with sticky notes attached that pointed out strong or weak points. She noticed that students would browse and even talk together and sometimes go up to look more closely while they were working. (This idea came from a Chicago teacher interviewed on National Public Radio. Whoever you are, we thank you!) Similarly, Betty shared many demonstrations on the overhead, and she encouraged students to "shop" for ideas in a file or a notebook in a corner of the room that contained writing samples of student and published work, identified by genre.

Creating Rubrics

Betty created many rubrics during the year to reflect a new genre or project format, such as brochures, persuasive letters, interviews, and surveys. Sometimes students worked with her to create the rubric and sometimes not, but always she showed how their ideas were included in the criteria.

She talked them through the rubric at the beginning of or early in the assignment. Students looked at what was expected before they did the work. Betty spent more time with criteria *before* students started to work than afterward.

These sessions were nonthreatening because the students' achievement was not yet in jeopardy. Betty tried to ensure that students were prepared for expectations—and even had an opportunity to influence the expectations—before they tackled the job so that they had a better chance of being successful. Sometimes students were more motivated because they knew better how to proceed.

Rubrics seemed to make assignments more concrete and manageable for students. They provided a common language to talk about the work and a framework for questions and concerns. And they certainly made it easier for Betty to remain consistently focused as she graded assignments.

Criteria for good work can change as students grow. At the beginning of the year, for example, the standards for public speaking were rudimentary, but by spring more advanced criteria were needed. Students were more confident as speakers, and their experience enabled them to envision a more effective speech. Now they could think about consciously planning a speech to meet criteria such as using a quote or other reference to an authority, referring to a map or visual, or providing a provocative introduction. Similarly, the first written reports of the year were expected to be informative and readable, but later in the year strong organization and development of ideas were added to the assessment.

Student Self-Reflection

Exit Slips as Informal Communication

There will never be enough time in the middle school day for students to let you know what they are thinking. Exit slips are short informal communications, written perhaps on a half-page of used photocopier paper. They invite students to tell you the little things that get lost in the fast-paced schedule of the day—or the things they hesitate to say face to face. They helped Betty keep her finger on the pulse of student engagement—who was frustrated, who was excited, and who had made a new discovery. The exit slips made teaching much easier because they let Betty know what gave students trouble and when they need encouragement. It seemed important to keep in touch if she wanted to help each student become confident. A little word at the right time meant a lot. Sometimes students wrote,

"I really didn't try," or, "This was easy today." These slips are actually an invitation to assess oneself in an informal way, but Betty didn't label it assessment—just "feedback."

At the end of the first week of school, for example, Betty invited students to write a note about how things were going for them. Instead of a written prompt, she made it a personal invitation:

> Write to me about what you have learned this week. It will help me plan for next week. Tell me also something I can do to help you learn better. What is hard for you, or how we could change things to help you. So, three things: how's it going, what you've learned, how I can help you.

In the next few days, Betty made a point of mentioning student comments to let students know she was reading the exit slips and using their responses.

The notes helped her support students who were taking risks to change as learners. She remembers: "I would sometimes discover that a student was trying something new and feeling really insecure, so I could add a word of encouragement. I also picked up on little personal items and could take an interest." The few minutes of class time needed to write the notes were repaid again and again by not wasting time on problems that could be solved.

Some exit notes didn't require a response from Betty. But sometimes students did need a personal response, such as when they apologized or mentioned a major new direction in their work. This touching note created a bond between Betty and the student early in the year: "Things you can do to help me: • understand my feelings • tell me the *truth* about my work • give me tips." Betty wrote back: "I'll try to. Keep talking to me and keep me posted."

Sometimes Betty gave specific prompts such as "What I've learned this week . . . " or "A question that I have . . . ," or asked about specific assignments, such as "Tell me two prewriting strategies that you have learned and will use in the future. . . . Tell me how your library search is going. What search strategies have you used and what have you found?"

Self-Reflection throughout the Year

Students often reflected on their learning, responding to a set of questions. When a teacher asks students to write what they think about their own work, it conveys to them that the teacher is not the only one who gets to say, "This was a good lesson." Self-reflection was also a way to teach students what was important about their learning. When Betty asked, "What changes have you noticed in yourself this marking period as a member of the community?" students were reminded to think about their responsibilities to the group. It was important to make self-reflection a positive experience. If Betty graded self-reflections, the grades were based on participation, not on what was written. After several months of periodic reflection, students became less anxious and more thoughtful about looking at themselves as learners.

Often the reflection was followed by goal setting for the next unit or the next nine weeks, as in the following list of questions from a first-nine-weeks-grading-period reflection form:

Thinking about Your Learning: First 9 Weeks

- What activities or topics have you liked best in this unit?
- What new skills or strategies or activities have helped you learn and improve?
- When do you most feel you are a valued and contributing person in this class?
- What is confusing or difficult for you?
- What do you feel you could do now or that you know now that you didn't a month ago?
- Any other concerns or comments?
- 2 or 3 goals for the next grading period:

Making Reflection More Useful

Sometimes asking students to reflect seemed ineffective because their comments were vague or commonplace. Here are some suggestions Betty has found to be helpful in creating better reflection questions:

- Draw from other teachers' reflection forms, but let your ideas and questions guide you in creating your own form, adapting the items to your program.
- Think about how you would like to use the information, and don't overload yourself and your students with responses that are not useful to you.
- Think about how you yourself would develop as a learner if you were asked the same questions.
- Don't be afraid to ask big, thought-provoking questions—whether or not you think students can answer them. The process of addressing the big questions of life, repeated over time, shapes students' thinking into a more thoughtful mode.

The following list outlines some ideas for enriching the process as students respond to the questions:

- Talk students through the questionnaire before they start. Be personal. This is something *you* (the teacher) want to know and that *you* will use, not impersonal paperwork.

- Ask students to have their portfolios on hand or gather a pile of work from throughout the year to remind them of the work they have done.

- Ask students to pull their desks together in small groups, not to do the survey together but to chat and share as they work. This exchange will introduce new perspectives and remind students of what they have forgotten. When the surveys are completed, if there is time, let students share them in their small groups.

- Give students feedback the day after they've completed the forms. Share your reactions. Tell them how their responses were helpful to you or might be to other students.

How Reflections Are Used

We discovered that what students wrote on the reflections was not the heart of this activity. More significant was the thinking that occurred as they answered the questions. Minimal responses from students who had made important strides in their learning were discouraging: "I learned a lot about people in this period of history. It was a good unit. I liked the novel I chose." We had to remind ourselves that the process of reflection made the students more self-aware and gave them more control over their learning, no matter what they had written on the paper. Students could then use their reflections to set goals for the next marking period and copy the goals into their notebooks.

Holding a discussion after students wrote their reflections helped them expand their thinking. As they listened to one another's answers, they made connections to their own learning and perhaps stretched their academic ambitions. When, for example, Betty asked students to reflect on themselves as problem solvers, it was evident that surprisingly few students understood what problem-solving behaviors were. The discussion of suggested behaviors (use resources, stick to the topic, be specific, and [in the science lab] use trial and error, follow lab rules, and follow directions) seemed to help students pin down what they were expected to do as "good problem solvers."

End of the Year Reflections

At the end of the year, students were ready to be free of school, and a reflection was not likely to influence their future work. But Betty found that when she asked students what stuck in their minds about the big purposes and themes of the year, their responses helped her prepare for the next year. And perhaps it kept the "big ideas" of inquiry, collaboration, justice, equity, and tolerance on their radar screens a little longer.

She asked broad questions such as "What does inquiry mean to you now?" and "What did you learned about justice and injustice in the world?" The positive responses helped Betty find the energy to implement the big projects again the next year. Some of the quieter students surprised her with their comments about their inquiry, such as:

> We spent more time writing up things and working together. It's not only more fun, it's more real.

> Using a variety of sources helped me meet people in my family so I could interview them.

> I learned how horrible people can be and how we all have to speak against racism.

> The injustice in the world is still with us. We need to learn from history and avoid World War III.

> This year was interesting because it takes you back in history and better prepares you if it happened now.

Portfolios

Portfolios were an important collaborative assessment activity. Selecting from their own work to show how they met expectations involved a high level of student ownership of their learning. Generally, students created or modified their portfolios three or four times a year, at the end of each nine weeks. They were given parts of several days in class to go through their work, usually sitting in groups on the floor so they could consult with one another, while Betty circulated, probing, counseling, and reminding students how choices might be made and how each of the portfolio requirements had grown out of class activities. Students provided a written summary as well as using sticky notes to verbalize the criteria for their choices. Although time-consuming, the process was worthwhile.

Betty's students were not ready to jump into compiling a portfolio at the beginning of the year. She created more informal portfolio guidelines in the fall and more demanding ones in the spring. For the first nine weeks, for example, students might write an informal letter to parents (or grandmother or other caregiver) using a guide and including their best piece of writing, along with goals for the next nine weeks. Or a "then-and-now" comparison of two pieces of writing could be a good occasion for pinning down characteristics that were present or absent in their writing.

Specific guidelines in the form of lists of items to include (one of your poems, your report, two of your most thoughtful literature log entries, and so forth) or questions to answer were needed to direct the students' portfolio searches. Betty found professional resources that helped her create efficient and thought-provoking procedures. Samples are given in the Materials for Teachers section of this chapter.

Students gradually came to feel more ownership of the criteria during the year through repeated comparisons of expectations and their achievements. They also saw that Betty used their ideas to modify assignments. For some students, their own expectations for themselves were more demanding than those of the school. When the social inquiry units became a larger part of Betty's curriculum, she included in portfolio guidelines more questions about research strategies, inquiry stance, risk taking, and understandings of society.

Many of the less able students continued to have difficulty keeping track of papers to use in a portfolio. Betty admits that some classes defeated her intentions to involve them in portfolio reflections, so she asked them to do simpler self-assessment projects, such as then-and-now comparisons.

Assessment Letters to and from Parents

When parents were the audience for student self-assessment, the assessment process took on a high level of authenticity, and students took it more seriously. In the third nine weeks of one year, parents received a letter and a portfolio of their child's selected work with a statement of the criteria that were used to evaluate it. Here is part of Jessica's heartfelt letter:

> The purpose of my portfolio is to give a sample of all my best and favorite writings I did this year. As I put my portfolio together I realized just how many types of writing there are. I understood that writing is not that easy and it takes time to make your piece good.
>
> I hope you will recognize my spelling corrections, and that I've become a better speller, and I now have better writing skills. I also hope you realize that I tried to do some longer, harder pieces.

The students asked their parents to write back after viewing the work. With this packet of information, parents became better informed about what was expected of their child in seventh grade and felt more confident about responding. Many of the parents wrote back to the students, and, thankfully, all wrote positively. (See a sample parent response in Figure 3.2.)

Betty had structured the parent-child exchange to emphasize the students' positive achievements. Weaknesses were generally pointed out by the students themselves in their letters, so in a way they were "in charge" of the assessment instead of parents who criticized while students tried to defend themselves.

Jean, I liked the surprise ending. As we think of treasure stories, we rarely think of other than silver or gold. The message was quite clear—people are truly treasures and parents among the best of treasures. I thought your use of dialogue and variety of voices added the interest factor.

And you did well in your use of punctuation. I thought the story was well developed. It appeared to have been written by a much older student! Yes, I agree, perhaps more clarification of the whereabouts of the parents would have been nice.

Figure 3.2. Letter about Jean's story from her mother.

Last Thoughts

When we reflected on how the classroom community had grown during a year, we saw that some caring and collaborative interactions had become habitual ways of living for the students. And more of the marginal students were active and seemed to feel they belonged. Student leaders created a bustle of initiative. There were indeed happy moments when everyone was glad to be together in the room.

Nevertheless, the classroom was still far from the kind of world Betty wanted to live and work in, and she suspected students would agree. We wondered what it would be like for a entire middle school to work toward Ayers's ideal of "an environment that is abundant with opportunities to practice social justice" (Ayers, Hunt, & Quinn, 1998, p. xxxii). A large school such as Betty's would be resistant to change, but within a school a group of teachers working collaboratively could create an island of caring and respect. Students might be invited to think in a manner similar to this message Betty saved from an old peace calendar: "Think about the kind of world you want to live and work in. What do you need to know to build the world? Demand that your teachers teach you that" (Kropotkin).

Additional Literature for Students

Multicultural Memoir, Autobiography, and Biography

Angelou, M. (2002). *I know why the caged bird sings.* New York: Random House.

Blos, J. (1990). *A gathering of days: A New England girl's journal.* Orlando, FL: Harcourt Brace.

Bridges, R. (1999). *Through my eyes.* New York: Scholastic.

Bruchac, J. (1997). *Bowman's store.* New York: Dial Books.

Conrad, P. (1991). *Pedro's journal: A voyage with Christopher Columbus.* Boston: Houghton Mifflin.

Denenberg, B. (1997). *So far from home: The diary of Mary Driscoll, an Irish mill girl, Lowell, Massachusetts, 1847.* New York: Scholastic.

Filipovic, Z. (1994). *Zlata's diary.* London: Penguin.

Fleischner, J. (1997). *I was born a slave: The story of Harriet Jacobs.* Brookfield, CT: Millbrook.

Fritz, J. (1982). *Homesick: My own story.* New York: Putnam.

Giblin, J. C. (1997). *Charles A. Lindbergh: A human hero.* New York: Clarion Books.

Gold, A. L. (1997). *Memories of Anne Frank: Reflections of a childhood friend.* New York: Scholastic.

Graham, R. (1991). *Dove.* New York: HarperCollins.

Hansen, J. (1997). *I thought my soul would rise and fly: The diary of Patsy, a freed girl, Mars Bluff, South Carolina, 1865.* New York: Scholastic.

Hart, E. T. (1999). *Barefoot heart: Stories of a migrant child.* Tempe, AZ: Bilingual Press.

Hunter, L. (1992). *The diary of Latoya Hunter: My first year in junior high.* New York: Crown.

Jiang, J. L. (1997). *Red scarf girl: A memoir of the cultural revolution.* New York: HarperCollins.

Jiménez, F. (2001). *Breaking through.* Boston: Houghton Mifflin.

Lasky, K. (1996). *A journey to the new world: The diary of Remember Patience Whipple, Mayflower, 1620.* New York: Scholastic.

Lester, J. (1968). *To be a slave.* New York: Scholastic.

McGill, A. (1999). *Molly Bannaky.* Boston: Houghton Mifflin.

Myers, W. D. (1999). *The journal of Joshua Loper, a black cowboy.* New York: Scholastic.

Myers, W. D. (1999). *At Her Majesty's request: An African princess in Victorian England.* New York: Scholastic.

Severance, J. B. (1997). *Gandhi, great soul.* New York: Clarion Books.

Silverman, R. (1997). *A Bosnian family.* Minneapolis, MN: Lerner.

Simon, C. (1997). *Jane Addams: Pioneer social worker.* New York: Children's Press.

Stewart, W. (1997). *Aung San Suu Kyi: Fearless voice of Burma.* Minneapolis, MN: Lerner.

Talbott, H., & Greenberg, M. (1997). *Amazon diary: The jungle adventures of Alex Winters.* London: Viking/Puffin.

Turner, A. W. (1999) *The girl who chased away sorrow, the diary of Sarah Nita, a Navaho girl.* New York: Scholastic.

Turner, N. E. (1998). *These is my words: The diary of Sarah Agnes Prine, 1881–1901, Arizona Territories*. New York: Regan.

Warren, A. (1996). *Orphan Train rider: One boy's true story*. New York: Scholastic.

Wassiljewa, T. (1999). *Hostage to war: A true story*. New York: Scholastic.

Diverse Stories of Family Experience

Coman, C. (1995). *What Jamie saw*. New York: Puffin.

Couloumbis, A. (1999). *Getting near to baby*. New York: Putnam's Sons.

DiCamillo, K. (2001). *Because of Winn Dixie*. Cambridge, MA: Candlewick Press.

Ellis, D. (2000). *The breadwinner*. Toronto: Douglas & McIntyre.

Fox, P. (1999). *Radiance descending*. New York: Dell.

Hamilton, M. (1999). *The Garden of Eden Motel*. New York: Greenwillow.

Hobbs, V. (2000). *Charlie's run*. Thorndike, ME: Thorndike.

MacLachlan, P. (1988). *The facts and fictions of Minna Pratt*. Dubuque, NY: HarperTrophy.

MacLachlan, P. (1991). *Journey*. New York: Delacorte.

Meyer, C. (1997). *Jubilee journey*. San Diego: Harcourt Brace.

Myers, W. D. (1994). *Somewhere in the darkness*. New York: Scholastic.

Naidoo, B. (1999). *No turning back: A novel of South Africa*. New York: HarperTrophy.

Paulsen, G. (1999). *Alida's song*. New York: Delacorte.

Sanders, D. (1990). *Clover: A novel*. New York: Fawcett Columbine.

Sanders, D. (1994). *Her own place*. New York: Fawcett Columbine.

Voigt, C. (1984). *Dicey's song*. New York: Ballentine.

Nonfiction: Growing Up, Family, and Family Origins

Ancona, G (1989). *The American family farm: A photo essay*. (Text by Joan Anderson) San Diego: Harcourt Brace.

Birdseye, D., & Birdseye, T. (1997). *Under our skin: Kids talk about race*. New York: Holiday House.

Branch, M. (1995). *The water brought us: The story of the Gullah-speaking people*. New York: Cobblehill/Dutton.

Dolphin, L. (1997). *Our journey from Tibet: Based on a true story*. New York: Dutton

Gaskins, P. F. (1999). *What are you? Voices of mixed-race young people*. New York: Holt.

Giovanni, N. (1999). *Grandfathers: Reminiscences, poems, recipes and photos of the keepers of our traditions*. New York: Holt.

Greene, B., & Fulford, D.G. (1993). *To our children's children: Preserving family histories for generations to come.* New York: Doubleday.

Harness, C. (1995). *Three young pilgrims.* New York: Aladdin.

Lansky, B. (1998). *The very best baby name book in the whole wide world.* New York: Meadowbrook.

Lansky, B., & Sinrod, B. (1990). *The baby name personality survey.* New York: Meadowbrook.

Levine, E. (1997). *If your name was changed at Ellis Island.* Boston: Houghton Mifflin.

Peavy, L., & Smith, U. (1999). *Frontier children.* Norman, OK: University of Oklahoma Press.

Philip, N. (1997). *In a sacred manner I live: Native American wisdom.* New York: Clarion.

Rochman, H., & McCampbell, D. (1998). *Leaving home: Stories.* New York: HarperCollins.

Wilson, W., & Papadonis, J. (1996). *Ellis Island and beyond.* Portland, ME: Walch.

Wolfman, I. (1991). *Do people grow on family trees? Genealogy for kids and other beginners.* New York: Workman.

Magazines and Web Sites for Memoir and Family Origins

Biography Magazine (A&E Television Networks)
http://www.biography.com

Someone Born on this Day
http://www.ed.com/bio.html

Today in History (American Memory, Library of Congress)
http://lcweb2.loc.gov/ammem/today/today.html

Additional Readings for Teachers

Beaver, T. (1998). *The author's profile: Assessing writing in context.* York, ME: Stenhouse.

Bertrand, John E., & Stice, Carole F. (Eds.). (1995). *Empowering children at risk of school failure: A better way.* Norwood, MA: Christopher-Gordon.

Charney, Ruth S. (1992). *Teaching children to care: Management in the responsive classroom.* Greenfield, MA: Northeast Foundation for Children.

Frost, Helen. (2001). *When I whisper, nobody listens: Helping young people write about difficult issues.* Portsmouth, NH: Heinemann.

Grant, J., Heffler, B., & Mereweather, K. (1995). *Student-led conferences: Using portfolios to share learning with parents.* Markham, Ontario: Pembroke.

Green, A., & Lane, B. (1994). *The portfolio source book.* Shoreham, VT: The Vermont Portfolio Institute.

Lawrence-Lightfoot, S. (1999). *Respect: An exploration*. Reading, MA: Perseus Books.

Mueller, P. N. (2001). *Lifers: Learning from at-risk adolescent readers*. Portsmouth, NH: Heinemann.

Northeast Foundation for Children. *Responsive classroom: A newsletter for teachers*. [NEFC is a private nonprofit educational foundation. This excellent newsletter, full of ideas from classrooms through middle school, is free to teachers. Write Northeast Foundation for children, 71 Montague City Road, Greenfield, MA 01301 or go online at www.responsiveclassroom.org.]

Yancey, K. B. (Ed.). (1992). *Portfolios in the writing classroom: An introduction*. Urbana, IL: National Council of Teachers of English.

Materials for Teachers

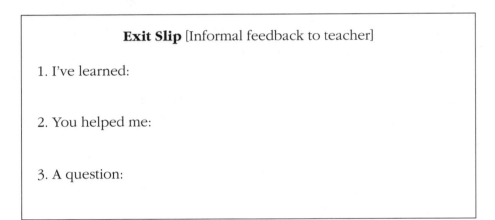

Exit Slip [Informal feedback to teacher]

1. I've learned:

2. You helped me:

3. A question:

My Goals for Second Nine Weeks

Name _____Date _____

Goals for writing this nine weeks:

1.

2.

3.

4.   ▶

Goals for reading this nine weeks:

1.

2.

3.

4.

Student signature _____

Teacher signature _____

Thinking about Your Learning [choose from this list to vary the reflection opportunities for students]

Name _____

What activities or topics have you liked best?

In what ways can you see yourself learning and growing? How can you tell?

What skills or strategies or activities have helped you learn, improve, or discover?

When do you most feel you are a valued and contributing person in this class?

What is confusing or difficult for you?

What do you feel you could do now or that you know now that you didn't a month ago?

How are writing conferences helpful for you?

with other students

with the teacher

Why is it valuable for students to save all parts of their writing, such as notebook entries, brainstorms, webs, drafts, responses, and finished graded pieces? ▶

What makes people valuable class members?

How would you rate the job you are doing?

Any other concerns or comments?

Building a Portfolio

First Quarter

What is a portfolio?

So far this year you have been asked to collect and save your writing. This writing includes your journals, reading responses, learning logs, and various pieces of writing at different stages, such as brainstorming and web prewrites, and also drafts and revisions. You have them in your notebook sections, in your class folders, and on disks.

Collecting your work is only the beginning. A portfolio is far more than merely building up a mass of work. A portfolio is a group of *selected* work—selected for different reasons to demonstrate your growth in different abilities. Creating a portfolio means thinking about the best features of a paper, an assignment, or a project, and then judging your work against those ideal standards.

How do you create a portfolio?

First, as you have already started to do, you save your work. If you haven't been keeping a running list of reports, tests, writing assignments, etc. on a sheet of notebook paper so that you'll have a quick overview of your work, you should do that now.

A second step is to find a general way to organize all your papers, putting sticky notes on places in papers where you thought you did a good job or tried something new. Also look for your weakest work that shows what you would like to improve.

Third, when you receive a list of portfolio requirements, you should group your completed assignments under the various categories given. This will help you study and consider which of your pieces of work might best fulfill a particular requirement of the portfolio.

Finally, write a reflection of how you made each choice, what you saw by looking at your work, and why or how your work completed the requirements of the portfolio.   ▶

What is self-assessment and how is it part of portfolios?
Learning to judge your work is called self-assessment. Understanding what makes a good piece of work and carefully examining your own work against the requirements or criteria of a model assignment take honesty and practice. Self-assessment is similar in some ways to reflection, but in assessment you have various standards and criteria to think about and compare your work to.

Remember, different portfolios will have different criteria or requirements, but all portfolios involve collecting, examining, making observations about, drawing conclusions about, and finding connections in your work, your learning, and your growth. You must be involved in thinking about and judging your own work if you want to improve. We all feel proud and successful when we improve.

First-Quarter Assessment Letter to Parents

Purpose: To explain what you've been doing and learning in language arts class.
Audience: Your parents or other adult.
Tone: Friendly, personal, and informational.
Format: Correct, friendly letter; see your text and other resources for format.
Content: (What this letter should include)*
　　First: An interesting opening and explanation of the purpose of the letter.
　　Next: A discussion of:
- ✓ The most important topics and ideas we have studied and used.
- ✓ The activities and types of activities that are frequent in this class.
- ✓ Something you have learned about:
  study habits
  reading strategies
  researching
  the writing process
- ✓ At least three new or improved skills that you are proud of.

▶

✓ Enjoyable books, stories, assignments, and projects that helped you grow.
✓ A connection between something in language arts and any other part of your life.
✓ The effort and work you have put into this quarter.
✓ Your goals for future report periods.

Then: A closing.

Finally: Enclose your best piece of writing with an explanation of why you think it's good.

*You may include or add anything else that is relevant to this class, your learning, and your growth.

Third-Quarter Letter to Parents

Purpose: To keep your family informed about your work and progress in language arts and to reflect on your growth.
Audience: Your parents or other adult.
Tone: Friendly, personal, thoughtful, informational.
Format: *Correct,* friendly letter; see text and previous letters you've written.
Process: Look through your notebook and folder to reflect on your accumulated work this year. Think of important accomplishments, skills, and knowledge connected to all aspects of your work in various classes this year. Look in your notebook and on the walls for lists of criteria.

As you study your work, make a jot list of examples and ideas about each of the following areas:

New subject knowledge and understanding.

Connections between subjects and between school and life.

Understanding and creating relationships with people: teachers, old and new friends, classmates, parents, and siblings.

Accepting responsibility for and/or leadership in work, learning, and behavior.

Being a good friend and better-informed community member.

Five new and/or improved skills that are helping you.   ▶

Now plan the organization of your letter.

Content

>Write about at least five (5) things you now know about being:

>>A writer

>>A reader

>>A researcher

>>A learner

>>A valuable, contributing classmate

>>A good friend

>Write about things you have enjoyed and/or felt proud of.

>Write an explanation of what has been difficult for you and how you have tried to or did overcome it.

>Write about plans, changes, and futures you now see for yourself.

Don't forget a last paragraph with a closing.

Parent or Other Adult Reader's Response to Writing

Name of Reader_____   Date _____

Name of Student Writer _____   Relationship _____

Title of Piece _____   Type of Writing_____

As you read this piece, consider the following features of good writing:

>Interesting topic

>Good beginning (states topic, purpose, and/or catches attention)

>Organized (paragraphing; definite beginning, middle, end)

>Details, examples, and description

>Smooth and flowing (sequential, logical, uses transitions)

>Sentence completeness and variety

>Specific and vivid word choice (possibly sensory or figurative language or dialogue)

▶

Correctness (spelling, punctuation, usage, capitalization)

Voice (sounds like a real person experienced and wrote this for a definite audience)

What did you notice that you liked?

Was there a message, purpose, or appeal that was clear in this piece?

What did you think showed the author had grown as a more skilled or capable writer and user of language?

What would you have liked to see the author add, develop, or change?

How would you rate this author's accuracy in language use and correctness of language conventions?

Did anything about this piece or the assignment surprise you?

4 Inquiry: Noticing, Questioning, Searching, and Caring

Inquiry is a deliberate exploration of the delicious tension that unsatisfied curiosity creates in all of us.

Caroline Owens, "Inquiry Is . . . What?"

CHAPTER OVERVIEW

After providing a real life example of student-centered inquiry at work in one of Betty's classes, this chapter begins with a conceptual framework for classroom inquiry. The nature of student inquiry in a socially conscious curriculum is explored, including the ways in which an inquiry stance grows out of and contributes to different kinds of instructional activities. What kinds of questions do students raise about social issues, and what do you do with them once they are asked? How do questions turn into organized investigations? How can a teacher consciously stimulate students who are not eager to raise and pursue their own questions? And how do you encourage inquiry while still meeting grade-level requirements?

Betty found that she had to work hard at the beginning of the year to overcome student inertia, and we discuss concrete strategies for building the habits of inquiry into literature responses and journals. We then offer sections on the inquiry processes of interviewing and I-Search projects (or expert projects), with suggestions for coaching lessons, response to student work, and assessment.

A Story of Student Curiosity

It was a sunny southern October day as the bus pulled off into the weeds at the edge of a country road not too far from our suburban school. The doors opened and fifty seventh graders piled out. The sheer joy of being outside sent them swarming over the field and the small cemetery we had come to visit, leaping and calling to each other. Betty was afraid their exuberance would turn disrespectful and offend our guide. But soon the students began to move around the gravestones, kneeling to look for dates and other clues about who was buried here. "Hey, look! This one's really old! I can't even see a date. Here's one from the forties! Oh, no, a baby! Come here, Mrs. Slesinger, I think this must be a mother and a baby."

Students had suggested this field trip when they were reading *The Secret of Gumbo Grove* (Tate), a historical novel featuring South Carolina coastal African American heritage. At first they weren't very sympathetic with the teenage protagonist Raisin's investigation of the gravestones of Gumbo Grove, a small African American enclave surrounded by the beach tourist businesses geared to the white residents. Raisin might believe she can find clues to the past of her community, but, really, cemeteries are dull, just a bunch of stones. The students perked up when Betty shared what she had learned about local gravesites. An anthropologist had informed teachers about where Union soldiers had camped and were buried near their school. "Right here, Mrs. Slesinger? I want to see that." The shadowy romance of the past began to capture their imaginations. What secrets might their local gravestones reveal? Ron asked, "Why can't we visit a cemetery around here, Mrs. Slesinger, and see if there are any old-time graves?"

Unable to resist this early sign of an inquiry stance, Betty began the tedious task of organizing a trip. Mrs. Baker, the team custodian, overheard us wondering what to do and told us about her African Methodist Episcopal (AME) church that had an old cemetery in the country. Then Leigh, in the honors class, heard about the planned expedition and offered her father, a Lutheran pastor, as a tour guide of the oldest neighboring Lutheran cemetery. The students were ready to go! A list of their questions was turned into a data collection sheet (see Materials for Teachers at the end of the chapter). Then, paperwork and permissions completed, two classes of seventh graders, Mrs. Baker, and Betty ventured out in search of secrets of the past.

When Allison suddenly looked around the open field and asked, "Why isn't there a church here?" Mrs. Baker explained that her church had moved closer to town long ago, but some of the families had continued to bury their members here. Sure enough, students found dates as old as the 1800s and as new as the Gulf War. They saw that many of the markers were sunken and crumbling with age, and they knelt down, running their fingers over the worn stones and bronze plaques to tease out their secrets. Without an active congregation to give regular attention to the site, weeds and tree roots from the surrounding pasture and woods had encroached on the stones.

Clutching their clipboards, the children piled onto the bus, which deposited them at the local Lutheran church. The minister took the group inside for more lessons in the history of their community. This church had also moved, but not by choice of the parishioners. When the TWA built a dam and created our huge local lake, vast new resources of electrical power were created, but hundreds of families who had lived in the now-flooded valley were uprooted. Two years before, one of Betty's classes had studied the lake's history, so she was ready with photos and articles that showed the wooden buildings down in the valley and the half-finished dam.

Perhaps due to different traditions or the greater affluence of a white South Carolina congregation, this cemetery was formally laid out with stone paths, well-tended shade trees, and orderly blocks of stones. But the past lingered here in a corner filled with the worn stones from the old flooded cemetery. Now the students were more experienced cemetery inquirers; they quickly found the oldest and newest deaths and began to use dates and ages to figure out causes of death. They recorded the epitaphs that caught their interest, as well as biblical quotes and sentiments that seemed exotic to their modern eyes.

Betty took their data sheets home and compiled statistics—such as years with high rates of death combined with the age of deaths—to help students piece together some significant insights about human life revealed in the cemetery data. In the follow-up discussion, students could see a cluster of adult male deaths around 1939 (workers on the dam, including non-church members), a cluster of deaths of people of all ages around 1918 (influenza after World War I), and male deaths from the Vietnam War. They could see the decrease in children's deaths in modern times. They realized that their town was more than its glitzy mall; it had a history, and people had struggled to make a community there. Ultimately, they saw that it is possible to learn about social conditions from the artifacts of history.

Then students returned to their novel reading with increased interest to see what the protagonist Raisin would discover in her town's graveyard, and their newly gained firsthand perspectives found their way into more energetic literature log entries.

How We Understand Inquiry

Inquiry is not a specific kind of assignment. Rather, it is a stance that, as the chapter epigraph by Caroline Owens states, is brought into operation by the "unsatisfied curiosity" of a student. When people are curious, they think differently about the world around them because they are looking for clues and hints that will provide answers. We would all agree that inquiring is a natural process of humanity, but teachers know that it is not a natural process at all in a middle school. If you want your students to follow the paths of their curiosity, you have to work hard to make it happen.

Although in the long run students will find that active learning is deeply satisfying, in the short run they find it difficult to open up to all the uncertainties of new classroom roles. By the seventh grade, students have become comfortable keeping their wondering in the closet. They find it hard to abandon their successful strategy of risk avoidance. The relaxed lounger who knows how to get by, the disorganized kid who happily announces that he has no paper, the neat and organized note-taker, the bright memorizer, the fast finisher—all of them have a lot to lose. By middle school, students know that the penalties for trying and failing at school are real and painful. It is better to hold back and be safe.

Those of us who have tried to create active classrooms in the middle school know the frustration of student resistance, and we frequently yearn to be third-grade teachers with only one class and no student hormonal extremes. In the pressures of middle school, teachers find it hard to give up their successful routines and strategies for something new that might not work. On days when it is difficult even to get students' attention, inquiry in the middle school classroom can seem like an unrealizable dream.

Although the principles of inquiry are the same for all ages, adapting them to the schedules, curriculum requirements, and developmental characteristics of middle school felt like pioneering. The work of many others helped us see what we might do. We began by borrowing powerful models and examples of inquiry from elementary school teachers. The work of Carolyn Burke, Jerry Harste, Donald Graves, Kathy Short, Karen Smith, Heidi Mills, and Tim O'Keefe was particularly helpful. Middle school perspectives from Nancie Atwell, Ken Macrorie, and Jeffrey Wilhelm were also important. Betty felt her way in small steps. We had to let go of a tendency to blame the developmental stage of the students when the going was difficult. Yes, seventh graders are often selfish, materialistic, forgetful, and emotionally unstable, and prefer above all else to socialize with their friends. It isn't easy to envision a classroom full of powerful inquirers when what you actually see before you are the slackers and the cautious note-takers.

As Betty began changing her assignments in the direction of question asking and individual construction of ideas, we came to understand better the vulnerability of adolescent learners, and we began to view their inertia in the light of their many fears. We recognized the benefits of their boundless energy and quick empathy for those in need. A few successes, especially the World War II unit, gave us the energy to seek ways to extend the excitement to other topics and units of work. Each year Betty added and altered strategies. Gradually, throughout the school year, curiosity and initiative became more normal ways of learning. Many students were truly interested in trying to understand this strange and troubling society we live in, and with Betty's praise and encouragement, students found the courage to move forward.

When Inquiry Is Authentic

The process of inquiry is a fluid and interconnected whole that is intimately connected with people's lives. New experiences that are intriguing or troubling lead to wondering and searching for ways to understand. The impulse to understand is ultimately an individual one, but it is stimulated and nurtured by social interaction. Individual inquirers are stronger when they belong to a group of learners who are also asking questions and who respond, extend, and challenge one another.

Effective classroom inquiry requires more than simply following an impulse to question. Finding answers and achieving new understanding depend on having access to many different sources of information, knowing how to use these sources, knowing how to connect fragmented insights, and having opportunities to test tentative conclusions with others. Inquiry depends on having a chance to follow new questions that arise and on caring about the answers. Inquiry will persist when students feel that both the process and the results make a real contribution to their lives.

The framework for classroom inquiry presented in Figure 4.1 represents the principles we worked with as we thought about how to make inquiry happen in Betty's classroom—intriguing or puzzling experiences, encouragement of individual perspectives within an active learning community, access to multiple sources and kinds of sources, strategies of investigation and analysis, utility of results, and openness to new investigations. This framework was radically different from the standard language arts curriculum. How was Betty to "cover" the language arts standards for seventh grade and still be true to her beliefs about the nature of authentic inquiry? The curriculum model described in Chapter 1 provided an organizational structure for planning such a challenging agenda. This model helped Betty know when to encourage individual investigations and when to plan teacher-guided whole class inquiry sessions. It helped her see that some investigations are brief and tentative, while others are more extensive. Sometimes investigation involves asking questions about language patterns in spelling; sometimes it's a group survey about racism; and sometimes it's a field trip to the cemetery.

Our inquiries come from our experiences. The questions on which our inquiries are based come from observations and experiences, especially when our lives rub against the lives of others in literature and reality. The roles we see in our future stimulated questions for inquiry.

We begin our inquiries as general explorations. At first the search may be unfocused, but then patterns or questions emerge that target our attention to certain aspects of our inquiry.

The driving questions are our own. Even though others may support or limit the scope of our investigations, gathering information is a highly personal process that is propelled by individual curiosity.

We use many different sources of information. Most of us begin our inquiries by probing the resources available close to home, including our colleagues, and then broadening our search to include visits to other sites, reading additional texts, and consulting with experts in the field.

Others have a part in our work. Fellow learners and friends are sources of stimulation, information, response, support, and challenge as we struggle to understand the object of our inquiry.

We use our findings. Inquiries arise from real situations, and the results make a dynamic contribution to our lives through real actions and new relationships.

Inquiries arouse further curiosity. One question rarely stands alone. The findings of an inquiry allow us to enter future investigations with greater knowledge of both our subject and our resources, making each related inquiry easier and more productive than those that came before.

Figure 4.1. A framework for classroom inquiry. Adapted from Caroline Owens, 1996.

Packaged versus Authentic Questions

A packaged curriculum that encourages student investigation based on short-term, teacher-structured, "higher-order thinking" assignments seriously limits students' potential for inquiry. Betty tried special programs that were planned to lead students systematically from factual thinking to questions of synthesis and evaluation but found these hierarchical plans for stimulating questioning too constricting. She tried using the end-of-story questions in the literature book, but few of them were valuable for stimulating thinking. Canned "questioning" programs usually require from students instant responses to small bits of information, when what students need is time for important questions to emerge. We saw that thinking at higher levels developed from personal questions, accumulated knowledge, and opportunities to use this knowledge in various ways, not from one-shot activities.

In a unit of inquiry, students needed to come to questions on their own timetable. It's not a matter of moving up Bloom's taxonomy step by step. We watched some students leap to deep searching questions almost as soon as they approached a new topic, while others lingered to gather facts before they raised analytical or broad conceptual questions. And students needed to move back and forth between literal and critical questions throughout a unit of inquiry. Learning returned to the factual and experiential level when new information was needed to make connections, inferences, and judgments. At any time, students might need more information to make connections and thoughtful extensions. They did not stop needing facts just because they had developed a critical stance to write an editorial.

Using the Results of Student Inquiry

Questions emerged and led to further learning in many different ways. Betty used the students' questions to stimulate discussion, guide research, and lead to new integration of understandings. She wanted questions to be *useful.*

Betty initiated discussions with questions and made a habit of soliciting new questions as students discussed, but she did not tell them what questions were important. She frequently shared her own wondering. She decided to nudge the students into more assertive inquiry by requiring them to ask questions as part of their literature journals and reflections. We wanted to know what the students would be curious or concerned about as they came up against troubling issues of human life.

We worried that requiring student questions might destroy their authenticity, but on the other hand, the requirement might help overcome student inertia until a desire to investigate could develop. Betty did not want to create a curriculum in which only the most academic students participated. After the first marking period, which Betty felt was a struggle, students seemed to accept that they would write down their wondering in their journal entries, and they freely raised questions in literature discussions. Questions were encouraged in all of their work, not just within the units of social inquiry. Betty wanted to make questioning a habitual way of working together.

When students were engaged in the inquiry units, their questions were a thread that tied activities together. Again and again, the results of individual research were shared in various ways with peers so that each student made a contribution of expertise to the entire class. When they shared, they all benefited from one another's work, including the less able students. The process seemed more authentic, more like what happens in the real world.

Sharing individual research became a major strategy to keep a whole class of students with different levels of ability active as learners. It also

provided a structure that honored both individual initiative and cooperative responsibility for learning. In the descriptions of two inquiry units
(Chapters 2 and 5), readers can see some ways that student research was
integrated with the other processes of learning. Following is a summary
of strategies to help students share the results of their investigations with
one another:

- Compile a list of questions about factual background raised by
  students in their literature journals, and assign two to three questions per student for research to be shared with the class.

- Have students browse in informational books and write on sticky
  notes questions to be assigned for research. Leave sticky notes on
  book covers if the browsing continues over several days.

- Involve students in creating a knowledge wall, where facts can be
  posted in categories as questions are answered. Include a section
  for new questions.

- Help students create a class encyclopedia, with information gathered on subtopics entered under categories. Make the encyclopedia available—on either hard copy, an accessible computer, or a
  computer disk—as context for student writing projects.

- Put a compiled list of information, gathered from individual "what
  I learned" exit slips, on an overhead. Share with the class to discuss, categorize, rate by importance, web, or use as a support for
  writing. Distribute copies as test study guides.

- Have students share research findings in small groups. Create a
  composite list of key ideas to be shared with the rest of the class.

- Involve students in sending information outside the classroom to
  someone who needs to know.

- Have students create visuals of the results of surveys and questionnaires, share them with peers and other classes, and display
  them in the hallways.

Inquiry and Curriculum Requirements

It seemed that the more Betty moved her curriculum from personal
authoring cycles toward societal investigations, the more excited the students got about being effective readers and writers. Problematic social
realities captured their interest, and they wanted to communicate their
opinions to others. These students, poised on the brink of adulthood, were
more eager to explore the contradictions and mysteries of adult life in a text
set than they were to move from story to story in the literature anthology.

Shifting the focus to social inquiry did not crowd out the required curriculum. Conflict and survival in times of social crisis had a strong authentic

pull on student engagement. The habit of recording questions as they read helped weaker students persist through difficult texts, and hearing their peers' questions helped them find their own. Reviewing their questions helped Betty know what kind of support students needed, so many of the students improved as readers as a result of taking more control of their learning. And students found that they *needed* the skills of the language arts curriculum to learn about and express their strong feelings about social issues. When, for example, they took a critical stance toward issues of their own world of schooling and wrote letters to school administrators, they were suddenly interested in paying attention to the format, punctuation, sentence construction, and other skills of the seventh-grade curriculum. It was actually easier than before to teach some of the required language arts objectives.

Kinds of Questions

A curriculum that addresses social issues should provide a fertile environment for the sometimes messy process of wondering. In the flow of journals that passed through Betty's hands each week, she could see that students were raising questions. And in discussions, the pursuit of ideas seemed stronger. It was not, however, easy to tell what the questions meant to students' learning. We had to relax and trust in our belief in the value of personal inquiry.

Sometimes questions emerged that were so obviously significant that they influenced subsequent student work. Betty remembers the day that Jack, after a discussion of *Roll of Thunder, Hear My Cry* (Taylor), blurted out, "Is there ever a good reason for segregation?" The class was silent at first, and then students tentatively began to think back over all their amassed knowledge for answers. Jack's question was an important moment that raised the level of the conversation. Next year, at the end of the Depression-era unit when the class was reflecting on all they had learned, Colleen was trying to think about the large cumulative effects of economics on society when she said, "I have to ask one more question. So, how long was it until we really could say we were out of the Depression?" This question provided a perfect entrée into the World War II unit, which was the next planned topic that year. It also offered an opportunity to talk about cause and effect on a large historical scale.

During the World War II unit one year, we monitored as best we could the students' written work, discussions, and conversations (Busching & Slesinger, 1995). As we reviewed the piles of photocopied journals, papers, and reflections and listened to tapes of discussions, we began by assuming that we should categorize questions in terms of Bloom's taxonomy. Soon we realized that the so-called "level of thinking" represented in the taxonomy revealed only the *form* of the question, not the *kind* of thinking the student was doing. It was more productive for us to try to figure out how the questions were being *used*. Therefore, what the students were doing with the questions became the focus of our study. We found the following eight different kinds of questions asked during that inquiry unit, and continued to find these kinds of questions as students inquired into social conflicts and problems:

Kinds of Questions Asked by Students

Unfocused information-seeking questions. Asked whenever a new text/video/interview puzzled or confused students. These questions revealed to us the benefits of students being simultaneously engaged in factual and in fictional texts. Examples: Where in Germany are they? Who were the people that spoke differently? [about the town in the book *Rose Blanche*] What does the star symbolize? What happened in the camps? What was a sharecropper? What caused the Dust Bowl?

Required questions. Asked to fulfill an assignment. Students confessed that they asked these questions in response journals at the beginning of a novel, before they were engaged with the characters. Examples: Is it safe for someone so young to be flying that much? How long will his luck last? [about a character in a novel about World War II pilots]

Focused information-seeking questions. Asked when students had a base of understanding and were looking to fill in the holes. These questions revealed to us that facts offer conceptual power and do not always precede theories. Specific factual questions can provide the basis for testing broad theories and beliefs. Examples: Who helped the Jews, and what happened to them? Why is there a neo-Nazi movement, and what does it want? How were Spitfires different from other aircraft? What race do you think Cassie's teacher was? [in *Roll of Thunder*] Why was Black Thursday important? What is trading on the margin?

Questions of connected understanding. Asked when students were extending an already rich understanding of the topic. These questions probed into motivations and causes and tended to ask "how" and "why." Examples: Why did Germany go to war again so soon after World War I? How can you invade if you don't have any bases to supply you? Why didn't the police stop the nightriders? Do you think the Logans [in *Roll of Thunder*] were strong in dealing with their problems?

Speculative questions. Asked when students had built an understanding of events and wondered how events could have been different.

These questions are important for a democracy because they encourage citizens to imagine different outcomes. Students who can imagine different historical results may be able to imagine changes in the present. It is the recognition of alternatives that lead citizens to question the status quo. Examples: What if Dunkirk had failed? What if the Confederates had won at Gettysburg?

Questions of psychological imagination and moral commitment. Asked when students had constructed an understanding of events and were emotionally involved. They showed empathy for characters and outrage against injustice. Students were trying to construct understandings of humanity that encompassed both kindness and brutality. Examples: How could Nazis threaten people so horribly? How could anyone follow a man who burned books? Are we really that inhuman? Why did the author write this book?

Unspoken questions. Seemed to be on students' minds when engagement with a topic had connected with personal fears too difficult to state openly. Underneath some journal entries or private conversations with the teacher seemed to be questions about perceived prejudice against themselves or fears of homelessness and abuse. Examples: A student who privately shared with Betty in her journal that her father had lost his job, and she wondered if they could become homeless. The boy who asked Betty one to one as he was leaving class if kids could scapegoat other kids like the Nazis did the Jews.

Questions of a literary nature. Asked as a stylistic device to enliven essays and stories. These questions often dramatically focused reader attention on the central concerns of student papers. Examples: Dear Anne [Frank]: When did you begin to write your journal? Did anyone inspire you to write? To end an essay: The end. Or is it the beginning?

Questions to focus research. Asked as a way to structure a survey or interview. Students worked to find personally relevant questions to ask in their own school or community. Examples: What can you and others do to stop hatred? What is the connection between rap music and violence?

The First Steps of the Year: Activating the Inquiry Impulse

At the beginning of the year, Betty looked for moments when the students were emotionally engaged and someone had raised a good question or suggested a new perspective to reflect back to students the effective strategies of empowered learners. She hoped this would increase their awareness of what inquirers do and help them value their own ideas. Each instance was a small opportunity to strengthen or weaken the impulse to wonder and question.

Inquiring into the New Middle School Context

Taking advantage of student uncertainties in a new grade, Betty created a small project around school life in order to teach some inquiry strategies and help students feel a sense of community. She started in a simple way by inviting students to write a question about her or the class in their exit slips at the end of the period. After several days, she categorized the questions and answered them on a chart—what she liked to do away from school, what her husband did, why she made them keep journals, and so forth.

Students saw real results from their questions: their teacher paid attention to what they wondered about. There was indeed social utility in asking questions. They learned about Betty as a real person, with individual preferences and life experiences, and as a lover of literacy. Perhaps they felt more comfortable in the class. This personal interaction gave Betty the opportunity to present her beliefs about responsible and active learning while she answered questions about her assignments. Her responses introduced a language that would enable the class to talk about learning—*resourcefulness, support, collaboration, wondering, initiative.*

To extend the questioning and interviewing process, students then paired up with someone they didn't know and asked each other the questions they had prepared, writing informal reports. Once the reports were completed and edited, copies were placed in a three-ring binder for the class. Kids passed it around in their free moments and became better acquainted with one another. So, with these initial examples of what Betty hoped would become habit—actively following their curiosity—students had begun in the first few days of school what would be a yearlong dialogue about their learning.

To encourage more reflective dialogue about school and students' concerns, Betty assigned students to observe and critique how their school operated and how kids acted. Some took notes, and a quickwrite helped them gather their thoughts. In the discussion of their observations, students were able to voice many complaints about the behavior of abusive students and about what was expected of them in seventh grade: how big and heavy the literature anthology was; kids who made the bathrooms disgusting for everyone else; people who always wanted to borrow stuff; line cutters; kids who said ugly things to others; kids who fought; teachers who gave major tests when another teacher's big project was due.

Students then turned these observations into poetry. To warm them up, Betty read some humorous poetry and led a short discussion of the qualities they had noticed. Some of the students who had been busily exuding nonverbal rejection of school woke up long enough to write some

What is a middle schooler
I was asked one day.
I knew what she was
But what should I say?
She is as shiny as the sun,
She is a thinker who flies.
She is not sure at all
For she lies and lies.

Amelia

Figure 4.2. A student poem revealed the underlying tensions of a middle schooler.

lively complaint poems. Most of the poems were light and playful, but others revealed hints of the anxieties that students carry around with them (see Figure 4.2). Betty thought that the opportunity to vent openly and share at least hints of deeper concerns created a sense of safety in the classroom community that could give students confidence to join in a dialogue of inquiry.

Activating an Inquiry Stance through Literature

Betty introduced students to several novels and short stories at the beginning of the year to initiate a discussion of how different people learn in different ways and how learners can be supported or hindered. Through imaginary characters, students encountered some of the controversies about learning in our culture. Daniel Keyes's *Flowers for Algernon* not only shows the heartrending struggles of Charlie as he finds, but then loses, his intelligence, but also the rather brutal attitudes of others toward him. Ron Jones's *The Acorn People,* equally touching, follows a cabin of physically handicapped kid campers through the summer. Some have no legs, others are incontinent or unable to feed themselves. After their initial disgust, our students cheered as this crew of society's misfits overcame repressive edicts from the camp director.

Besides the emotional draw of these novels and the social issues they highlight, their journal-type formats provided models for students' own response notebooks. As students read, they were learning inquiry strategies for literature journals and discussions. They were surprisingly anxious about sharing their questions and interpretations publicly. Discovering that other students had similar reactions to the readings, however, encouraged the more reluctant students. All of them needed Betty to join in the conversations to show explicitly that she valued their questions and comments.

The students were simultaneously strengthening their own learning strategies and taking a critical look at how our society treats people with learning problems. As they discussed the ways characters solved problems, students analyzed themselves as problem solvers. Betty listed their ideas on the overhead, and they thought about goals for themselves in this new year of middle school. Each student made a personal list of goals, and sentence strips of their "hints for improvement" were hung from the ceiling. Starting with a discussion about someone else's problem, and then thinking how they might solve their own problems, was more palatable for these self-conscious students than having the teacher point out their weaknesses.

Other texts that raised issues of the social limits imposed on learners were Kurt Vonnegut's "Harrison Bergeron" and Karen Hesse's *Music of the Dolphins*. Through texts such as these, students could explore personal issues of learning such as what makes people lose confidence in themselves. It set the stage for them to think about their own learning (reflection) and to document their growth over time (portfolios). They also confronted society's definitions of ability and how society can support or diminish a learner's possibilities. Students were exposed to different kinds of intelligence and ability as Betty presented Gardner's range of intelligences and pointed out that the standardized tests students took in school tested only that narrow range of verbal ability traditionally recognized as academic indicators of intelligence. She wanted them to be better informed about the testing structures that ruled much of their school lives and to value their other abilities.

Journals—the Backbone of Inquiry

A strong democracy needs a multitude of strong voices. To have a voice that makes a difference in society, citizens need more than concern and awareness: they need the confidence and the skills to speak out. Once Betty starting thinking about the implications of nurturing the public voice of students, the role of the focused journal—or research journal or writing notebook—in her classes loomed larger than ever before. Journals can give students a safe place to develop that ability for speaking out.

Betty viewed journal keeping as a long-term process of changing habits—habits of noticing and thinking, habits of believing in themselves, habits of using time well, habits of writing. Students need conscious, channeled habits of the mind and literacy that will push them toward inquiry and self-examination and help them connect with the world. Betty wanted them to do more than complete an assignment or jot down private thoughts. She wanted them to use the journals as a place to stretch their thinking and to value the process of "growing" ideas.

As discussed earlier in the chapter, students' journal entries were the foundation for many other classroom activities. Students used their response journals for many purposes—to accumulate background knowledge ("List the facts about Gary Paulsen's life that you think influenced what he writes about"); stimulate discussions ("Write questions about *When the Stars Begin to Fall* that would help a reader think more about the characters"); and prepare for more formal writing ("List facts from your article about homelessness to use in your opinion paper").

In the social issues inquiry units, response journals were the backbone of the first three phases of work: Entering into the Topic, Guided Explorations, and Focused Engagements. There was never enough time for long, satisfying discussions of all the articles, stories, novels, Web sites, poems, and songs students discovered during their inquiry; brief journal responses, completed in class or at home, enabled the students to recapture their thoughts for the integrative, more finished writing and for projects at the end of the unit.

Getting Started with Journals

Needless to say, most of Betty's seventh graders did not share her lofty aims for journal writing or her love of notebook keeping. Early entries tended to be minimal. Students tried to make artistic titles stand for ideas and filled the air with their complaints when Betty called them on it. Almost none of them came to her experienced in using writing as a process for generating and developing ideas, and they lacked an awareness of what writing could do for their learning. Few of the students had saved and reflected on their writing over time. They did not understand that writing mirrors and enhances what they know, think, and feel, and that writing gives them a voice in the world. Some students were overwhelmed and at a loss. They had never been expected to generate so much written material themselves.

Betty offered the students a variety of activities that would push them toward belief in themselves and the value of their ideas:

- **She provided materials with which students could personalize their notebook covers.** We were amused to see most girls' notebook covers filled with photos of togetherness (pets, pals, siblings, kindergarten graduation, birthday parties), whereas most boys made robust covers featuring jazzy images of sports and music groups, with more symbols than photos.

- **She shared herself as a notebook keeper.** Betty read from her entries from a summer literature class and from discussions with Beverly. She shared *why* she had made certain entries.

- **She gave encouragement, suggestions, and lavish praise for progress.** Now was the time for recognition of any steps toward insightful and individual ideas.

- **She led brainstorming sessions to help students generate lists of possible topics.** Although the memoir and autobiographical pieces students were reading in their anthologies were helpful demonstrations, Betty wanted more variety. She shared samples of famous journals and talked about the reasons why these people kept journals.

- **She continually gave minilessons featuring appreciative analysis of interesting entries.** In these coaching lessons, Betty could show her belief in the students' potential, conveying positive expectations for growth rather than negative assessments. She showed (with anonymous samples or by permission) how students could ask questions, verbalize confusions, try out different points of view, practice skills and literary elements, and make assessments of their learning.

- **She wrote personal responses to journal entries.** Her responses showed appreciation for their insights, altruistic impulses, and signs of growing maturity. She often asked questions and gave reading suggestions.

Learning from Published Journals

Students were interested in excerpts from famous journal keepers such as Anne Frank and Christopher Columbus (see Additional Literature for Students in Chapter 3). Betty invited the students to look with her at how the person kept a journal and how the content was influenced by the purposes for the journal. *Flowers for Algernon* and *The Acorn People* are both written in the form of diary entries and are full of honest inquiry into life circumstances as the characters raise questions about how people are treated.

One of the most compelling diaries available in the classroom library was the wartime diary of Zlata Filipovic, a young Bosnian teen. This diary helped convey the potential of a personal journal to make a lasting contribution. Zlata says that she was inspired by the diaries of Anne Frank and Adrian Mole, and she shares what her diary meant to her:

> I started writing my own diary before the war in Bosnia because I wanted to have a place to record my childhood and create something that I could look back on and laugh, cry and reminisce. I wanted to see myself grow through my writing. I never dreamed that my childhood would be cut short. (Freedom Writers, 1999, p. xiii)

As students listened to the courage of these writers to reveal their intimate feelings and adversities, they may have gathered courage to make their own entries more honest and heartfelt. In one entry, Betty read:

> A time I really grew up was when I realized that my mother didn't have enough money to buy us everything we need. Like, I wanted some Adidas shoes and some hair paint, but I wasn't going to ask my mom because I knew that it was going to hurt my mom's feelings because she didn't have the money to get them for me.
>
> [Betty's response: *You love your mom and respect her if you realize this, and you are grown up!*]

Eyes on the World: No Longer a Personal Journal

After the first few weeks of writing about themselves and family events, students were pulled into other subjects in the inquiry units. Students made entries about topics in the news, for example, when they were conducting a media watch, and later they looked for people who contributed to or threatened our democracy, as described in Chapter 8. They reacted to their literature from and about World War II and the Depression era, and they wrote about their school surveys on racism.

Quality of Entries

Coaching lessons to help students make their thinking more compelling continued throughout the year. In the Materials for Teachers section at the end of the chapter is a list of alternative formats for stimulating different kinds of thinking or preserving thought. These are alternatives writers can reach for when needed, such as using multiple sign systems and genres to find different perspectives on a topic. Sometimes Betty gave such a list to students as possibilities to be placed in a notebook for future use.

To encourage students to value their journals, Betty would mention that discussions seemed livelier because they had prepared ideas ahead of time. She helped students hunt through their journal entries to find ideas for finished pieces of writing. Reflections and goal setting also went into the journals, and sometimes they served as planning for projects such as interviews or puppet shows.

Managing the Burden of Response

Although teachers know that response is needed to keep student journals alive, 70 to 125 students writing in journals was a monumental and frustrating load. Betty recalls, "More than once I've wanted to give up on the journals. Fortunately, I've always reconsidered. Instead of abandoning them, what I need are ways to simplify procedural problems."

Betty experimented with a variety of management routines, such as using a journal crate for each class and keeping them in the room, or using three-ring binders so that individual pages can be turned in rather than whole journals. Literature study groups sometimes kept one group log. Betty sometimes checked and responded to the journals of only one or two classes a week, doing several entries for one student at a time. Or she asked students to reread the last five entries and mark the page of the most significant to share with her. Students responded to each other's journals or took them home for parent response. When students brought journals to a literature discussion, Betty's personal response was not always necessary.

Honors classes tended to need little or no help with journal management, whereas other classes benefited from strict monitoring. Betty used a variety of grading routines, usually with a point system that at the beginning of the year gave credit for simply doing the entry and that later added points and criteria for quality entries.

Interviews: Inquiry across the Generations

Students found great satisfaction in the face-to-face interactions that interviewing promotes. There were endless possibilities for discovery and for expanding students' personal contacts with active adults—authors, lunchroom cooks, historians, health care activists, city council members, and even homeless people. It was time-consuming to scout out and set up visits from experts, but the benefits make the effort of tracking down willing visitors worthwhile. Both parties can be energized by the surprises of cross-generational communication. When it was impossible to include all the students in a session with an expert, those attending could be responsible for collecting new information and sharing it in published notes, newspaper format, or simple oral summaries.

Interviews: A Personal Experience with Social Issues

The beginning-of-the-year peer interviews were important for community building and for helping the students learn good questioning and organizing skills. Interviews became a primary research methodology, repeatedly used during the year, so students developed confidence and competent techniques. Interviews allowed less book-oriented students to become actively involved in learning.

When she reviewed a set of family interviews that students had gathered during the World War II unit, Betty appreciated the educational power of interviews: "I just sat there, reading and rereading, with the students' work spread out all around me. There was so much informational learning there! The scope and detail of many interviews really exceeded the contents of their social studies texts." Descriptions of the war abounded, not just in the main World War II countries such as Germany and France, but also in countries more peripheral to the war such as China, Greenland, Ceylon, and Greece. Students found out about air raids, blackouts, rationing, war bonds, and collecting aluminum. They learned that the war effort was about more than soldiers; it also included lumberjacks, mill workers, farmers, and other ordinary citizens.

Like all of us, the students were hooked on stories, and the emotional pull of their family stories drew them into an exploration of history. Some of the students became personally interested in the World War II study only when they discovered their family connection. Now they were insiders in history and they liked the feeling. Now Tom paid attention to where Poland was: his grandfather had walked on muddy roads there. These were not just personal histories, but history in a larger sense. They were not just history, but history living in the lives of real people. Students' relatives had spanned the globe during the war years, and their stories brought to life parts of the world that to the students were just pink and yellow spots on the map. Fragmented facts were connected into larger cultural forces. Betty began to see interviews as a major part of her instruction, instruction through the power of preadolescent inquiry, independent of the school, with parents as learning resources.

Interviews seemed to be the glue that united feelings and ideas and helped students care about history. After the interviews, when we asked students if any of the novels they had read had exaggerated conditions, there was general agreement that they had proof of similar events in the lives of relatives and friends. "I talked to real people that actually lived through the things that happened," Becca reflected. "It's really true, my great-uncle was there," Jake blurted out one day.

Relationships with Relatives

Several parents made a point of thanking Betty for these assignments because they stimulated positive family interactions at home. Some families were fragmented by divorce or work schedules, or struggled with chaotic schedules. It was not easy to maintain warm relationships with their volatile preadolescent children. "It seems hard even to have a positive conversation," one parent confessed. "I'm either trying to get him to pick up his room or turn down the music. But when he had to do the interview, and my

dad began talking about going off to France, Joe and I were both fascinated. I went to dig out some old photographs. It was just a happy family
time." Relatives appreciated being asked to be learning resources and being brought into their children's school lives.

Students also seemed pleased by their new connections to family
members. They excitedly shared letters they had received and reported
that they were allowed to call relatives long distance. Matt said, "I don't
mind this assignment because at least it gives me something to talk to my
parents about at dinner." Some of the students provided loving tributes to
their relatives while recounting the stories they had been told, as in Jake's
reflection:

> . . . I learned from my grandfather that if you listen to someone who
> has been around you can learn a lot. He taught me that listening is
> just as important as talking.
>
> In just one hour I learned that if he could, he would talk forever
> about his memories. He taught me why World War II was fought
> and that his part in it was as a B-24 radio man. He also taught me
> about myself—like what was happening when I was born and how
> I was named.
>
> Then he told me about World War II, a terrible racist war, a war
> when the Nazis were in power over Germany and Hitler, a cruel
> man, was their leader. He told me that the war affected him greatly
> as it did many people. He also said that the war had some good
> results. Many democratic countries were formed and great focus
> was put on human rights.
>
> After I finished my interview with my grandfather, I learned a
> lot, but most of all, I learned how much I loved him.

Justin shared some changing feelings about his international heritage:
"Learning about my grandmother's life during the war has given me an
understanding of who she is and of my Japanese background. Now I realize the importance of carrying on the traditions of my heritage."

Life Lessons

We believe that the focus on periods of social turmoil was part of the success of the interviews. The war and Depression periods were both memorable times, times when lives were in crisis and social issues were revealed
in strong contrast. Maya's grandfather wrote her, "Your assignment was like
opening Pandora's box. It made me think about events that made a lasting mark on my life." People living today are proud of how they were able
to endure. And they usually have great stories to tell of turbulent times.
Grandparents seemed to realize that unless their grandchildren understand
what they had gone through, they could never really be known for who

they were. They used the interviews to pass on life lessons about responsibility and character that their grandchildren would probably have rejected if conveyed directly.

I-Search and Expert Projects

Students carried out individual research projects in a number of ways. Sometimes they researched a set of factual questions at the beginning of a social issues unit (see Chapters 2 and 5), and other times they conducted a larger inquiry project. I-Search (Macrorie, 1988) (sometimes called an expert study, as described by Short, Harste, and Burke, 1996) is a personalized approach to research that fit with our beliefs more closely than a traditional research paper. I-Search starts with questions of personal interest and involves extended inquiry using a variety of sources: print, online, and human. Writers not only research a topic, but also research their own inquiry process.

The writers, the "I's," must notice how and why investigative decisions are made. They report (and thus reflect on) how the topic was found, how the search for resources and information developed, what problems emerged, what decisions and changes were made, and, finally, what the researcher learned and thought about the subject and the search itself. I-Search and expert projects encourage the use of nontext resources such as interviews, films, maps, and surveys, moving the investigation from a dead, theoretical exercise to a lively, real life activity. These individual inquiry projects help writers better understand the decision-making processes of authentic research with opportunities for surprises and discoveries.

From Choice to Engagement

Research topics for I-Searches came from many sources. Betty offered students techniques to help them find a focus but did not assign topics. Sometimes an I-Search grew out of a social issues inquiry unit, but not always. Some grew out of a genre study or a novel study. Reading back through their literature journals helped students recall what had engaged them. Since they had raised many questions in these journals, students found topics of real interest. Holly had always been curious about snakes, and this was her chance to find out more. The novel *When the Stars Begin to Fall* got Tess interested in water pollution, and Liz wanted to know how people other than the Jews were treated during the Nazi occupation. "I had never really thought about this and it truly opened my eyes!" she reported.

One year the first research projects emerged from students' abilities and life experiences that made them an "expert" on a topic. At first the most obvious areas of expertise were talents in sports, instrumental music, and dance. Then some students realized that they listened to and knew about popular music, and others chimed in with pet expertise, cooking expertise, building knowledge, and international living experiences. Two girls couldn't think of anything and were depressed by their classmates' many out-of-school activities. Finally they recognized that hair styling and making hair accessories were areas of expertise. They brought in an array of ribbons, beads, glue gun, mousse, and other styling aids and did demonstrations of putting hair into different styles and making hair decorations such as special headbands and braid keepers. Several girls in the audience placed orders for their personalized, one-of-a-kind products.

The variety of topics added zest to sharing sessions. Even the gifted kids had rarely picked their own topics, and students enjoyed having the opportunity to do so. Maya reported on her self-assessment form at the end of the nine weeks: "I-Searches were my favorite project. I had only picked a topic once before. If you're involved, you learn more." Carl said, "It makes me want to learn more and it makes me want to go to school."

Sharing Herself as a Researcher

To get the students started, Betty read bits from her own I-Search journal and paper, a project done in a summer humanities institute. After reading a diary of a South Carolina plantation owner (Theodore Rosengarten's *Tombee*), she had wondered what farming was like for those who did not own slaves, and had enlisted the help of the state historical archives in locating sources. "I wasn't sure that I would find anything, but I found a diary of a man who founded a cooperative here in South Carolina, and there was a whole network of these farmers who belonged in a cooperative grange," she told the students. Looking at Betty's journal helped students visualize how a researcher kept a record of new information and new questions. Alternatively, Betty could have begun a new search and shared her processes with students.

Coaching the Researchers

Betty coached the students in a variety of research strategies. She showed how to keep double-entry journals, with one side showing "research processes" and the other recounting "what was learned" (Atwell, 1990). As students worked, Betty taught toward their work with minilessons on writing and research skills from the required language arts curriculum, such as gathering ideas without copying, identifying most important ideas, summarizing, combining information from several sources, and using bibliographic format. As the students wrote papers that reported on both the search and the results (and in some cases, made public presentations with artifacts and visuals), Betty continued to coach them in relevant communication skills.

Informed Opinion and Commitment

Some students developed strong opinions about their topics based on the factual evidence they gathered. Trey's long, informative paper on coyotes ended with: "I learned a lot about coyotes. I think many people think coyotes are bad. I do not agree with them. Coyotes are helpful. I think coyotes should be protected, not trapped." Therese researched the job of a pharmacist and was struck by how important the code of ethics was to the pharmacist she interviewed: "A pharmacist should never knowingly condone the dispensing, promoting, or distributing of drugs or medical devices, or assist therein, that are not a good quality, that do not meet standards required by law, or that lack therapeutic value for the patient." Louis studied his grandfather, who had taught himself to be a tax consultant after having survived polio. Louis's report was a lesson to the others about how someone educates himself, lives his principles, and continues to learn every day.

Research: A Stance, Not an Assignment

Because researching information was an important ability from the standpoint of the language arts curriculum and also foremost in our own vision of preparing students for democratic citizenship, Betty planned two or three I-Search projects during the year. Students had the opportunity to grow from their first efforts as novice inquirers into more able researchers. The I-Search emphasis on making the processes of search the object of attention was an asset when Betty was trying to teach students to take a critical stance toward sources of information.

Some of the students seemed to be acquiring an inquiry stance that might serve them well in the future as citizens. They were learning that sharing information with others was a form of making a contribution to the community. We hoped they would become citizens who have questions and concerns and go on to investigate or speak out. Many of the students commented on how their research skills were growing, and they set goals for themselves to keep expanding their skills, such as: "Next time I hope to be able to use the Library of Congress Web site." Researching was becoming an ability to be acquired, valued, and nurtured, not just something to do to finish an assignment.

To encourage the view that inquiry is a stance of effective people, Betty added questions to her end-of-the-grading-period reflection forms, such as these:

> Do you think you are a curious person?
>
> What are some things you have investigated in the past?
>
> How are you growing as a researcher?
>
> What projects this nine weeks helped you connect information or skills?
>
> Now what is inquiry for you?

Inquiring Authors; Inquiring Characters

Nonfiction books that illustrate authentic instances of inquiry can inspire young inquirers and demonstrate some of the many paths that curiosity has taken in the real world. Students can learn how to ask good interview questions through Pat Cummings and Linda Cummings's *Talking with Explorers* (questions and answers organize the text) and will also read about how childhood curiosity can lead to an adult career. Wilborn Hampton's *Kennedy Assassinated! The World Mourns: A Reporter's Story* follows the actions of a fledgling reporter who suddenly is thrown into an event of great importance. Peter Sis's strangely beautiful picture book *Starry Messenger* hints at the determination of Galileo, who would not give up his search for the basic laws of nature even in the face of political oppression.

Young adult literature is full of characters who investigate, and Betty tried to bring as many of them as possible into the classroom. She used some of these as read-alouds to stimulate inquiry, and others were available as individual book choices. She mentioned the inquiring characters in book talks and recommended that students notice the techniques for investigation used in the book. Eleanora Tate's *The Secret of Gumbo Grove* set off the students' explorations of cemeteries described at the beginning of this chapter. P. J. Peterson's *Would You Settle for Improbable?* follows a boy from a juvenile center as he tries to fit into a suburban school, each chapter featuring a new journal assignment from the off-beat student teacher in their English class. Katherine Paterson's *Park's Quest,* Jean George's *Who Really Killed Cock Robin?,* Lois Lowry's *The Giver,* Carolyn Meyer's *Rio Grande Stories,* and Beverley Naidoo's *Journey to Jo'burg: A South African Story* all provide a wide assortment of characters who are searchers and askers of questions.

Concluding Thoughts and Concerns

How boring the field trip to the cemetery would have been if it had been planned by a teacher and assigned—two lectures by elderly persons and a requirement to gather facts and dates about dead people! The trip could have been about material to be memorized, repeated on a test, and forgotten. Instead, the students were "scratching an itch of curiosity" and were actively engaged in on-the-spot research as a result of their questions. The inquiry strategies begun early in the year continued in many different forms as the year progressed. Rachel expressed her satisfaction at following a trail of her wondering when she reflected, "We work together a lot to learn information and we see that it's not just what the book or the newspaper said but what it meant to us." Many students were led from the exploration of social issues to express strong personal convictions. When Becca looked back at what she had learned in seventh grade, she applied the problems of people in the Depression times to her own life: "I enjoyed learning all the facts and I learned that life is too short to hold grudges, and that you need to walk more miles with people before you criticize."

Additional Literature for Students

Fiction: Characters Who Inquire

Bauer, J. (1999). *Backwater.* New York: Puffin.

Creech, S. (1994). *Walk two moons.* New York: Scholastic.

George, J. (1995). *The firebug connection: An ecological mystery.* New York: HarperTrophy.

Lowry, L. (1993). *The giver.* New York: Houghton Mifflin.

Nixon, J. L. (1996). *Search for the shadowman.* New York: Dell.

Web Site

American Family Immigration History Center [Includes data and brief descriptions of immigration by time period, as well as sample family histories.] http://www.ellisislandrecords.org

Materials for Teachers

Cemetery Data Collection Form *(duplicate to include 4 reports)*

Name_____ Period _____

Fill in information for as many categories as possible for at least 4 grave sites of individuals or family plots with several grave markers.

Last or Family Name	First Names	Dates	Headstone (Size, Material, Features, Condition, other)	Gravesite Upkeep & Location in Cemetery
		1. From_____ To_____		
		2. From_____ To_____		
		3. From_____ To_____		
		4. From_____ To_____		

Total Family Time Span: From _____ To_____

Epitaph or Quote on Headstone:

Mention of Special Events:

Your Interpretations and Conclusions:

Guidelines for I-Search Investigations

The first list assists the search itself and can be given to students with a space for their response to help them plan and organize their search. Some students needed to work on this form as a group activity and others could work on it independently. The second list gives the general organizing categories for the final papers and was also usually run off on a single page with space for notes or an outline.

Sections or Paragraphs of Your Final Paper

Getting started

Finding relevant resources

How I went about my search

What I learned (or didn't)

What my search meant to me

Answer these questions as your work on your I-Search:

What is your topic?

How did you decide on your topic?

What do you already know about this topic?

What are your questions?

What texts will assist your search?

What nontext resources will you investigate?

What are some of your problems as you search?

What can you do when you are stuck?

What surprises did you find?

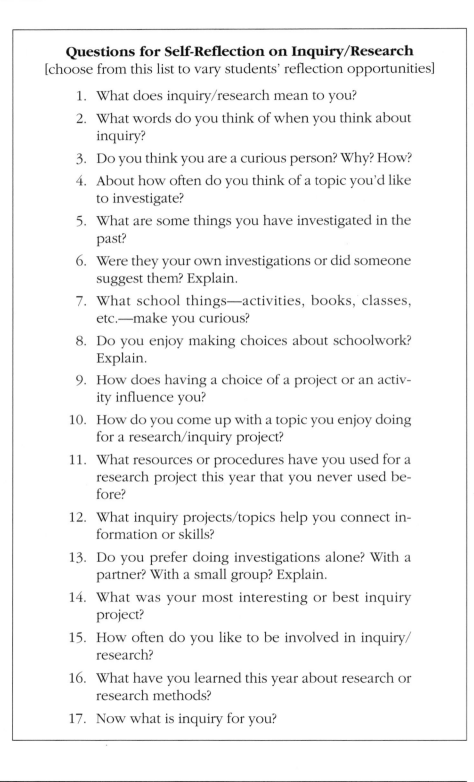

Questions for Self-Reflection on Inquiry/Research

[choose from this list to vary students' reflection opportunities]

1. What does inquiry/research mean to you?

2. What words do you think of when you think about inquiry?

3. Do you think you are a curious person? Why? How?

4. About how often do you think of a topic you'd like to investigate?

5. What are some things you have investigated in the past?

6. Were they your own investigations or did someone suggest them? Explain.

7. What school things—activities, books, classes, etc.—make you curious?

8. Do you enjoy making choices about schoolwork? Explain.

9. How does having a choice of a project or an activity influence you?

10. How do you come up with a topic you enjoy doing for a research/inquiry project?

11. What resources or procedures have you used for a research project this year that you never used before?

12. What inquiry projects/topics help you connect information or skills?

13. Do you prefer doing investigations alone? With a partner? With a small group? Explain.

14. What was your most interesting or best inquiry project?

15. How often do you like to be involved in inquiry/research?

16. What have you learned this year about research or research methods?

17. Now what is inquiry for you?

Reflecting on Your Learning This Year

What books, articles, and poems were most memorable for you? Give a reason for each choice, please.

What topics or styles did you like writing about? Please explain why.
       Topic or Type of writing: Reason:

Which writing are you most proud of and why?

What were the projects/activities that really meant something to you?

What things from class/school have tied into life outside of school for you?

What new or deeper understandings about our society and the way things are done do you now have? Please explain a bit.

What new or deeper understanding do you have about people, both in and beyond school and also out in the world?

What changes have you noticed in yourself this year (whether or not they are obvious to others)?

      As a reader and writer:

      As a learner:

      As a member of a community (classroom, team, school, community):

---

5 The Depression-Era Inquiry Unit: Expanding a Novel Study

Well, son, you should know that the ocean of life
Ain't never completely placid and crystal clear.
In my time the pool was sometimes dirty
From what others left behind.

Tess, taking the voice of Papa from
Roll of Thunder, Hear My Cry (Taylor)

CHAPTER OVERVIEW

The Great Depression was a time when economic forces, natural disasters, and institutional discrimination plunged our country into dramatic, even cataclysmic, disruption. The heartrending stories of struggle captured the students' imagination and thus provided a good forum for exploring universal issues of human life. Who in our society has access to resources, and how are resources allocated? When resources are scarce, who gets shortchanged, and why? In periods of tumult and conflict, social relationships stand out in sharp relief and therefore are more accessible to inquiry by young people.

   This chapter traces the work of students one year as they engaged in a monthlong study of the Depression era. It is organized around the immersion model's phases of inquiry presented in Chapter 1. Figure 5.1 is an overview of that model as it unfolded in this particular unit. This unit demonstrates how that model can be adapted to a novel study format in which information is partnered with appealing fictional characters to create student caring and concern and new understandings of historical and social issues.

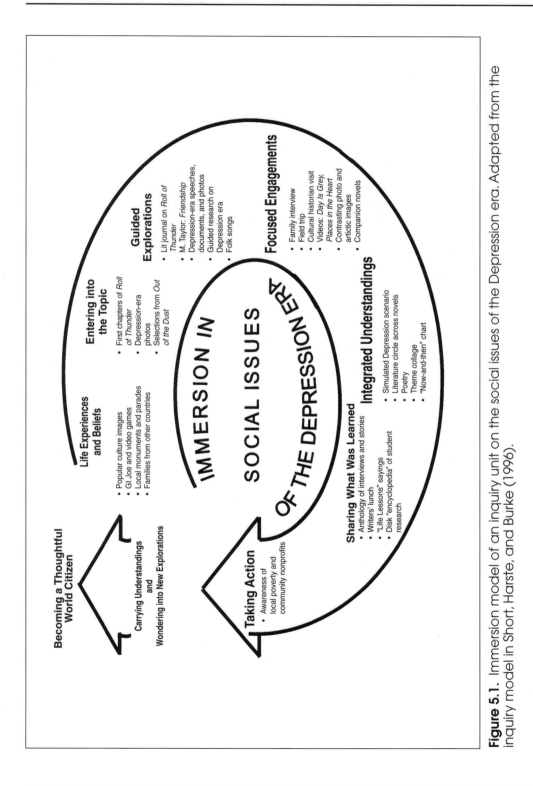

Figure 5.1. Immersion model of an inquiry unit on the social issues of the Depression era. Adapted from the inquiry model in Short, Harste, and Burke (1996).

Entering the Topic

It was February, and the eighth-period class had begun to read Mildred Taylor's *Roll of Thunder, Hear My Cry,* a moving novel set in the segregation and poverty of the rural South in the 1930s. Betty had long wanted to teach Taylor's novel because of its warmth and exciting action, and because the strength and tenacity of the Logan family held potential for breaking racial stereotypes.

The first chapters of Taylor's novel caught the students' interest. The ugly conflicts between blacks and whites and Cassie's fierce pride created intense class discussions. But when Betty looked at students' response notebooks, her satisfaction quickly wilted. Cathy's entry was representative: "If I had been the Logans, I would have just moved away from there. It doesn't seem like a very nice town. I wouldn't have let them treat me like that."

What had happened? Betty knew Cathy to be bright and a thoughtful reader. Just a few weeks before, in response to another book, Cathy had offered insightful interpretations. This text shouldn't have been too complex for the students, yet most of the responses assumed that the Logan's problems were the fault of some people who were not "nice." Other students had written: "The Logans had a lot of problems because of a few bad people in their neighborhood, and Momma should take a job as a school bus driver for the white students as a way to work herself back into teaching."

Need for More Social Context

Once we took the time to mull over what had happened, we realized that once again we had assumed too much. To us, the societal context was clearly "in the text." Incidents of racial conflict and the restrictions of black citizens under segregation were richly described in Taylor's compelling voice. After all, her ability to bring these incidents to life was the reason Betty had chosen the book. On rereading with more discerning eyes, however, we saw that, yes, the incidents were richly described, but explanations of the pervasive economic crisis of the country and the systemic nature of segregation and discrimination were missing. Naturally the students could not understand that when Mrs. Logan was fired from her job, the campaign of the white community to deprive the Logans of their land had succeeded. In the segregation and hard times of the Great Depression, Mrs. Logan would have no other good employment alternatives—no other teaching job, nor, in fact, any other job. Naturally students had missed the import of why Big Ma rather than a doctor in a hospital emergency room sets Papa's broken leg, and why Papa couldn't report to the police the deliberate "accident" that caused his injury.

Without additional context on that time period and some background on the devastating social and economic conditions, most students didn't have a clue that there was more to this powerful story than the hardships happening to one nice family. The class had no way of knowing that the Logans' lives were a reflection of national policy, local tradition and law, weather conditions, and a world's economic depression, not isolated incidents of ill fortune. Not surprisingly, they focused narrowly on conflicts among individual characters in the story.

Yes, they had heard of open segregation, but they went to school with people from various races and cultures and in some cases lived with them. They had little sense of a society that mandated and strictly enforced segregation. Some students had vague notions of inequality from sermons or television, but even apartheid had been legally abolished before these children could read, and their suburban world displayed little overt segregation. No doubt the minority students knew of and had experienced discrimination, but they were quiet, probably too unsure to share their knowledge. (Even they, however, seemed without factual knowledge of this repressive era.)

The students believed times had changed. The general consensus of the class seemed to be that since the civil rights movement had overturned the laws of segregation, there was little reason to worry now. Certainly, their school experiences had not helped them delve into the history of these conflicts or its legacy in our own time. So, armed with the insights we had gained by observing students' responses, we got to work and created a set of materials and experiences designed to open up students' inquiry into the social issues of the Depression era.

Creating a Socially Conscious Text Set

We believed that our role was to create opportunities for students to consider new ideas and experiences, not to promote our own beliefs, so we worked to surround the core novel, *Roll of Thunder,* with materials that reflected multiple perspectives, different voices from the times, information, contrasting stories, and commentary. We wanted each item in a text set to hold a special value or validity that would help students see the topic in a different way.

Informational books that were rich with photographs as well as factual background confirmed the authenticity of the problems at the heart of *Roll of Thunder.* James Agee and Walker Evans's *Let Us Now Praise*

Famous Men and Milton Meltzer's *Brother, Can You Spare a Dime?* were popular. Depression-based Internet sites are increasingly valuable sources, such as the WPA archives at the Library of Congress site that provide interviews, pictures, poetry, newspaper clippings, and so forth. Betty and the students gathered artifacts and original documents from these and other sources. Many informational sources, including encyclopedias and a documentary video—*The Shadow of Hate,* from the Southern Poverty Law Center, featuring actual footage, newspaper accounts, and recreations of hate crimes in our country—constructed a context for the times. Other useful texts, as well as more recent novels, nonfiction, and other resources, are provided at the end of the chapter.

Companion novels written at various reading levels allowed students to confirm their emerging sense of the times and extend their vicarious experience to different regions of the country and other lives. Poetry by Langston Hughes offered an expression of the feelings and themes of despair and hope. Woody Guthrie's folk songs chronicled the depth of people's struggle along "that old dusty road" to California. Speeches by Franklin Roosevelt were bright windows onto the economics and government policies that underwrote the issues of people's lives.

Guided Explorations

Guided Research

Working individually or with partners, students skimmed informational books, including indexes, to suggest possible questions and topics about the 1930s. (They needed instruction about the use of indexes, including cross-references.) Betty offered her suggestions to round out the list. Each student investigated a small, manageable piece of the Depression context, using some class time, some library time, and some homework time. Words such as *hoboes, orphans, migrant workers, tenant farmers, Wall Street, bank loans,* and *Jim Crow* took on new meaning. In the computer lab, students entered their information and sources under headings such as migration, farming, education, collapse of money, segregation, government action, and family problems. Finally, all the entries were consolidated under headings on a disk, printed out, and shared in class. Students proudly called this work their Depression Encyclopedia. The hard copies and duplicate disks were available for access throughout the rest of the unit. As a result, their writing and discussions were rich with information.

Betty then posted a chart of student questions that were not yet answered: "What was a sharecropper?"; "What was a Bear?"; "Who were the Okies?"; "Why was Black Thursday important?"; "What is trading on margin?"; "What caused the Dust Bowl?"; "Why were there so many ho-boes?" If a classmate submitted an answer, supported by a specific source, the answer was printed in next to the question, and students received recognition and extra credit for their search. This chart was posted on the wall for most of the unit, and it promoted interest in research and clarified many issues and events. The accumulating mass of facts reflected the students' growing authority on the topic. An informational source might confirm or explain a fictional event, such as the white children riding on the bus while the Logans walked to school, or that the Night Riders, who terrified black families in *Roll of Thunder,* was another name for the Ku Klux Klan. Thus the teacher guided student research at the beginning of the unit and gradually encouraged students to take more initiative as their background enabled them to focus their inquiry efforts.

As students researched, they learned that almost everyone had been affected by the Depression. Many entries ended up being more than merely factual as students added their own feelings and opinions. They showed a growing awareness that social conditions, not individual irresponsibility, created hardships. After looking for information on unemployment and homelessness, Robert reported:

> During the Depression, money meant food in your mouth. Back then, there were no existing support groups for the jobless or home-less, so many people had to live on the streets. Because of the generosity of people who were willing and who could give money or food, other men were kept alive.

Students were extending their points of view and challenging stereotypes. When Louis researched the topic of hoboes, for instance, he was able to understand that they were not just tramps who refused to work and expected handouts. Students uncovered details of the harsh regime of terror African Americans faced during this period: of more than one thousand lynchings, fewer than fifty victims had been charged with crimes. Some students began to see the institutionalized nature of discrimination when they investigated such subtopics of discrimination as Jim Crow laws and the Ku Klux Klan. Sam wrote: "The KKK had the power to do whatever they wanted to, and they did. The local police couldn't do anything about them, or maybe they could and just didn't want to. Sometimes one of the police, himself, was a Night Rider."

During the Depression, one of the government's New Deal WPA projects put the literary community back to work. Reporters, writers, photographers, and painters were employed to be eyewitnesses of this devastating period of U.S. history. Their poignant interviews, photos, and first-hand accounts enriched the information and statistics the students were gathering. One student showed that verbal descriptions don't always provide enough information when he asked in his journal, "What color was Cassie's teacher?" Returning again and again to photos of the period helped students keep in mind what the 1930s were like. Document reproductions, news clippings, speeches, and census records added to the sense of reality.

Other Shared Literature

Many kids were puzzled by the black-white relationships in *Roll of Thunder*. Why would Cassie's white friend demand that Cassie step off the sidewalk to let her pass when they met in town? How could she want to be friends with Cassie but act like that? Betty read aloud to the class Taylor's book *The Friendship* as a way to open dialogue about the complicated personal relationships of segregation. In this story, two African American children accompany an elderly neighbor to the local country store. Perhaps failing to size up the potentially hostile situation, or possibly determined to keep his pride, the old man greets the white shopkeeper by the friendly and personal nickname of their closely spent youth. Ordered to use a formal title, the black man will not acquiesce. Finally the owner (caught perhaps in the bind of saving face in front of his peers) pushes the old man down the steps. Several times during the story, Betty stopped for the students to talk so that they could imagine the contradictions of a segregated society and the emotional costs of negotiating them.

Focused Engagements

Living History: Depression-Era Family Interviews

Just as the WPA workers had done in the 1930s, students went home to gather personal stories of the Great Depression. Peter's interview, replete with compassionate feeling and rich detail, confirmed for the class the hard times of this era. His grandfather had been a sharecropper, splitting 50 percent of what his family farmed with the landowner. He'd had to kill his pet dog because his parents could not afford to feed it, and he'd been responsible for a lot of chores such as feeding all the animals and killing and plucking the chickens (for 21 cents a week). The closing of Peter's interview showed the level of students' background information on this period. He expressed appreciation for the role of the New Deal government in pulling the country out of the Depression, commenting, "I am glad the Federal Reserve Bureau was made."

Students were surprised to find that their elderly relatives had been grateful to live on farms during the Depression: "Even if you had no money, you had food and shelter" was a repeated sentiment. One grandparent mentioned "the luxury of Ivory soap, especially since you were always filthy from working in the garden or hog shed." Several reiterated that their only safety net was their neighbors, on whom they depended for help. Their diversions were playing checkers, doing puzzles, riding the bus into town, or listening to the one radio station that came in from Atlanta; yet no grandparent mentioned boredom. Students recognized their own lives as affluent, easy, and even exciting by comparison.

The interviews also elicited family stories, stories handed down through several generations. Like Mildred Taylor, who says that many of the events in her stories come from family tales her father used to tell, students discovered amazing family stories. Sixty years ago Mandy's great-uncle, working as the newspaper editor, was driven out of his small Florida town because he printed remarks about a particularly unjust trial of a black defendant. Laura learned that the homemade doll that sat on a chest in the hallway of her family's home had been made in the thirties out of scraps of cloth from a distant cousin's mending basket. Robert's great-grandfather, a locomotive engineer, died a hero, saving scores of lives by derailing his freight train to avoid an oncoming passenger train.

Many of the facts students gathered from print resources—especially the prevalence of extreme poverty—were substantiated by the interviews and family stories. Students began to see that their classroom texts reflected reality: the Logans, like their relatives, were people caught in specific historical conditions.

Songs, Speeches, and Original Documents

When Woody Guthrie's twangy voice filled the room with his mournful chronicles of struggle, students knew what he was singing about. Because they knew what lay behind the poetic images, the songs evoked empathy for families, gathered by campfires, who had struggled across the mountains to California in their broken-down cars, only to find bitter disappointment. Guthrie's songs, sometimes ironically humorous, also helped to highlight some of the main themes of this period for the students, who now had enough background knowledge to follow his meaning. In a similar way, they listened with interest to quotes from speeches by Eleanor Roosevelt and Franklin Roosevelt and could understand some of the economics and policies. Roosevelt's commitment to rebuild America was inspiring: "to eliminate special privilege in the control of the old economic and social structure by a numerically very small but very powerful group of individuals . . . [and] to widen the distribution of wealth and property." Betty and Beverly ruefully reflected that this is not how presidents speak today.

Local History and Field Trips

Just prior to the thirties, a Tennessee Valley Authority project brought electricity and running water into our locality by building a giant earthen dam on a nearby river. In fact, the students swam and fished in this lake, but few realized that filling it had meant flooding many farms, sharecropper shacks, sawmills, churches, and cemeteries. A few of the old farms and their outbuildings still survive on the edge of the lake, testaments to a time when cane syrup mills, springhouses, and water wells were important in people's lives.

Using books and artifacts from a community history project, Betty reviewed the town history of the 1930s with her classes, creating in them a stronger sense of place. Now the students understood why, until the Lake Murray Dam, their relatives had no electricity, central heat, or running water in their homes, and why their chores had been to chop wood and haul buckets of water. Here was evidence that some people in our town had once lived very much like the Logan family in *Roll of Thunder.*

Field trips put students in touch with remnants of the Depression still found in their community. As described in Chapter 4, they examined local cemeteries to investigate life spans, causes of death, occupations, and family size. Learning the background of the lake helped explain to students the causes of death (e.g., malaria, accidents, knife wounds) they saw recorded on old grave markers and in the obituaries of the huge crew of men who built the dam. One Saturday, with mothers as volunteer drivers, about half of one class inspected a site built by the Civilian Conservation Corps (CCC). The remnants of the CCC camp confirmed the effort by the Depression's New Deal government to reemploy the population. Not only was there a plaque on the park entrance sign that noted the CCC's contribution, but also the buildings where the young men lived had been kept as a reminder of their efforts.

Guest Cultural Historian

Now that the students had a base of information, Dr. Jane White visited the classes, bringing an ethnohistorical perspective on the changes the Great Depression made in people's lives. Dr. White brought copies of census tables and migration maps for students to study and asked them to make hypotheses about the waves of movement in this decade. When students compared county census reports of the Chicago area with those of rural Alabama, they saw that Cook County residents increased as Alabama counties emptied. Archival photographs of men waiting at small rural train stations and families in front of their old, loaded-down cars and trucks provided visual illustration of the statistical story. Students could fill in the blanks from their fiction and nonfiction reading.

New questions, fueled by empathy, surfaced: "Why would they think that jobs were better up North? How could they get there if they were struggling to even buy corn meal?" Then they looked at Dr. White's photos of workers in various jobs in Detroit and Chicago, and the class sorted out the "worst" jobs. When they found a predominance of blacks in these jobs, they had to consider why. Other photos of cities helped students realize that rural areas weren't the only depressed locales in the country.

The Artist's Eye

Dr. White also wanted students to think about unexamined attitudes toward groups of people. Since perceptions are influenced through visual representation, she asked the students to analyze the differences in the portrayals of African Americans by two black artists: William H. Johnson, who painted more than sixty years ago, and Jonathan Greene, a contemporary artist. Johnson's paintings are done mainly in neutral colors, and the people in them seem somber and stiff. On the other hand, Greene's pictures are vibrant with colors and patterns. His African Americans are portrayed happily relaxing with friends or dancing, and if doing household chores, they are in bucolic backyards and cheerful rooms. Dr. White asked, "What do we see people doing here? Why do you think the artist painted this way? What might we believe about these people from seeing these pictures?" The students articulated the differences and speculated about the changes that time, protest, and new legislation have meant for minorities.

This contact with an expert added authenticity to the students' inquiry. Dr. White's enthusiasm and expertise were motivational. Students saw her excited by the same information they were using in class, and she modeled how research continues throughout life in recognized academic disciplines. She was an expert who made learning bigger than school assignments.

Additional Literature Perspectives

When students finished reading *Roll of Thunder,* each of them selected another novel of the Depression era to read independently at home and discuss in small groups. Robert Burch's *Queenie Peavy,* Linda Crew's *Fire on the Wind,* Vera Cleaver and Bill Cleaver's *Where the Lilies Bloom,* Karen Hesse's *Out of the Dust,* Zilpha Keatley Snyder's *Cat Running,* and Irene Hunt's *No Promises in the Wind* were all popular choices. By this time, the students had some understanding of the variety of ways that poverty can shape a life, and they had an inkling of society's role in creating poverty and racism. Most of them were reading beyond the surface story as they followed the struggles of people caught in constricted circumstances.

Visual Representation of Story

The emotional impact and visual context of videos helped students make deeper connections between social and economic facts and the stories of peoples' lives. The film *Places in the Heart* expanded the boundaries of discrimination to include people with handicaps and women, and represented the anguish of that era. Clips from this dramatic movie were used in class: the lynching scene, the contrasting funerals of the blacks and the whites, and some segments depicting the treatment of a blind man and of women, as well as the featured incidents between a white widow struggling to keep her farm and a migrant African American hoping to help himself by helping her. Later, the entire movie was shown after school. With parental permission and bags of popcorn, more than half the class stayed for the movie, bringing friends for whom they answered questions and clarified confusing scenes. Class members were now the "experts" in the facts and practices of this period.

The ending of *Places in the Heart* is a fascinating example of the way that power and economics can influence artistic expression. The warring town in the movie is made whole again in a fanciful scene with all those who have died, been driven away, or are at odds with one another gathered together at a church service serenely singing the closing hymn. Even students could think of reasons why Hollywood would create this scene to avoid a more critical view of our society. But it also provided an opportunity for students to envision a better world, a world they would be willing to work to create.

The Sky Is Gray, a half-hour video based on Ernest Gaines's short story, also shows the grinding burden of poverty. The African American mother and son are barely surviving as sharecroppers. The father is away, perhaps recently drafted. The strong mother is determined both to keep the family afloat and to teach James, a boy about twelve years old, how to become a man in these hard times. Although she easily could have done it herself, for example, she forces James to kill the quail he trapped so the family can have a decent meal.

On a raw winter morning, James and his mother make a trip to town to the dentist. It sounds like an ordinary, unimportant event. But when you are black, have only a few coins for food, have rarely taken a bus to town, and have never seen a doctor or eaten in a restaurant, a simple medical visit can turn into a day full of humiliation. The students were stunned by the limits of this family's life. Poverty and segregation meant more than not having material things. They meant pain and discomfort; they meant lack of control over your life and disrespect at every turn, even for children. The video is quiet and subtle but deeply moving, and it stimulated thoughtful written comparisons of the two films.

Moving to Integrated Understandings

Peterson and Eeds (1990) remind us that talking about layers of meaning is important because that is where the author's message lies. Recognizing underlying themes required higher levels of thinking from the students and was essential to addressing social implications of the books. Betty's role was to raise questions, elicit student questions, and provide activities that helped students think about themes. The diverse text set of stories, information, videos, documents, and so forth provided contrasts and supportive information to stimulate student ideas. When two texts addressing the same theme were discussed, it was easier to find the message underneath the plot, mood, symbols, and context. Time was at a premium, and long, satisfying discussions were not possible. Concrete activities helped students focus and also provided the intellectual stretch of switching ideas from one medium to another.

As they finished their companion novels, students worked in groups of three or four to develop large charts that compared the same elements in the diverse novels they had been reading—characters, their problems, solutions and outcomes, and era context clues. Using their charts, the class discussed differences and similarities in these novels. Betty shared pictures or bits of information when students needed more background. For example, Jerry Stanley's *Children of the Dust Bowl: The True Story of the School at Weedpatch Camp* was especially useful for the California farmworker context.

Theme Collages

Betty hoped that creating a visual of their core novel *Roll of Thunder* would push students beyond "what happened." She wanted them to draw on their accumulated store of stories and information. The project could also provide opportunities to explore how authors use symbols, metaphor, and analogy to convey layers of meaning in their work. Familiar with collage making from their work with Betty's teammate Sandra Vann, students set to work assembling photos, drawings, symbols, key words, items, clippings, colors, and so forth to represent important ideas—not the plot—of Taylor's story. Making and presenting these collages brought the big ideas of Taylor's work into focus—the hardship and violence of prejudice, the value of owning and appreciating land, the power of a loving family, the power of unquestioned status quo, and the strength of individuals who choose to break the code.

Students shared their collages in small groups and also wrote explanations for their selected representations. To highlight the central purposes of the assignment, using a rubric they rated their group's collages on the presentation of themes. Betty added an item to the generic rating form to emphasize how visuals can promote thought: "Explain what about this collage made you think of new ideas or see something in a new way."

An interesting incident occurred when students posted their collages on the classroom walls. As students were changing classes, Betty overheard a girl from another reading class say to her friend, "Does Mrs. S. know that's up there?" pointing at one collage with cutout pasted letters spelling out "Kill the Nigger." No one in her class, nor Betty herself, had felt the need to call special attention to this remark because they all knew the context of the racial slur (a quote from *Roll of Thunder,* the cry of an angry white mob yelling as T. J. was dragged from his home). Betty's students knew that the words did *not* express the feelings of the boy who had made the collage. No one, including Betty, had thought about other interpretations and their potential to offend.

Betty made sure that all classes understood the full meaning of the poster. On reflection, she was pleased the girls had been offended by such a remark. She was also pleased that her classes had recognized the epithet as a message from the author, Mildred Taylor, that the ugly truths about racial intolerance need to be spoken in order for people to combat racism forcefully. Yet now she knew that both she and the students needed to be more careful with outsiders who might receive very different messages from their work. She took the poster down before the next parent night.

Poetry, a Medium for Big Meanings

Students had focused on the traits and roles of the key characters in their reading logs, and Betty wanted to see if they could extend that thinking to consider the relationships between characters through the medium of poetry. Poetry would allow the expression of important thoughts that students could not yet express in essays. Although they identified closely with the characters, students found it difficult to move beyond feelings to the larger, more cognitive view often needed for essays.

Reviewing poems in their literary anthology warmed up students' poetic vision. Then, using Langston Hughes's "Mother to Son" as a model of an "advice" poem, Betty explained how they would write their own poems using talk to show the relationship of one character to another. The kind of advice given in their poems would depend on the results of their thinking deeply about this relationship. Not surprising, like "Mother to Son" most of the students' poems concentrated on themes of love and struggle. This activity was not just about imitation or modeling; it was an invitation to trying on ideas from notable authors in order to create a new idea. Students learned lessons of poetic craft, and they were also pushed to use new thoughts and language. The most obvious language explorations were with dialect, but the general concept of a poem in the form of talk also stimulated students' creativity.

Tess created a poem with lovely words and an extraordinary extended metaphor to show the complex predicament of an African American father contemplating the life his son must face. The tone is serious and caring, just like the narrator, Papa.

Advice from Papa to Stacy

So, boy, I hear you've been strugglin'
Heard you're close to givin' in.
Well, son, you should know that the ocean of life
Ain't never completely placid and crystal clear.
In my time the pool was sometimes dirty
From what others left behind. And sometimes,
I would step in a weak spot and be sucked right in.
But all I could do to save my life
Was to thrash and pull and fight for air.
I escaped each time, but others aren't always so lucky.
But, boy, you know how to fight the pull of the current.
You have it in your genes to always fight
And keep your head held high above the water.

In the following poem about the characters in *Queenie Peavy* (Burch), Lydia sent a blunt message from a daughter to her father who has returned from a long prison term. She chose to take Queenie's point of view, capturing with surprising sensitivity the tension of a child who wants to love, wants to understand, yet resents her father's absence and the stigma that his crimes have brought on her.

Don't You Know?

Listen to me now,
'Cause I'm sure you do not know
How bad life's been.
I'd like to show you somehow.
I've been the outcast,
'Cause you've been servin' time.
I've had to live a lifetime of *your* crime.

And now you come back, 'spectin it all,
Like I'm s'posta come to you in a call.
Don't you know I'm trying and tellin' it true,
But it's not that easy to come to love you.

Chart of Then and Now

To connect information from the 1930s to contemporary events, small groups created charts depicting changes in living from the Great Depression to recent years. Students used obvious categories such as transportation, clothing, cooking, and education, but they also thought about social issues. They recognized parallels between homelessness then and now, and noticed that, just as the soup kitchens of the Depression helped people survive, so do the missions and shelters of today. The students were horrified by the activities of the Ku Klux Klan and dismayed to learn that the organization still exists today.

Sharing What Was Learned

Writing New Endings for Novels

Having read two novels, *Roll of Thunder, Hear My Cry* and another of their choice with a Depression context, students chose one of these for which to write their own believable "final" chapter using their knowledge about the period. They showed skill at embellishing their texts with the objects and customs of poverty—cold kitchens before the stove is lit, horse-drawn wagons, primitive jails—but most succumbed to far more happiness for their characters than would have been possible in those years. It was evident that the kids continued to yearn for a more just world.

Students still found it difficult to believe there was a time when many people lived without the most basic rights. Tina, for example, could make strong inferences about how life in the thirties would sober and age a black child, so she makes her Cassie compassionate and thoughtful:

> He looked so helpless right there. I felt like reaching out to him and giving him a hug, holding him, comforting him, just as his mother had on the night of the incident. . . . T. J. and the jail had taught me a lot. The jail was no longer like a vacation to me, it was a place to tear apart lives.

Although Tina describes the starkness of the jail and T. J.'s bad physical condition and shows Cassie hoping he will die rather than face a lifetime there, she doesn't make the 1930s world of legislated discrimination as bleak as it actually was—a time and place where T. J. would have been lucky to make it to jail, or to a trial.

Entering into the Lives of Depression-Era Citizens

Some students still seemed to lose sight of how the desperate conditions of the 1930s were systemic and nationwide. So Betty developed a writing assignment to take students into the point of view of people in pivotal roles during the Depression (see the Materials for Teachers section at the end of the chapter). Each case involved a person who had to make decisions based on social and economic conditions. Students chose from a group of five scenarios written by Betty:

- a banker caught between his principles and calling in loans
- a mother desperate for work
- a father out of a job
- a farmer who has lost his formerly prosperous farm
- a son of a sharecropper contemplating leaving home

As students developed appropriate personas for these people, they brought their bits of knowledge of 1930s economic and social circumstances into a living whole. They had to do more than just describe a life; they had to demonstrate how people might have made decisions. Anita used the "son of a sharecropper" scenario as the seed for her story. The plot reflects her own drive and positive outlook but is detailed with facts she has learned—the siblings sick but no money for a doctor, no shoes or books with which to attend school, credit cut off at the store, Philadelphia as the dream city of many southern African Americans. In the end of Anita's story, her protagonist has come to the end of his endeavors to keep his family going:

> I go straight to bed without dinner. As I lay on my pallet made of cornhusks; the rest of my family surrounds me in our small house. The only thing I can think of is my Uncle Louis and his grand life in Philadelphia. He is a teacher at a black university, and he is the only one to finish college in our whole entire family. He comes on special holidays and brings us wonderful gifts. One time . . . he told me something I will never forget. He told me to aim for the moon, even if I don't make it I will land amongst the stars. I miss him and hope he is right. Maybe I can go to Philadelphia . . . so I can help my mom and siblings. . . . [I]n a deep sleep I dream of all the wonders in life.

Lee created a more pessimistic story about a family that has lost its indebted, eroded farm. Encouraged by newspaper ads and rumors, they decide to try to make it to California, "the promised land." Problems leave them stranded in the Midwest, and the father dies of exhaustion. Eventually, relatives help them return to South Carolina.

With a scenario, students don't have to construct an entire plot; they can concentrate on solving a life problem. In these assignments, most of the students created options that would be realistically available to their characters and gave them personality and courage. Most of the students focused on family strength and togetherness, perhaps reflecting the values their relatives emphasized when talking to them about getting through the Depression. Only a few students addressed racist incidents.

In addition to sharing their work in presentations and displays, students presented a disk copy of their Depression encyclopedia to the library for other students' research, and they read their work at a writer's lunch, a periodic gathering of kids who wanted to share pieces.

Betty asked each student to write a saying that reflected "lessons learned" from the Depression. The results listed below demonstrate both knowledge and compassion, both financial wisdom and personal principles of living:

Lessons to Be Learned from the Depression

Don't take things for granted.

Accept things as they are, BUT work to change things.

Help people in need, for you may need help one day.

Don't make fun of those less fortunate.

Act on your beliefs, not because of what others are doing.

Treat people equally, not by appearance or skin color.

Remember the hard lives many people had, and still have.

Don't waste; conserve and appreciate what you have.

Don't invest in just one thing.

Land is valuable.

Since money often runs out, people with money are not better than others without it.

Betty bound anthologies for the students that included their family stories and interviews, as well as their "Depression Lessons." Copies were given to Ms. Vann, the other language teacher, for her class when they began reading *Roll of Thunder, Hear My Cry*.

Taking Action

No important action project grew out of this unit. In most years, due to the pressure of time the class jumped right into the World War II unit. One year, however, the class was able to follow up on their concerns about the Logan family sacrificing their forest in order to save T. J. The whole team took a field trip to a nearby national forest for a day's activities, learning about the importance of trees and their influence on people and the environment. Betty was able to tie this information into the Logan family's feelings about their land and the importance of ecological sensitivity.

Life Lessons: The Value of the Depression-Era Unit

As the students cycled back into the topic through diverse perspectives during this immersion unit, the mix of fiction, family histories, poetry, visuals, and informational sources provided access to new understandings and helped shape students' feelings and convictions. They were engaged with the voices and perspectives of the times, not just to learn about the issues involved, but also to understand how life was lived in times of crisis. They saw that social issues are not just "things out there"; they are "problematic concerns that permeate the lives of people" (Totten & Pedersen, 1997, p. 23).

Students gained insight into the crippling effects of poverty and the covert and overt terror of segregated society in the 1930s. Their awareness and rejection of racism was expressed strongly in their reports and journals, but when it came time to sum it all up, they focused on the issue of family strength in the midst of struggle. We were pleased that their study had come a little closer to home than the usual humanities study. Through a historical study, students learned not only about their country and culture, but also about their own families and local history. Remnants of that historical life surrounded them, in the soil of the fields and the customs of the people.

Additional Literature for Students

Fiction of the Depression Era

Adler, D., & Widener, T. (1999). *The Babe & I.* San Diego: Harcourt Brace.

Cleaver, B., & Cleaver, V. (1989). *Where the lilies bloom.* New York: HarperTrophy.

Cochrane, P. (1996). *Purely Rosie Pearl.* New York: Dell.

De Young, C. C. (2000). *A letter to Mrs. Roosevelt.* New York: Dell.

DeFelice, C. (2001). *Nowhere to call home.* New York: HarperCollins.

Gaines, E. (1985). *The autobiography of Miss Jane Pittman.* New York: Bantam.

Hesse, K. (2001). *Witness.* New York: Scholastic.

Levine, G (1999). *Dave at night.* New York: HarperCollins.

Moss, M. (2001). *Rose's journal: The story of a girl in the Great Depression.* San Diego: Harcourt Brace.

Peck, R. (1998). *A long way from Chicago: A novel in stories.* New York: Scholastic.

Peck, R. N. (2000). *A day no pigs would die*. New York: Random House.

Porter, T. (1997). *Treasures in the dust*. New York: HarperTrophy.

Recorvits, H. (1999). *Goodbye, Walter Malinski*. New York: Farrar, Straus & Giroux.

Richard, A. (1971). *Pistol, a novel*. New York: Dell.

Taylor, M. (1975). *Song of the trees*. New York: Dial.

Nonfiction: The Depression and Its Issues

Bartoletti, S. C. (1999). *Kids on strike*. Boston: Houghton Mifflin.

Christensen, B. (2001). *Woodie Guthrie: Poet of the people*. New York: Knopf.

Downing, D. (2001). *The Great Depression*. Chicago: Heinemann Library.

Farrell, J. (1996). *The Great Depression*. San Diego: Lucent.

Tillage. L. (1997). *Leon's story*. New York: Farrar, Straus & Giroux.

Related Books

Atkin, B. S. (1993). *Voices from the fields: Children of migrant farmworkers tell their stories*. Boston: Joy Street.

Hart, E. T. (1999). *Barefoot heart: Stories of a migrant child*. Winter Springs, FL: Isis.

Jiménez, F. (1999). *The circuit: Stories from the life of a migrant child*. Boston: Houghton Mifflin.

Menzel, P. (1995). *Material world: A global family portrait*. (Text by C. C. Mann.) San Francisco: Sierra Club.

Parker, D. (1998). *Stolen dreams: Portraits of working children*. Minneapolis, MN: Lerner.

Springer, J. (1999). *Listen to us: The world's working children*. Toronto: Douglas & McIntyre.

Taylor, M. (1981). *Let the circle be unbroken*. New York: Scholastic.

Taylor, M. (1990). *Mississippi bridge*. New York: Puffin.

Walter, M. P. (1992). *Mississippi challenge*. New York: Bradbury Press.

Photographs, Film, and Video

Donovan, A. (Producer), & Benton, R. (Writer/Director). (1984). *Places in the heart*. Culver City, CA: Columbia TriStar Home Entertainment.

Green, W. (Producer), & Lathan, S. (Director). (1980). *Ernest J. Gaines's The sky is gray* [Video]. Malibu, CA: Monterey Home Video.

Guggenheim, C., & Carnes, J. (1995). *The shadow of hate: A history of intolerance in America* [Video]. Montgomery, AL: Teaching Tolerance.

Welty, E. (1989). *Eudora Welty: Photographs*. Jackson: University Press of Mississippi.

Music and Poetry

Crosby, B., Kemp, H., & others. (2001). *Brother, can you spare a dime? American song during the Great Depression* [CD]. New York: New World Records.

Guthrie, W. (1969). [Recorded by Country Joe McDonald.] *Thinking of Woody Guthrie* [CD]. New York: Vanguard. [Songs of particular interest: "Pastures of plenty," "Talkin' Dust Bowl," "Going down the road," and "Roll on Columbia."]

New Lost City Ramblers. (2000). *Songs from the depression* [CD]. Washington, DC: Smithsonian Folkways Recordings.

Rash, R. (1998). *Eureka mill.* Corvallis, OR: Bench Press.

Speeches and Primary Document Reprints

Jackdaw Publications
Offers packets of ready-to-use, original-size historical documents with intriguing text and suggested activities. Also includes photo collections. Contents include world history, U.S. history, and several Depression-era packets.
www.jackdaw.com

Parks and History Association
FDR Speaks: The FDR Memorial Collection. (1997). Washington, DC.
This collection of twelve pamphlets reprints Roosevelt's most influential speeches.

Perspectives on History Series, Discovery Enterprises, Carlisle, MA
Beyer, J., & Weisman, J. (1995). *The Great Depression: A nation in distress*

King, D. (1997). *The dust bowl*

Mofford, J. (1997). *Talkin' union: The American labor movement*

Yamasaki, M. (1997). *Movin' on: The great migration north*

History Web Sites for the Depression Era

Library of Congress American Memory Collection [Over 160,000 photographs available from the Great Depression to World War II. Special topical collections for teachers.]
http://memory.loc.gov/

The New Deal Network (initiated by the Franklin and Eleanor Roosevelt Institute). [This is a database of over 20,000 photographs, political cartoons, speeches, letters and other historical documents.]
http://newdeal.feri.org

The Woody Guthrie Foundation and Archives [Includes information about the Depression era.]
http://www.woodyguthrie.org

Materials for Teachers

Depression Scenarios

Choose one of these scenes and its characters to develop into a believable story about the Depression. You must include specific facts and people and events from your *nonfiction* research, trips, interviews, encyclopedias, etc. to make your story detailed and credible.

1. You are a banker in the small town of Walterboro, SC. You have the reputation of being friendly and fair to your customers and of giving them good advice, but you always respect the bank rules and maintain your honesty. You live a comfortable life in a large, well-maintained home with your wife, two school-age children, and a housekeeper/cook. Now with the Depression, you are responsible for pressing people who are your neighbors and acquaintances to pay their loans and mortgages. Most of these people are now unemployed and their debts have accumulated. The value of stocks and bonds is insecure. The bank may not be able to pay out people's savings.

2. You are a mother who works in a textile mill in Great Falls, SC, about seventy miles north of the capital, Columbia. Your husband also worked at the mill but was recently dismissed and blacklisted for supporting the labor union's effort to improve living and working conditions and increase wages. Because the mill owns the house you and your young children live in, as well as the only store you have to shop in, you have no choices. You must take your ten-year-old son out of the school he was sometimes able to attend two miles away and put him to work in the mill. At least you have not been evicted. Your husband has left—walking, hitchhiking, and hopping trains to Columbia to look for work.

3. You are a husband and father, a former millworker (see #2). Although it has taken you more than a week, you have finally reached Columbia to look for work. Along the way, you met other men trying to reach the big city, and you have camped together and shared meager food and supplies. Although you are no longer allowed to work in a textile mill, you try for days to get other jobs,

▶

but there is little except for occasional work at the railroad station unloading and sweeping out boxcars. You can't earn enough to support yourself, let alone your family. You know many men are leaving the city to try other areas by hiding in freight train boxcars. You have also seen posters recruiting men for a new government organization called the CCC to build parks and bridges around the state.

4. You are a cotton farmer in Marlboro County, SC. You have only about forty acres; besides the family's kitchen garden, you have always planted tobacco and cotton because they are cash-producing crops. But repeated plantings of the same crops have made the land less productive. In addition to the mortgage on the land and equipment, you also owe the bank for the money you borrowed to buy fertilizer. Your bill at the local general store is large, so you have no more credit. Now your crops fail because of drought and the boll weevil. The bank takes your land, house, and outbuildings. After an auction of your animals and belongings, you have enough to settle your bill and possibly get the family to California where you hear there is fertile but cheap land.

5. You are the son of a sharecropper who farms for a big landowner near Bamburg, SC. You have six siblings. The land your family works is where your great-grandparents were once slaves. Although you and your family work hard and long every day, you barely survive after the owner receives his share of the corn, cotton, and bean harvests. Besides the fieldwork, you hunt, fish, and help with the vegetable garden to help feed everyone. No one in your family has been able to go to a doctor or dentist, and none has made it to high school. You quit school in eighth grade because your shoes wore out and it took more than a half-hour to walk each way—time you could have spent doing chores. As you lie on your cornhusk pallet at night, you hear the distant whistle of the night freight train as it slows for the crossing. You think of your uncle now up north in Philadelphia.

6 Literature: Expanding the Lifespace of Students

Literature responds to the human record of history and evokes further responses in young readers by . . . putting a human face on the history. It also helps us to see what might be.

NCTE Committee on Teaching about Genocide and Intolerance

I like stories that go deep into a topic like Flowers for Algernon *and* Roll of Thunder.

Tina

CHAPTER OVERVIEW

In this chapter, we discuss the contribution of literature to a socially conscious curriculum, including issues surrounding teacher text choices. We show how text sets are developed around social issues and historical periods, and how texts, information, art, and music interacted to stimulate student inquiry about society during immersion in an inquiry unit. One section describes strategies to help students take a critical look at the author behind the message. The chapter ends with a description of some of the key engagements used to activate readers and provide a structure for the exchange of ideas.

Critical Literacy in Action: A Literature Circle

As they came into class, students pulled their desks into a literature circle. They had just finished reading a novel that made connections between environmental issues and the marginalization of families in poverty. They had made entries in their literature logs and discussed them in small groups. But this was the first time they had all come together to talk about what the book had meant to them. Everyone knew what to do; the responsibility of preparation for literature circles and active participation in them had been practiced and discussed over several months. Matt and Adam, the discussion leaders, had prepared questions the night before, and they led the discussion, with Betty and Beverly sitting outside the circle as occasional contributors.

When the Stars Begin to Fall (Collier) is the story of the White family, who are outcasts in their isolated, economically depressed town, living in a run-down farmhouse with a littered yard. Refusing to take a regular job ("I will not be a slave."), Mr. White ekes out a subsistence living for his family by doing odd jobs and by other activities of suspect legality. The mother, while loving, is in a chronic state of depression and inactivity. Harry's older sister turns to boys for attention and affection, letting them sexually exploit her, and eventually runs away. The family is labeled as "trash" by the rest of the community and is treated as such.

The lead character Harry spends his free time hiking alone in the woods to escape his family and the scorn of neighbors. After he spots some suspicious effluent in the river adjacent to the local carpet factory, Harry is determined to prove it is pollution, both to contribute to the life of the town and to redeem his family in the eyes of others. While he eventually is successful in gathering evidence, as the town's main employer the carpet factory holds the town officials hostage. Even the local newspaper editor, who has supported Harry, will not publish the evidence of pollution. The book doesn't deliver a lone ranger ending. Harry is threatened by the factory director and forced to suppress his findings. He must console himself with the prospects of joining the air force and leaving his town and family when he graduates from high school.

As Betty was browsing through the class sets in the seventh-grade bookroom, she noticed *When the Stars Begin to Fall* first because of the author. She knew that James Collier was adept at capturing issues in a good story and that he carefully researched the background for his books. She remembered that this book had caught the interest of a few students last year as an individual choice. The words *community* and *carpet factory* on the back cover blurb reminded her of a chemical fiber plant near the school that was the center of a chemical pollution controversy, and after a review, she decided the book was just what she needed as a focus of discussions about critical issues of citizenship.

Issues of family dysfunction, environmental community activism, stereotyping, economic oppression, and exploitation are all intertwined in the personal development of Harry White. This combination was just what we needed to engage students in sorting out personal and societal forces in their lives. Through the lives of Harry and his sister, students could identify with marginalized points of view and see how personal values are part of a cultural and economic context. The students could begin their reading while Betty collected newspaper articles, Web sites, and other sources to create a text set with different perspectives on the issues embedded in the story. The novel was a natural next step on the students' journey to explore what democracy means to peoples' lives.

Betty had the sense from their journal entries that the suspenseful action and the social issues had captured the students' imaginations. They had found Harry worthy of respect despite his outward deviation from the norm, and they were even sympathetic toward his sister, understanding that she wanted desperately to escape her social isolation.

The students gathered for literature circle, and the student leader, Matt, opened the discussion with the question: "How is Harry different from the other students in his school?" Alexis attempted to characterize the complexity of Harry's character: "We think he's different, [but] he doesn't want people to think his family is different. He's the only one trying to do everything. He's the only one that cares." The acquiescence of the rest of the family to their outcast status bothered and puzzled the students. Hale's query "Why doesn't the rest of his family care about what people think about them?" elicited a rash of inconclusive explanations that led the group to their real concern: how can people call other people such an ugly word as *trash?*

Les was adamant as he interjected that a person can't really be trash. "Trash is something you throw away. Everyone has something good about them, so nobody can be trash! They could have some bad qualities, be, like, a little dirty, maybe steal, but nobody is trash." The group was very intent, hunched and leaning forward over their desks. Many nodded in agreement, and others were poised to jump in.

Jack began to list the negatives of the White family, perhaps excusing, or just trying to work out in his mind, the basis for community rejection: "I just think people thought that about them because of their house, the way they lived, where they lived. I think the parents may, I mean, his dad stole things, so. . . . The children didn't do that. Well . . . Helen does later."

The students knew very well how people were treated as outcasts in their school and also in society by adults. But they seemed to be struggling to go beyond the usual definition of outcast status. They seemed to be trying to articulate an important distinction. Perhaps there was, for some of these students, a shared effort to restructure their moral code. They sensed that it was wrong to reject a person based on material possessions, but they weren't sure where the boundaries of disrespect should be drawn. The question of what makes a good person was being put to a test, and it was evident that they cared about finding some answers. As the discussion continued, students built on one another's insights, but wouldn't let go of the central point.

Other students chimed in, and the topic veered onto stealing and bad reputations, how people judge one another by the house they live in, and whether Harry and his sister would have been better off if they had been placed in a foster home, which sparked disagreement.

Addy would not allow the initial discussion of "trash" to be dropped. Twice more she brought the group back to reinforce Les's point about not judging people by outward characteristics: "People can act 'trash-y,' like, if they are mean to other people or they do things like steal or deal drugs to get money, but no one *is* trash." After a pause, Addy launched into surprising insights about cultural relativity: ". . . and also like Adam said about going into a foster home, in some cultures that's how everyone lives." This last comment was met with puzzled silence and some "huh's" and giggles. The other students didn't get it. When Betty asked her to explain a bit, Addy continued, "I mean, like in villages in, like some faraway land, everyone lives like it's common for them though."

Alexis helped Addy with a related thought, that in some cultures the *ideal* is to live without material things, not making an impact on the earth. "Yeah, if they lived in some little village nobody ever heard of, in some village, like in Africa or something, they would live like that and it would be normal and not trashy." These girls seemed to be more aware than the other students that different societies operate differently. At any rate, this idea was quickly dropped, and the students went back to their central concern—the ostracizing of a family they had come to empathize with.

Les returned yet again to the distinction that seemed to be so important to the students, and others agreed: "It's what they *do* that makes them become trash. Trash isn't what they *have,* it's what they *do.*" Now other students who had been quiet jumped in to defend the White children, pointing out that they couldn't help smelling when they had no washing machine and their water was cut off, and having a depressed mother who didn't cook or clean for them. Tina, who knew someone in depression, came to the mother's defense: "Maybe she knew her kids were miserable but she didn't think she could do anything about it so she just sat around." Amelia added her insight about the difficulties of getting out of a bad relationship: "Maybe before she married, she had her own good life, or he might have said, 'I'll beat you if you get a divorce.'"

Adam, in his role as discussion co-leader, sensed an end to this topic and offered another prepared question: "How important is money in this story, and why?" Russell raised his hand and said with feeling, "If you believe you have to have money, you'll probably not be happy being a good, moral person." Jack's hand was up now, and he defended his father as a good man who made all his money by himself and wanted to keep it. It seemed that Jack needed to make some kind of bridge between his father and the rejection of materialism that had emerged in the discussion, and he added, "You need morals to make your money worth more." After a few more comments, the discussion continued at a quieter pace, focusing on other topics, led by the student leaders' questions.

From time to time, a significant discussion such as this one grew out of the day-to-day exchange of ideas around the texts students were reading. Betty wanted students to move beyond the text into larger questions; she wanted texts to be "sites for cultural conversations." Although students did identify literary elements and often began discussions by clarifying the characteristics of the characters, the setting, and the plot, she wanted them to develop an understanding of how the world works and how it *might* work. Books such as *When the Stars Begin to Fall* allowed students to speculate about how people make judgments about others, specifically the damage to our society made by judgments based on external characteristics. And they did raise their thinking to the level of ethical treatment of others, with many expressions of compassionate concern. Students were beginning to notice the ways in which social customs and power affect ethical decisions. When they talked about principles they believed in, we hoped that the "lifespace" they envisioned for themselves as adults was expanding to embrace a more active role of citizenship.

Literature: A Repository of Cultural Values

Beverly: Why do you think James Collier might have written this book?

Tina: So students could have the kind of discussion we've been having. So people will talk about these things.

Literature allowed these mostly affluent, suburban students to get inside the lives of others, including those whose lives were more threatened by social and economic conditions. Each book, each story, offered a different world of meaning, and as they read, students could view the workings of society through the eyes of authors who portrayed that society.

Students need to see their own lives interpreted and validated in the books they read, and they also need to see the wide panoply of humanity, not just to watch these characters enact their lives, but also to see *into* their lives. Through books, students can develop strong bonds with diverse individuals they would be unlikely to meet in their actual lives, or could never know well. Books can overcome the strong social barriers that keep adolescents boxed up in their own particular social group.

Literature is a repository of new and alternative ideas and values that expand the life boundaries of students. Living in someone else's life, even vicariously, can help readers grow beyond themselves and help them discover what they may be seeking in life, or help them identify what they are missing. For students who are trying to unravel problems and conflicts between people, discussions of literature can offer a safe space for open discussion of confused feelings, without the direct confrontation of peers. Powerful stories arouse the kind of compassion for others it is necessary for people to feel in order to care about social issues, and when stories are surrounded by informational material, students can also become better informed.

The power of a story, especially a novel, is its capacity to recapture some of the wholeness of experience. The process of coming to understand the dynamics of a particular time and place inevitably fragments the intricate connectedness of life. Life itself has an unbreakable unity, but when we name and describe its elements, we lose track of that unity. The conceptual process of coming to understanding guarantees that we break up the unity of life that we experience as a whole. An author of fiction tries to recreate the integrated flow of experience as it might have been lived (Paterson, 1981, p. 11).

Teachers will find stories from every corner of our country and the far reaches of the globe. And each year more documentary material is available. It is now possible through the abundance of compelling socially conscious literature to bring into classrooms the lives of marginalized and voiceless peoples, the lives of people who protest injustices, and the lives of people who come together to work for humanity.

Teaching about Social Issues in Language Arts Classes

The NCTE Committee on Teaching about Genocide and Intolerance developed important guidelines for teachers who wish to introduce older students to society's conflicts and issues through literature. The committee recognized the two-sided power of books to influence—and to expand—humanitarian impulses and also to distort reality in negative ways. Our work has been guided by these nine "curricular premises":

> Language has been used throughout history in the service of deception, manipulation, and domination of individuals and groups. It can also be used by victims, advocates, and activists as a means of resistance, education, and liberation.

Language thus functions as a social and historical medium that can limit or expand human possibility, depending on the way language is organized to mark, mythologize, or delimit what it means to be human.

Literature goes beyond representing a culture or a period. It is universal, transcending time and place, and as such has a lasting, shaping influence on readers.

Similarly, other media such as newspapers, films, art, and music can be used to influence human activity. [In classrooms] they can also be used to examine the context of a historical event and the factors that helped to shape it.

Literature teaching therefore can be viewed as a transformative social practice through which students (along a developmental continuum from primary through secondary levels) can imagine how things could be otherwise and come to recognize that the possibility exists for a better world.

Literature functions not only as aesthetic, but also as social discourse. Texts play with meanings in a way that reflects and shapes cultural practices and—in many ways—represent the emotional and cultural memory of humankind.

Literature engages the human character. It not only evokes a response, it also helps to illuminate history because it frequently serves as a response to it. Literature responds to this human record of history and evokes further responses in readers by bringing people to life and by putting a human face on the history. It also helps us to see what might be.

Literature resonates, helping us to see and know ourselves. It often does more, but it should not do less.

Through writing, students can analyze, refine, and clarify their own emotional responses to issues and engage in the critical reflection that leads to personal transformation. (Danks & Rabinsky, 1999, pp. 2–3)

Readers and Cultural Messages

When we began to look to literature to introduce students to social realities, we discovered that certain cautions were important. Apol (1998, p. 34) advises that a text should not be viewed as a reflection of reality, not even one particular reality. A text inevitably promotes a certain version of reality from a particular author's perspective, and it positions readers within that version of reality. The author Katherine Paterson (1981, pp. 72–73) recalls being startled when an admirer praised her for conveying so well the dreams and fears of people in medieval Japan in *The Sign of the Chrysanthemum* (1988). She knew that, although she worked to make her historical novels true to their time, the dreams and fears of the characters were a reflection of a twentieth-century author. "My books are not Japanese novels. They are Western novels about Japan," she notes.

Like a thoughtful author bringing a period to life, teachers are faced with a paradoxical decision-making process. On the one hand, we want the author to infuse hopes and dreams into the book, and we want students to see characters in cultural contexts. Yet a realized character is "realized" through the filter of one author's culture, experiences, and psychology. It is important not to ask too much of one text as an interpreter of cultural experience, and we need to make sure students understand the subjective nature of any text.

In a sense, a novel is situated in three cultural contexts—the culture of the setting, the author's culture, and the reader's culture. All three of these contexts contribute to what a child learns about society from a novel. Our solution to the dilemma of "reality" was to expose students to alternatives in all three of these cultural spaces. Through a wide variety of sources, Betty brought many different lives from the Depression era or the World War II era into the classroom so that the particular time and place was not defined by one life or perspective. She looked for thoughtful authors and those who had done thorough research or had firsthand experience, and thus included perspectives from autobiography, biography, newspapers, databases, maps, poetry, and fiction. And last, she provided opportunities for dialogue so that students were exposed to their own many cultural perspectives as they constructed a shared sense of the text.

Accessibility of Social Context

When students had difficulty seeing the societal conditions of the Depression era as a context for the events in *Roll of Thunder, Hear My Cry,* we began to understand how much of the novel's context was merely implied. For instance, near the end of the book when Papa sets his cotton field on fire to save T. J. "from the mob," the students needed to research facts about lynching and also have Betty's assistance to connect that information with the text in order to think about T. J.'s probable fate. Now we realize that students will miss much of the social implications of a book without additional background. We wonder how valid the engagement with social struggle can be if the "story" constructed by the students is limited to personal conflicts caused by "mean people."

At first glance, *Roll of Thunder* and *When the Stars Begin to Fall* seemed of similar difficulty. Neither had technical vocabulary nor difficult stylistic elements. Both showed social inequities and control by a dominant class. But in *Stars,* the social issues were spelled out overtly in scenes depicting unfair harassment and exploitation of Harry and his sister Helen.

Also, students could fill in the blanks from their own school experiences, whereas the historical period of *Roll of Thunder* was more foreign to them. Students knew what it meant when the newspaper editor in *Stars* said: "I still have to live in this town." They easily related events in this book to their concurrent study of the media, especially newspaper clippings highlighting a local exposé of a fiber plant that tried to hide its pollution. The issues were, for the most part, accessible to this group of students, and they were able to inquire into the larger issues of marginalization, as shown in the opening narrative of this chapter.

Just because a novel is set in a period of history does not mean that it reveals the social forces of that time. Both *No Promises in the Wind* (Hunt) and *Bud, Not Buddy* (Curtis), for example, show boys on the road during the Depression. Widespread poverty is apparent in both books, but *Bud, Not Buddy* overtly depicts more of the issues and social movements of the period, whereas *No Promises* offers a mostly personal experience of poverty. Neither book reveals patterns of racism or race laws in the northern states, but *Bud, Not Buddy* includes a racial confrontation, while *No Promises* gives no hint of discrimination even when the boys end up on the New Orleans waterfront. Similarly, *Esperanza Rising* (Ryan) includes an extensive description of how a farmworker strike might be planned and defeated, whereas Hesse's *Out of the Dust* features individual struggles against adverse conditions.

Reading with a more discerning eye for the explicitness of social messages will help teachers better match students with the books they need in order to learn about society. A compelling book such as *Out of the Dust* will be even more powerful if surrounded by information explaining the pervasiveness of the natural and economic forces behind the conditions of life depicted. As students share their interpretations of the texts they are reading, teachers will discover what additional resources are needed.

Issues That Touch a Nerve

Sometimes books will open up personal conflicts among a group of students. A friend in Los Angeles told us that conflict resolution activities would be needed before a book depicting African American discrimination, such as *Roll of Thunder,* could be read in her racially polarized classes. Teachers should consider whether tensions in a group will be aggravated or healed by any particular book. Children whose families have been damaged by the Holocaust, for example, might not be able to enter into the World War II literature as easily as Betty's students did. They were horrified but not personally threatened.

Betty was surprised that few students wrote about racial conflict in their final projects. Certainly their factual reports gave strong descriptions of these discriminatory and violent conditions. Living in a southern state, however, students may have backed away from this conflict because it came too close to home. Students may have found it hard to be explicit about black-white conflicts with friends of a different race sitting next to them. And perhaps the available literature itself was less direct than it might have been. There were no novels of a lynching, nor stories of white families who stood up against segregation and were run out of town, powerful actions that might have prompted more students to address racism in their projects.

Rethinking the Classroom Library

Betty was committed to providing as large a selection of books as possible in the room for students' personal choices. She wanted a diverse collection in order to entice all the students into enjoyment of reading—fiction and nonfiction, boy books and girl books, tough books and tender books, easy books and challenging books, fat books and thin books. She also worked to include many cultures, making sure in particular that the large population of African American students would find a home in the classroom library. Kimberly noticed this right away at the beginning of the year, saying, "You have these books here all the time, Mrs. Slesinger, not just during Black History Week!" Betty wanted the stories of growing up to show the surrounding culture as explicitly as possible, as in Gary Soto's *A Summer Life* and Russell Baker's *Growing Up*. She also collected provocative stories in which people create multicultural relationships across social boundaries, such as Bruce Brooks's *Moves Make the Man,* Edward Bloor's *Tangerine,* and Carolyn Meyer's *Jubilee Journey.*

The classroom library can support students by offering stories of young people who step forward to act on their beliefs. Ellen Levine's *Freedom's Children* and Casey King and Linda Osbourne's *Oh Freedom: Kids Talk about the Civil Rights Movement with the People Who Made It Happen* portray the ordinary people who took extraordinary action during this turbulent period. Novels with persistent activist characters such as John in *California Blue* or the students in Jean C. George's *Who Really Killed Cock Robin?* have the potential to influence students' values.

Students should have access to biographies of people who challenged their times, who crossed cultural dividing lines and forged new paths, such as Eleanor Roosevelt, Cesar Chavez, and Frederick Douglass. Likewise, Mary Anning, Maria Mitchell, and Marie Curie are three women who broke scientific barriers; Fannie Lou Hamer and Jane Addams fought for the rights of impoverished people. It is also important for students to read about people who worked together for causes, such as the neighbors in Paul Fleischman's *Seedfolks*.

Text Sets: At the Heart of Inquiry into Issues

Once Betty understood the potential of a text set to engage students in different points of view about social issues, she tried not to present a topic from one point of view or to let an important work of fiction stand alone. She viewed student learning as evolving, beginning with one text and open to challenge and reinterpretation by other texts. At each stage, understandings are temporary.

What Is a Text Set?

A text set is a collection of various types of texts related to a topic that invites multiple interpretations and responses from students. In our text sets, we included both print (books, letters, articles, and so forth) and nonprint (videos, graphics, cartoons, artifacts, and so on) sources. Texts sets are not random; they are not simply a collection of different texts on a topic. They are deliberately and thoughtfully chosen materials from reliable authors, artists, musicians, participants, and experts who offer different perspectives on a topic. Each item should make a valuable contribution: a different genre, a different style of writing, different life experiences, and alternative points of view. For text sets on social issues, teachers should look for different voices of the times, especially the "silenced" voices of our society.

Exploring multiple texts on a topic helped students gain an awareness of alternative views without having to dismiss their existing beliefs. New perspectives could test students' beliefs and perhaps move them to a more critical stance. Literature discussions comparing two different texts allowed students a safe space in which to evaluate life alternatives. They could compare different viewpoints without directly criticizing or passing judgment on one another's values or way of life. When the opposing arguments came from a text rather than the person at the next desk, the risk of offending classmates was reduced.

Sometimes the whole class experienced the same text (short texts to launch inquiry, core novels, pieces of art or music), and at other times students were offered alternatives so they could make choices to meet their needs or interests (companion novels, nonfiction sources for research). We found that when students read different texts, their collaboration increased.

Students had reasons to interact with one another as they shared new knowledge from different sources.

Finding Fiction for Social Issues

When we were looking for items for a text set, the topic became a filter through which to view the world. New possibilities seemed to be everywhere. As Betty searched for books about learning, she discovered the theme in books she was already using. When we started thinking about the Depression era, Beverly discovered that she had a reproduction of Woody Guthrie's journal that discussed the context of his songs. Betty owned other 1930s music, and friends told us about online sources.

Rereading texts with a sharper eye for social context, we found that justice was at the core of much of the required seventh-grade literature. Even the old anthologies stored in the book room yielded some valuable items. Connections between books read at different times of the year would sometimes highlight a theme. For example, when students read Dickens's *A Christmas Carol* (excerpted in a literature anthology) after the Depression-era unit, they saw the social inequities in what had been in previous years primarily a story of personal suffering.

It did not seem necessary to preplan a text set in its entirety before beginning a unit of work. The set evolved as additional sources came to light, as students' needs suggested new text choices, and as students themselves began to contribute ideas.

Components of a Text Set in an Inquiry Unit

Texts to Launch Inquiry

Students' initial questions were stimulated by experiences that gave them a taste of a subject—just enough to leave them wanting to know more. An enigmatic picture book, a set of photographs, or a film clip were a few of the enticing short texts that piqued student interest. We looked for an emotional hook in a text short enough that students could engage with the work and yet have time to discover and share their questions all in one class period.

When students formed emotional attachments to characters, they became interested in searching out the factual information that surrounded those lives. A simple story was often all that was needed. For example, the picture book *Polar, the Titanic Bear* (Spedden), an eyewitness account by one of the passengers who got on a lifeboat, led students to read more about the third-class immigrants on the *Titanic*. It would be hard to find a better launch for studying World War II than the haunting storybook *Rose Blanche*. Photos from *Now Let Us Praise Famous Men* and *Kids at Work*, combined with the first chapters of *Roll of Thunder, Hear My Cry*, captured students' interest in learning more about the Depression era. The picture book *Angels in the Dust* by Margot Theis Raven or a dramatic passage from *Out of the Dust* (Hesse) made vivid the struggles of kids their own age against the mounting horrors of the dry-as-dust land. Once the students cared about characters and had an opportunity to raise their own questions, they seemed more likely to pursue the lengthy engagement of immersion in the topic. The predictable framework of asking "what we already know" and "what we want to know" was a simple yet still powerful way to begin pulling their ideas together.

Core Novels

One way to approach a unit of inquiry is through a novel study. To serve as the center of an extended engagement by students, a novel should be substantive, engaging, and well researched. The following criteria should be used to choose a novel that will be at the center of inquiry into social issues:

Selecting a Core Text for a Novel-Based Inquiry Unit

- Conveys the societal context of the characters, with glimpses of its complexities
- Appeals to and is appropriate for boys and girls twelve to thirteen years of age of all races, cultures, and religions
- Reveals qualities of a fair and just society
- Encourages and demonstrates qualities of human dignity
- Expands reader's awareness and understanding of life
- Promotes wondering; is multifaceted
- Has style and skillful use of language and literary elements
- Reflects situations/problems students of our community might face or need to consider
- Provides evidence of research into the social context and/or personal experience
- Receives awards or recommendations from reliable sources

Alternatives to *Roll of Thunder, Hear My Cry* as the core novel for a study of the Depression era are other novels that provide the depth of meaning, writing craft, unresolved issues, and multidimensional cultural context we looked for—*Out of the Dust* and *Bud, Not Buddy* (for younger students). Others, such as *No Promises in the Wind, Queenie Peavy,* or *A*

Year down Yonder (Peck) were more appropriate as companion novels because they provided a more limited, less complex view of the period.

Integrating Fact and Fiction: A Stimulus for Inquiry

When the students read fictional and informational texts simultaneously, the interaction between emotional connections and background information created a strong desire to know more about distant people, places, and events. Tidbits of factual information provided the essential context that enabled students to engage with "difficult" fiction. And once they began to care about the struggles of a few people in a story, they wanted to know more about other people who lived at the same time. They wanted to know *why* events happened. Further inquiry was stimulated as they entered into additional experiences with photos, informational books, maps, timelines, other novels, poetry, and art to expand a connected understanding of their protagonists' world and situation. If connected knowledge is what makes life interesting and meaningful for adults, why should it be any different for children? Staying with a topic over a long period of time supported a process of connecting the factual context of a topic with the emotional and enigmatic energy of art, poetry, and fiction to build layers of commitment and understanding.

Poet and essayist Naomi Nye (1989) reminds us that fiction and nonfiction are in actuality quite closely related: "Fiction and nonfiction are more like a big family with members who all secretly get along" (pp. 532–35). Both use characters, conflicts, settings, points of view, theme, and elements of poetry as well. Also, facts are present in both kinds of writing, and, after all, aren't data sets and stories just different ways that human beings represent life experiences?

Because of the verisimilitude of the novels they were reading, students would often ask Betty, "Is this a true story?" And she might reply, "Does it fit with the reports you are reading about the Depression?" These incidents also provided opportunities to remind students of how novelists use research to make a story credible and interesting to readers. Mildred Taylor, author of *Roll of Thunder, Hear My Cry,* reports that her father's family stories were the seeds for many of her published stories. Through their own research and interviews, students began to understand just how Taylor and other authors wrote convincing books.

The Many Genres of Nonfiction

The ability to read nonfiction purposefully and discerningly is critical for informed citizenship. A population that does not read diverse perspectives and factual information weakens the nation's well-being. Such citizens may have opinions but will lack the background needed for productive public dialogue. Yet in our nation's classrooms, fiction stories far outnumber informational books, and anthologies are more likely to be filled with short stories and poems than articles, essays, and biographies. Nonfiction is still a stepsister to fiction and poetry.

Nonfiction may be difficult for middle school students because they are less familiar with it than with fiction and because nonfiction sprawls across many diverse purposes and organizational forms. Theoretically, providing information is a unifying feature of all this diversity, but in reality, readers are faced with a confusing array of forms such as news articles, reflective essays, biographies, photojournal articles, editorials, and so forth. Each has its own characteristic style, content, and organization. Students needed guidance in learning how to read various types of informative texts. Betty provided many coaching lessons and text annotation experiences to help students master these texts.

Using Nonfiction

After watching students *using* information sources, we began to see nonfiction differently. We had been critical of encyclopedias as dry and rather useless sources of learning. In our thinking about informational texts, we privileged literary nonfiction, written to interest readers by means of personal connections, arresting illustrations, and captivating images. Now that we have watched students at work who want and need information, however, we have come to see the value of utilitarian nonfiction texts. These sources—dictionary, atlas, encyclopedia, telephone book, manual, and the like—written for an audience who already wants the information, are dense with facts and usually feature indexes and other aids to finding pertinent information readily. Their prominence in the students' inquiry shouldn't have been surprising to us. Our own houses are full of such texts—bird identification books, gardening books, guides to classical music, TV guides, dictionaries, and road maps.

Because the encyclopedia was not the only source of information for students' inquiry, we could appreciate its qualities in a better light. When students had read multiple stories about the Depression era but wanted to know about the stock market crash, a brief, spare encyclopedia summary was useful. When students began interacting in the world, getting in touch with people in the community to make arrangements for service projects and finding out information from experts, the homely, basic, to-the-point telephone books, maps, and encyclopedias were often what was needed. Even brochures took on new significance as we considered the importance of citizens banding together to work for the betterment of their community. Shouldn't such groups have expertise in getting their messages out to the public? As David Bloome (1993) points out, these utilitarian written materials may be the "genres of democracy" that need a more prominent place in the curriculum.

Literary Nonfiction Choices

A wealth of appealing nonfiction books about social issues is now available for children and young adults, perhaps because of the spread of student inquiry in classrooms. Students were fascinated with Jim Murphy's *The Boys' War.* Milton Meltzer is a prolific author for young adults, with a long list of provocative books on social issues, including a new Great Depression book, *Driven from the Land: The Story of the Dust Bowl.* Russell Freedman is the talented author of several valuable books the students used for their research. The photos in *Immigrant Kids* gave students a realistic look at how some of their families may have entered the United States, and *Kids at Work: Lewis Hine and the Crusade against Child Labor* was another eye opener. His two Depression-era/wartime biographies, *Eleanor Roosevelt: A Life of Discovery* and *Franklin Delano Roosevelt,* are sources we would use in future units. Each is full of the social context for the Roosevelts' leadership and includes information about the people who worked with them rather than presenting them as solitary heroes.

Many of these newer nonfiction books have the potential to hook readers with vivid descriptions, conversations, photos, and personal narratives. They create an emotional impact and pull students into societal situations and problems. A compelling nonfiction book that tells a story, such as Jerry Stanley's *Children of the Dust Bowl: The Story of the School at Weedpatch Camp,* could very well be the commonly read core title for a unit of social inquiry on the Depression era.

The Author behind the Message

Authors have always had a prominent place in Betty's classroom. Visitors could see them smiling from posters on the walls, and they could read about them in the large file of articles and books in one corner of the room. In Betty's classes, students talked about authors, speculating on how an author came to write a book and what he or she was trying to do with words. As we considered the competencies of citizenship, awareness of the author behind the text became more important than ever. Without an awareness of the ways in which authors influence readers, acquiescing students might become gullible citizens. They need to ask why an author chose to tell a story from a particular point of view, or how the story might have been different.

The middle school curriculum requires lessons on analyzing the validity and accuracy of an author's information, but Betty found that the students' observations indicated a rather simple level of awareness. Brad noted that "this author did a lot of scientific study to gather much information about volcanoes." Laura wrote uncritically,

> I could tell the author had looked up the lives of a lot of spies and he appreciated them very much. Throughout the prologue and the chapters he encourages admiration for the spies by telling us of their dangers and how important they were to battles we were having. The author might be a history professor.

If students were not brought to an awareness of the range of opinions that entered their classroom through the texts they read, would they be aware as adults of the range of opinion expressed publicly? Who has access to the media, why, and how are issues critical to fairness and equity in modern society. The fewer the people who are able to voice opinions, the fewer the people who control the media, the less chance we all have to make our concerns and situations known. If only corporate interests and governments have access to the media, how will we know the life conditions of factory workers, custodians, housewives, dishwashers, slum apartment dwellers, and newly arrived immigrants?

Viewing Critically: Media Watch

Each year, Betty's students conducted a loosely related series of activities that focused critically on the media in order to help them understand the power of the media in our society and then to join their own voice to the public discourse. In this chapter, we discuss the study of propaganda techniques and the values they promote, and in Chapter 8 we describe the extension of this study into journals, connections with nonprofit agencies, and writing to "someone who needs to know." Each year the schedule was different, and activities varied, sometimes focused on television, at other times on magazines and newspapers.

After a brief guided study of propaganda techniques, students were assigned to watch for examples of propaganda by keeping a TV log for five days, identifying either advertising or type of program, the technique used, and the message conveyed. (At the time of this study, access to the Internet was not as prevalent as it is today, so students' resources were limited to television, magazines, and newspapers.) A group discussion of a startling ad helped get students activated. At first they were delighted just to be able to watch television as a legitimate class assignment. It seemed to be the first time many students had viewed television from a critical stance. Many of the "messages" they identified were concrete and superficial, such as our society allows body tattooing and piercing, it's great to be rich, most people like sports.

As they continued their watch, however, students were able to dig a little deeper into media messages. Betty was pleased to see that some students began to "read" the commercials for more than their intended messages and became at least somewhat aware of how the total impact of a commercial promoted social values. Materialism, equity, and other social issues entered the discussion. As students brought their critical assessments into class, Betty pulled out conclusions and copied them to use in discussions to deepen the level of dialogue. She wanted to give value to their work by putting it at the center of her teaching while at the same time demonstrating that in a community of inquirers conclusions are tentative and open to debate. She offered questions to help students in their analysis, such as "Why was the ad set in this particular location? What clues were the viewers supposed to pick up on? What background knowledge did the program assume viewers had? Who was the intended audience? What were possible purposes of the sponsor(s)?" Following are some examples of students' critique of media effects:

> They manipulate audience's feelings, sometimes using bribes of rebates and reductions.
>
> They try to make the audience think corporations care about creativity and helping, when all they really care about is money.
>
> They make it seem like you should judge a person by the way they look.
>
> They use soft, blurry, or fast-changing focusing to keep your eye attracted and make things look bigger, brighter, and better than they really are.
>
> They give obese people little respect.
>
> They make people look pretty selfish, wanting everything.
>
> They often make husbands and fathers look dumb and silly.

Alerted to the potential of tacit messages, some students found discrepancies between their own values and the social values of the media, such as:

> Americans like entertainment, even if it is basically brainless.
>
> Life is not fair if you judge by "American values."
>
> The U.S. portrays itself as an optimistic place in spite of having many reasons not to be.

Our society pushes people to buy things instead of thinking and
caring.

Many governments are corrupt; people need to view situations
more critically.

There are many types of injustice, like the question of life in
prison with no chance for parole.

The few minorities [in the mainstream media] show how our
society is racist.

To continue the dialogue and push students to a sense of media as
a national force that influences values and perceptions on a continuing
basis, Betty put the students in small groups to rate each of the statements
for validity using a 1 to 5 scale, giving examples of specific TV shows that
supported their vote. Then they theorized about *why* our culture enjoys
or accepts such attitudes and practices. Betty hoped that the entire sequence of research, exchange of perceptions, and dialogue about values
would give students at least a taste of the open exchange of "informed
opinion" that should characterize a democracy.

Author Stance and Democracy

As students read different perspectives on social issues during the year,
they continued their speculation about the author's stance and purposes.
Betty used a series of questions to activate more critical discussions and
journal entries. Peter's interest in how the media treated Dr. Jack Kevorkian
alerted some students to the slant the media could give a story. By the time
students read *When the Stars Begin to Fall,* they were thinking more imagi-
natively about author purposes and thought that Collier's purpose might
be "to get students like us to have discussions like this." Peter was more
explicit about his message: "The author shows us that our society judges
people by how they dress or smell, and [we] don't bother to try to communicate with them."

Informed opinions and social critique depend on the ability to look
at issues from diverse points of view. We hoped that students might become accustomed to consulting many sources in order to learn about a
social topic, examining and challenging those sources in a group of their
peers. Perhaps this stance might become a habit that continued into adulthood. The Depression unit seemed especially successful in awakening
students to the potential of getting many points of view on an issue. They
heard the striking voice of Franklin Roosevelt, and they learned the bank-
ers' point of view. They heard Woody Guthrie's voice raised in song, and
they shared the life stories of hoboes, farmers, small businessmen, and
sharecroppers. Through paintings, photographs, and repositories of inter-

views, students became informed about the plight of migrant workers, coal miners, sweatshop seamstresses, minority refugees, and child laborers.

Changing Readers: Authority, Connections, and Convictions

As students gained experience in discussing different social perspectives, they seemed to change as readers. Students who had been "outsider" readers, those who focused on the events and actions, showed signs of becoming "insider" readers, those who lived within the literary experience (Rosenblatt, 1995). The stronger students seemed to thrive on activities in which they talked across texts. As Jonathan so vividly put it, "Your mind blows up when you read a new book that you can fit into the last book." When Yvonne wrote to her disk pal recommending *The Road to Memphis,* a sequel to *Roll of Thunder,* she moved into issues far beyond the text:

> As I read this book I got a taste of what it was like to be a black person living at that time. No one treated blacks as if they were real people. The white people did whatever they wanted with blacks. At stores if the white owners didn't want to serve the black people, then they didn't. This kind of stuff is happening all over the United States right now. It might not be blacks that are treated unfairly, it might be another minority group. I encourage you to read this book because you, too, will see the world from a black person's perspective.

Yvonne's remarks are all the more powerful when you know she is of Eurasian descent and may have known discrimination herself.

Strategies for Active Reading

It took instruction and practice over time for the students to enter the realm of inference, comparison, and extension as they read, and some never did reach this level of active reading. Fall classes were full of coaching lessons and teacher support, and gradually the students began to work more independently. Betty had to be patient, especially with the regular classes, waiting for them catch on to the strategies and for improvement to show. Most of the active reading strategies Betty taught were accumulations of and adaptations from sources such as Keene and Zimmermann's *Mosaic of Thought* (1997) and Harvey's *Nonfiction Matters* (1998). Betty modeled her own reading, gave explicit instruction, guided them through short texts, and reflected with the students about their strategies.

Short texts such as the excellent short articles on social issues in *Read* magazine were used to highlight or practice reading strategies students would need if they were to be active inquirers (Harvey & Goudvis, 2000).

Special assistance was also given to instruct and guide students before, during, and after reading some of the texts in the inquiry units. Students practiced the usual strategies of reading repeatedly: activating prior knowledge, anticipating organizational patterns, monitoring meanings, providing self-help with problems, using graphic organizers, testing assumptions and predictions, inferring meanings, asking questions, synthesizing information, and reflecting on texts.

Literature Journals

Active response in literature journals/reading response notebooks helped the students interact with stories in order to construct their own worldview. The use of journals is described in more detail in Chapter 4, and their integration into inquiry units is demonstrated in Chapters 2 and 5. Occasionally Betty assigned a special format, but for the most part students were asked to respond to their novels and short stories in comfortable, predictable ways, including at various times some of these kinds of responses (but always the last two):

- Note information about the social context.
- Record important feelings and thoughts of characters and significant movements in the plot.
- Note and explain the use of literary elements.
- Explain how the author uses language.
- Raise significant questions.
- Reflect on significant applications to human life.

Many class periods began with a brief coaching lesson focused on a student's thoughtful journal entry, which was placed on the overhead. Betty might say: "Here is an entry by Liz that comments on Cassie's frustration and then extends into a discussion of how people can act positively on frustration, and how sometimes it leads to negative behavior. Isn't this an interesting comment! Liz is digging into the text here and using it to think about how we live our lives. Does anyone have a different example in your lit response today of how the book makes you think about your life?" An informal rubric with a point system (see Chapter 3) was occasionally used. Betty either responded to journal entries (usually with points contributing to a grade) or she had students use them in literature discussions.

Students' reading response notebooks provided a pulse point that Betty used to check the students' thoughts and needs; the notebooks allowed her to take the temperature of their book choices and reading engagement. Response notebooks, far more insightful and useful than perfunctory chapter checks to ensure students were doing their reading, furnished an opportunity to observe students' thinking. Betty often found lapses in student thinking that helped her plan a coaching lesson, such as how authors manipulate time in different ways. Best of all, Betty could personalize her teaching with her replies and respond appreciatively to an individual student's thinking, feelings, and growth.

Questioning the Text

Questions occur in reading when there is some kind of "disconnect" between what the reader expects—or believes—and a feature, a meaning, or an event in a text. Sometimes differences between two students set off a round of questioning. Hale raised the question, "Why doesn't anyone else in the family care what other people think about the family?" and thereby set off a probing inquiry in the literature discussion of *When the Stars Begin to Fall*. That dialogue was probably so intense because of the many disconnects between the students' lives and the White family's life, and also between how the Whites were treated and how the students wanted people to be treated.

Betty constantly encouraged question asking as a reading response. In fact, to push the more passive readers, asking questions was a required part of the literature response journal. At the beginning of a new book, student questions were primarily space fillers, but as students got deeper into the book, real questions emerged. In teacher-led book discussions, Betty invited students to wonder about an event or a theme: "Let's look at where Mildred Taylor shows us injustice and how she does it. Let's look more closely at this. . . . What do you wonder about this incident?" Here are some of the prompts Betty used to encourage students to raise questions in their literature journals:

> **Prompts for Asking Questions in Literature Logs**
>
> As you read:
>
> > Write questions about something that interfered with your understanding.
> >
> > What made you curious in this chapter?
> >
> > Ask questions to predict coming events and situations.
> >
> > Write queries or dilemmas on sticky notes and place in text.
> >
> > Keep a bookmark (3" is good) to raise questions as you read.
> >
> > While reading, write questions that a story's narrator or characters might ask.
> >
> > Ask a question about yourself that is prompted by the book.

More than *answering* questions about reading, *raising* questions while reading opened up readers to various possibilities and suppositions about the text. Students were involved in making meaning, not just reading words or finding an answer. Asking the students to raise questions promoted controversy and encouraged the expression of alternate ideas. And the long stretches of time focused on one topic allowed the students to grow into the kind of layered understanding that raises significant questions and guides the pursuit of significant answers.

Disk Pals

Betty used the disk pal activity as a reading response to promote peer dialogue about books. These written exchanges were often more focused and probing than the conversation students exchanged in literature response groups. (Today teachers would probably create listservs or discussion boards to support this kind of informal dialogue, but Betty had a disk for each book that students inserted into the computer to read, and then they wrote about that book on the same disk.) To enter a message involved a conscious decision to say something "important," whereas face-to-face conversation could flow without much attention to what was being communicated. We also discovered that the disk pal exchanges led reluctant students to persist in their reading. Betty usually created opportunities for disk pal dialogue around the companion novels that students selected themselves. About four or six students in each class would be reading the same novel at one time, and rarely was there time for much face-to-face conversation about these books.

In the following excerpt from a disk pal discussion, Doug asks, in a personal style, for clarification about the term "Seder" and the confusing repeated flashbacks in his book. We were pleased to see that even when he was not required to do so, he raised questions. Perhaps it was becoming a habit of thinking.

> Yo! Book Pal,
> I'm reading the same book you are, *The Devil's Arithmetic* by Jane Yolen. I am half way through it. So far it's a book I can't put down, can you? But what happens at the Seder? I was wondering if you know a little more about a Seder? Remember when Hannah didn't want to go? It's like all mixed up. Also in the fifth and sixth chapters Hannah is teleported into a new location. I would like to know if you have an idea what happened to her? Anyway it is a good book.
> Doug

Annotating Texts

Students needed demonstrations of how critical readers process texts. "If we want students to learn, we must show them how," says Stephanie Harvey (1998). Annotation was an intense reading response that made the reading process more conscious as students recorded their thinking during the act of reading. Using wide margins, a bookmark, or sticky notes, students wrote their annotations adjacent to and in reaction to specific features of a text during reading. Annotation promoted close attention to text by students as they reread, scanned, compared, questioned, connected, reflected, and responded, to mention a few of the processes of interactive reading. Stopping to express their thoughts in a brief note or symbolic form further slowed the reading process and made concentrated thinking more likely.

To introduce this strategy, Betty showed students an example of an annotated essay in the literature book. After trying their hand at it, the students worked with partners to compare their notes to Betty's annotations on a short photocopied article. Using an overhead transparency of the text, Betty then talked the students through the text, reinforcing the importance of paying attention to main points, supporting information, important vocabulary, and places where the text was confusing.

Betty planned periodic opportunities for students to use annotation for both nonfiction and fiction. Annotation took time, but it was a good way to call attention to the different ways in which information is organized and presented in different genres. One year the students kept copies of an Active Reader list of suggestions in their notebooks to use as prompts.

An Annotation Example

The more able readers frequently used annotation as a way to puzzle through their difficult texts. Kurt Vonnegut's "Harrison Bergeron" is a challenging short story set in the future where everyone has been made "equal." The government has imposed severe physical and intellectual limitations on the gifted and talented, such as weights to reduce strength, masks to hide beauty, and inner ear buzzers that scramble thinking. In the following student annotation, Amelia's comments give a sense of her thinking, but also of her disconnects as she reads a text that contradicts much of what she has heard and believes. She asks questions as she tries to understand the text and wants to know more. Her outrage at the punitive autocracy is clear from her comments, which are in italic next to the text selections.

everybody was finally equal.	*What does equal mean to you?*
Nobody was smarter . . . , better-looking . . . , stronger, or quicker than anybody else.	*How did that happen?*
the H-G men . . .	*Who are they?*
took George and Hazel Bergeron's fourteen-year-old son away.	*Why?*
ballerinas . . . were burdened with sash weights and bags of birdshot, and their faces were masked . . .	*I can't believe that.*
He began to think glimmeringly about his abnormal son who was now in jail, about Harrison, but a twenty-one gun salute in his head stopped that.	*Ouch! That would kill my ears!*
If I tried to get away with it [pulling out the headset and removing weights padlocked on George] . . . then other people'll get away with it, and pretty soon we'd be right back to the dark ages again, with everybody competing against everybody else.	*The Dark Ages!! ?? This sounds like a tyrannical, dictating government!*
Harrison Bergeron has just escaped from jail. . . . He is a genius, an athlete and is under-handicapped, and should be regarded as extremely dangerous.	*Not dangerous, but EXCEPTIONAL!*

Amelia's annotations helped her follow the complications of the plot, and the invitation to make her own response stimulated her voice of protest. Her annotations show, however, that she hadn't yet sensed the irony of the story. Insights into the author stance emerged later in the whole class literature circle, as students began questioning the basic premises of the social control mechanisms. Here are student-generated questions that led the group to realize the larger themes of the story:

Who can keep their thoughts long enough to think up all the rules and changes?

Wouldn't putting handicaps on the people make the levels of intelligence sink?

Why didn't they decide to bring everyone up in abilities and intelligence?

What was the purpose of their system?

Literature Circles and Response Groups

The literature discussions were one of the most satisfying aspects of "democratizing" Betty's classroom. In accordance with our belief in the quality of public discourse as one measure of civic life, we wanted the students to have many opportunities to write, talk, and present around substantive issues. The honors classes learned to hold literature circles as a whole class, since they were small and had experience with intentional dialogue through teacher-led discussions in the Great Books program. The other classes divided up into small literature discussion groups.

Betty talked with students about the expected outcomes of the discussion: they were to move beyond impressionistic conversation to connections, implications, and extensions into larger issues. Students prepared by annotating texts, generating questions, writing on sticky notes, or responding in their journals. Students who weren't prepared could not participate.

For the whole class literature circles, desks were drawn into a large circle, with Betty outside. Students signed up as partners to take the role of co-leaders, whose job it was to prepare questions the night before and call on speakers. Observing one such lit circle, Betty noticed how interested the students were in each other's comments. Even students who did not talk much turned their eyes from one speaker to the other and looked back at the book as another student was answering. Twice the discussion got heated, with everyone jumping in. She thought that the discussion was so focused because the story was truly puzzling to the students; just any story would not have had the same effect.

Some of the students' questions were specific, such as "When did this happen?" but most were good, substantive questions such as "Why do you think Marilyn kept remembering the box? What did the box represent in her life?" We observed that the discussion leaders never evaluated the comments the way a teacher might, such as, "That's a good answer." Nor did they ever criticize each other; instead, they listened and then offered alternatives.

Beverly also watched as Betty introduced a new assessment form for participants to rate the discussion leaders: "Now we are more experienced. I want us to be serious. We don't want to just talk off the tops of our heads; we don't want just to fill in the silence." She went through the four items on the form, explaining how they grew out of the students' work: "You can always suggest additions to these forms." Beverly considered this a good example of how Betty pulled students in to share decisions about the classroom. The form was handwritten, and it was obvious to the students that it represented ideas about quality discussions they had been trying to put into practice. The student assessment form was helpful because it brought a sense of value and closure to the activity. The students could assess themselves and not wait for her to do it (see the Materials for Teachers section at the end of the chapter).

Value of Literature Circles

The students seemed to like taking responsibility for framing the questions and running the discussion. It was, we thought, the kind of independence they yearned for and carried off well. They thought about their society and their own lives and pushed each other to new understandings. The small literature study groups were also valuable ways to share and stretch individual perspectives, and they created an energy that allowed the less able students to keep reading.

When Betty asked the honors classes to reflect on the circles, we could see that they valued the serious dialogue and the struggle to put their thoughts into words. One response seemed to sum up students' feelings: "When we do it ourselves, there is less pressure, but more communication, involvement, and respect." Betty asked them to reflect on their learning in a response form for homework, using these questions:

- What did you learn about yourselves?
- What new ideas did you think about?
- What did the group leaders do that helped make the discussion better?

Many students could identify ways they had grown, ranging from concrete specifics such as "There were more details than I had paid attention to" to larger dimensions of reading such as "If you participate you learn more" and "I was getting connected more to the book." Previously hidden from Betty was some private self-evaluation such as "People can tell when you haven't done your reading" and "I met my personal goal for the number of times I participated."

Students were deepening their awareness of what literature can do for a reader and sometimes thinking across texts. Some of the "new ideas" they were thinking about included "what the author used to make the story more impactual"; "the different ways there are to interpret a story"; "literary term stuff because I don't think about those unless I have to"; and "that the trial episode is kind of like the poem we read, 'The Road Not Taken,' and TJ's lawyer is taking a different path from the other white people there."

Teaching Literary Elements and Structures

The compelling life struggles of characters in the literature that highlighted social issues provided a fertile ground on which to teach literary elements. "Point of view" became more than a literary element; it was a perspective on authors and texts that was woven into discussions throughout the year. Because students were paying more attention to historical and social context, it was easier, for example, to teach the use of context to unlock the meanings of words and the larger messages of the author. Betty also felt that she was at least a little more successful in leading students to attend to the literary elements such as irony, allusion, and symbolism that helped them interpret characterizations and themes.

The strong emotions and harrowing conflicts of the characters made students more willing to return to the texts and helped them see why authors need symbols, metaphors, and other literary devices. In *A Summer Life,* for instance, Gary Soto uses the barrio environment in which his family lived to express the feelings of his younger self. The roaring train that cannot be derailed by a small boy might be the boy's desire to be more powerful; the scraggly (but loved) avocado tree helped students see the family's determined endurance; and the factory windows that rose above the small houses were a strong, dark symbol of society's oppressiveness in Soto's life. *Roll of Thunder, Hear My Cry* was rich with dialect, different points of view, and symbols, and the students, captured by the dilemma of the characters, were willing to look back at the text to uncover how these elements contributed to meaning.

The Devil's Arithmetic (Yolen) is a complex story that switches back and forth in time in a stream of consciousness style, and students needed help with it. But once students understood that authors often manipulate time to make a story more dramatic and interesting, they enjoyed the puzzle of it, and some were eager to incorporate the technique into their own work. Mandy, for example, manipulated time and place, switching her story from a concentration camp to a German village months later.

Betty had found it frustrating to teach irony and satire with the literature provided in the seventh-grade anthology. The selections did not lead students to feel the strong emotions or the critical stance that irony and satire express. Students were bored when Betty's curriculum was a journey through the anthology, and they were not invested in uncovering the layers of textual meaning necessary to an appreciation of irony or satire. But when the World War II study stimulated strong feelings that were difficult to express directly, students began to understand why writers reached for these indirect avenues to express their outrage.

Peer Teaching

One of the best lessons on satire was provided by a student. After Betty had introduced satire in a minilesson, Byron surprised her by bringing in a poem by Robert Nathan (1944) he had found on microfiche while researching his Holocaust project. He liked the poem's satire and asked to share the poem with the class on a transparency. This portion conveys its ironic tone:

They Know What They Do

. . .
We always believe the best,
Or what we are told. Probably they did not murder
The Jews after all, or even the Czechs, or the Poles.
There is no smell to it. The corpses are buried.
They are such nice people; they make such nice toys,
They make such nice little gingerbread cakes at Christmas. . . .

Byron had also planned questions to initiate discussion and a short writing response assignment for his classmates. Maddie was one of the students who caught the satirical message: "I think this poem means that Americans are too gullible and nice. Also that we don't want to acknowledge what we don't see (the bad part). The poet used satire, I think, to get the point across better and to make it a stronger message."

Last Thoughts

We were fortunate to find such an abundance of good children's and young adult literature through which to introduce social issues to our students. The classroom was quickly peopled by characters who sat on inner-city stoops, ran on trails through redwood forests, or hid in the darkness while the Nazis searched for them. The suffering of war, the burdens of poverty, and the injustices of intolerance and discrimination, thoughtfully treated, were accessible to the students.

Our fears that students would not like this issues-oriented literature were unfounded. In it they discovered the same courage that permeates an adventure book, but, even more important, they seemed to value the sense of reality that could—or did—touch their own lives. One of the group reports ended:

Blacks were treated horribly and this should never have happened. We hope that no ethnic group is ever treated this way again. Even though there are laws against this sort of thing, people still do it and not only to ethnic minorities. It happens at school to "unpopular kids" and it happens in the workplace, especially to women.

Students generated many passionate pleas to the adults around them for a better, more just world. Although only a few of those messages reached the outside community, they were heard inside the school. Yvonne, whose disk pal message was featured earlier, wrote a letter that was published in the school newspaper about what she had learned that year about injustice. Her last sentence asks, "In reading this paper, if you are seeing the world from other people's point of view, what will you do now?"

Additional Literature for Students

Social Issues in Fiction

Boyd, C. D. (1988). *Charlie Pippin*. New York: Puffin.

Bunting, E. (1997). *On Call Back mountain*. New York: Blue Sky Press.

Evans, K. B., & Dade, P. (1997). *You must remember this*. New York: Hyperion.

Haddix, M. (1997). *Running out of time*. New York: Aladdin.

Hesse, K. (1998). *Phoenix rising*. Littleton, MA: Sundance.

Meyer, C. (1997). *Jubilee journey*. New York: Harcourt Brace.

Philbrick, R. (1995). *Freak the mighty*. New York: Scholastic.

Philbrick, R. (2000). *The last book in the universe*. New York: Blue Sky Press.

Additional Readings for Teachers

Allen, J., & Gonzalez, K. (1998). *There's room for me here: Literacy workshop in the middle school*. York, ME: Stenhouse

Ammon, B., & Sherman, G. (1996). *Worth a thousand words: An annotated guide to picture books for older readers*. Englewood, CO: Libraries Unlimited.

Day, F. A. (1997). *Latina and Latino voices in literature for children and teenagers*. Portsmouth, NH: Heinemann.

National Council of Teachers of English and the International Reading Association. (1998). *Rationales for Challenged Books* [CD]. Urbana, IL: Authors.

Wilhelm, J. (1997). *"You gotta BE the book": Teaching engaged and reflective reading with adolescents*. New York: Teachers College Press/ Champaign, IL: National Council of Teachers of English

Magazines and Web Sites for Teachers

Booklinks
A publication of Booklist Publications, an imprint of the American Library Association. Features literature in use in the classroom.

Social Education
A publication of the National Council for the Social Studies. Each April/May issue includes a list of Notable Children's Books in the Field of Social Studies. Also available online.

The Children's Literature Web Guide. [A portal to other children's literature Web sites. Includes many lists of award-winning books, author Web sites, publishers, professional organizations, and book reviews.]
http://www.acs.ucalgary.ca/~dkbrown/index

Young Adult Library Services Association
[Provides lists of award-winning books, picks for reluctant YA readers, and other resources.]
http://www.ala.org/yalsa/booklists/index.html

Materials for Teachers

Lit Discussion Self-Assessment

Name _____

I participated about_____ times.

Check Yourself:
__ I took turns—not blurting or interrupting.
__ I referred to specific parts in story.
__ I connected to and/or added to others' remarks and ideas.
__ My responses were new and original (ideas not yet considered).
__ If I disagreed, I supported my argument with text.

Rank Yourself:
Stayed involved and focused throughout discussion
        1 — 2 — 3 — 4 — 5
Addressed remarks to the group (not only to teacher/leader)
        1 — 2 — 3 — 4 — 5

▶

Was polite and thoughtful to all members
     1 — 2 — 3 — 4 — 5
My voice was clear and easily heard
     1 — 2 — 3 — 4 — 5

By listening to the discussion today, I learned:

Something new I thought about today connected to the discussion or topic was:

Something I noticed about a good discussion or a good discussion member was:

7 Communication: A Public Voice

I discovered the beauty of writing—when one can pour oneself onto a great white emptiness and fill it with emotions and thoughts and leave them there forever.

Zlata Filipovic, *The Freedom Writers Diary* (Freedom Writers)

She tells us, "You have a voice—so use it!"

Krista

CHAPTER OVERVIEW

Following the family celebration story, we describe the curriculum planning we did in order to provide more abundant opportunities for students to use the communication skills needed in a democratic society. The next section explores how the socially conscious curriculum supported young writers in the classroom, with emphasis on author choice and control, richness of background information, writer's craft, and collaborative assessment. Next is a discussion of the kinds of writing—instrumental, report, letters, and even poetry—that emerged as more significant when the curriculum emphasis shifted to social issues. We describe how the students' stance toward society—empathy, critique, and commitment to a vision of a better world—was revealed in their writing. The chapter ends with suggestions for strengthening the place of oral communication in the busy middle school language arts curriculum.

This chapter focuses on communication crafted for an audience rather than on informal writing and speaking to collect and clarify thoughts. Even though the students' poetry, short stories, letters, and editorials were the result of a process that began with drafts, journal entries, and conversations, only the end of this process is featured here. Making this distinction is artificial, yet it enables us to provide a more extensive discussion of the different phases and purposes of communication.

A Classroom Story of Family Celebration

It was almost 5:30 on an evening in early October, and the classroom was filled to brimming. Guitars, animal cages, golf clubs, photos, pieces of clothing, and flags crowded the perimeter of the room. Stylish lettering on poster boards depicted family trees. Adding to the colorful atmosphere, some students wore costumes—a kilt, a sari, a West African dress, a combat helmet. Dominating one wall of the room, a large quilt displayed students' symbolic representations of their family values and history. Different histories made up one collaborative class.

Students were going public with the results of a monthlong autobiographical study that included family history and their perspectives on growing up. Parents and wiggling little brothers and sisters wandered through the displays, sipping drinks while they examined artifacts, read information, and questioned the "experts." A hum of voices and the smell of coffee hung in the air.

Then the audience settled as the authors prepared to take the mike. The expert projects came first. Some students shared their research on an area of expertise derived from their life experience. All eyes were on Caitlyn as she held up a tiny pink bathing suit and told about her first swim meet at the age of seven. Her parents beamed as Caitlyn continued to explain the commitment and perseverance that being a team member required: "Now I train at the university pool most mornings before I come to school and I'm so tired at night that it is hard to do homework. I have to make the most of my time in school. . . . And there are always the personal goals to improve on your own times." She described the way meets are planned and how judges award points, and then added that one of the hardships was "having wet, out-of-control hair a lot of the time."

"Ohhh," went the small children as Jack lifted a large boa constrictor from the cage. It was enormous in the small space. Jack basked in the recognition of his special expertise. He handled the snake easily and with respect, explaining its features and the care it required. His job at the Fangs and Thangs pet store and his research gave him specific information about other reptiles featured in his display. During this presentation, he talked as an informed zoologist, not the hang-loose Jack we had come to know.

Betty's heart went out to Paul, who struggled with middle school work, as he awkwardly stepped forward with his display of racing car models. Would he be able to present to this large audience? But she needn't have worried. Paul's mother was bursting with pride as Paul shared a wealth of information about the racing meets he traveled to with his father and uncles. Betty knew that Paul had stepped through a threshold of confidence this afternoon, gaining the respect of his classmates, who were rooting for him.

David held his personal family treasure chest awkwardly on his lap as he rolled his wheelchair to the front of the room. He held up snapshots and mementos as he explained his struggle to learn to walk again using braces. Few adults in the audience were without a lump in their throats as they heard about David's multiple operations at the Shriners Hospital.

Brice's video presentation moved both kids and parents. The video spared none of the heartbreak his family had endured—the younger brother born with brittle bone disease who died at the age of two, and the debilitating leukemia his father died of five years later. He showed the support of their church for his father, who had been a prominent minister. Brice had created a surprisingly mature artistic production with many cinematic touches, so creative that his peers believed he would achieve his up-until-now secret dream—to become a famous cinematographer.

As parents left, some of them shared with Betty how much these projects had meant to them—not just the presentations, but even more, the weeks of preparation when they had enjoyed working with their children in gathering artifacts, photos, and family stories. The inquiry into family history cut through the negative communication that so often poisoned family life during kids' middle school years. All the extra work for Betty had been worth it. The evening also strengthened the bonds of classroom community through a successful conclusion to the students' early-in-the-year struggles to become active inquirers and writers. The research had brought families together and given students and parents something positive to talk about. Family histories, triumphs, and values had been celebrated at the school. As Beverly said later:

> I think that this evening set the stage for the rest of the year. I think that the main reason parents didn't complain when students began to address controversial social issues was this first unit of family study. It was as if you celebrated their lives and values right at the beginning. After that, they trusted you.

Curriculum Planning for "Speaking Out"

We had many questions about how the writing curriculum should change as we put more emphasis on creating a classroom to prepare students for active and critical citizenship. What should a curriculum to develop the public voice of students look like? What were the goal priorities? How would it be different from the authoring cycle?

We knew that some things would be the same. Betty would continue to value and celebrate the students as growing writers, not just evaluate individual pieces of writing. She would nurture their ability to engage in self-evaluation. She would continue to have conversations about writing and what it means to be a writer and would encourage students to read like writers. She would continue to include oral language development. And planning would continue to be based on a sense of students' growth instead of a set of activities from the textbook.

Of course, this curriculum had the dual burden of meeting district and state standards and embracing the essential qualities of citizenship. We identified the central competencies of citizenship (as discussed in Chapter 1) as investigation, critical judgment, collaboration and negotiation, and a public voice. Betty wanted to provide opportunities for students to immerse themselves in these roles throughout the year, providing repeated experiences in order to build more confidence in their use, more understanding of their nature, more belief in their importance, and more strategies that could be adapted to different situations. From the beginning, we knew there needed to be more communication with people outside the school and more opportunities for instrumental writing—writing that accomplished something in the world.

The framework provided by a series of social inquiry units during the year would provide many different opportunities for investigation, and the various kinds of speaking and writing would, we hoped, become occasions for informed voices to be heard. Students would have time to gather information and experience a text set of human stories as they recorded and shared their initial reactions. In the late phases of each inquiry unit, as their ideas merged into larger understandings, students would be asked to produce more finished and more coherent communications. As the year progressed, the demands on their finished work would increase as students' capabilities increased. Thus, students would gradually develop more mature speaking and writing skills during the course of each inquiry unit, and through repeated experiences with critical communication tasks, they would develop a more mature and informed public voice throughout the school year.

Yearlong Curriculum Perspective

The following list details the growth indicators Betty used to guide long-range planning and reflection:

Guides to Student Growth in a Socially Conscious Curriculum

Students will grow as communicators:

From uncertainty to confidence

From having a voice to having a skillful voice

From favorite genres to multiple genres

From spontaneous reactions to informed opinions

From noticing to commitment

From indifference to caring

The curriculum will move:

From journals to crafted and polished writing

From speaking to peers to speaking to outside audiences

From sharing informally to presenting formally

From sharing ideas to public persuasion

From discussions to debates

From informal letters to formal, purposeful business letters

From commenting about the world to commenting to the world

From presenting information to informed critique and protest

As we watched students at work over the several years this curriculum developed, we made discoveries. We were surprised by how much importance speaking assumed once students became active investigators and communicators. And the utilitarian modes of writing, letters in particular, played a large role in student work. A reassuring discovery was that once the students had immersed themselves in a topic and had something to say, their work revealed to Betty which language skills needed to be taught. Our state standards place an emphasis on the skills of communication, and we were relieved to find that with this new curriculum, Betty did not have to slight the requirements. Students were more willing to try the nonfiction genres and even pay some attention to punctuation and usage when they were writing about "important" topics to public audiences. Knowledge about literary elements and text structure actually seemed useful to students when they wanted to communicate something they felt strongly about. Another major surprise for us was the emergence of student leaders and their need for training in public communication. These students, such as Addy featured in other chapters, taught us how much a traditional middle school curriculum may be holding back student leaders.

Conditions That Nourish Writing in the Socially Conscious Curriculum

Building a Community of Writers

As the opening story illustrates, we decided to begin the school year not with controversial social issues but with the students' own lives. Although students were interested in studying the world around them, we knew they also needed opportunities to focus on themselves and to explore who they were and what they wanted to be. They also needed to learn more about their classmates in order to build a working community. So the year began with autobiographical readings and novels that explored problems of growth and learning. The students, however, didn't focus entirely on themselves in this Growing into Me unit—the biography and memoir reading choices ranged widely across economic and cultural boundaries in order to expand the students' sense of being part of a diverse, multicultural world. A nascent sense of world citizenship was established as students researched and shared their family histories. Although some classes appeared on the surface to be rather culturally homogenous, their family histories extended around the globe and provided hints of diversity in economic status.

At the beginning of the year, most of the students were uncertain of their voice, some were terrified, and a few were comfortably confident. Most students needed time to build the confidence and expertise to grow into authorship. Betty did not ask them to do finished writing at this time because she knew that only a few students would be able to succeed. They did, however, write every day—quick formula poetry, reactions to read-alouds, exit slips, short rough drafts, and journal entries. At the same time, she taught minilessons on effective writing, usually featuring a sentence or a short journal entry from the students' work photocopied onto a transparency. Some students were astounded to see their ideas valued by the teacher and used as positive examples for their peers. Through these selections from students' own work, Betty showed the students mundane but necessary tasks such as homophone spelling and indentation, as well as more inspiring aspects of writer's craft such as how titles can attract an audience and how vivid, specific works can make an idea come alive. She featured journal entries that demonstrated an original point of view and chunks of the students' writing that were good examples of how the reader noticed significant details. Although at this time students received full credit for completing journal entries, Betty conveyed the idea that students should strive for interesting and thoughtful writing. She continued to teach language skills all year. Because she knew the students' weaknesses from reviewing their copious writing, she could tailor the language arts textbook and packets of worksheets to their needs instead of moving through the materials page by page.

Students had many opportunities in these early weeks of the year to share informally with one another in pairs and small groups, which allowed them to get to know one another and to build working relationships (see Chapters 3 and 4). Using checklists to guide students' tasks increased the usefulness of these conferences. Class time spent in peer conferences was also a conscious element of Betty's curriculum: students were exposed to many demonstrations of writing that stretched their knowledge of what good writers do.

Student Choice and Control

We had long valued individual choice and decision making as fundamental elements of authentic authorship. Given this commitment, it was important to step back to consider whether the curriculum structure of immersion in inquiry on a topic (even if it was very broad) diminished students' opportunities to search for and develop their own topics. As teachers we wanted to offer opportunities for students to grow more confident in finding their own direction as authors, and we also wanted to stretch the students' fund of available alternatives as writers. It is the teacher's job to do both—support decision making and push students into new roles and new territories of writing. As Linda Rief says (1999), "Despite the fact that I've just argued for free choice, there are times when we need to be pushed in directions we might not choose for ourselves. These directions give us a framework to our studies, yet allow us flexibility, as they push our thinking" (p. 4).

Yes, everyone studied World War II; everyone read about Anne Frank and wrote summaries and responses. Everyone looked at Picasso's painting *Guernica* together, and all wrote responses. All the students conducted interviews and surveys. Everyone wrote to a community leader or organization. But each student researched different topics and questions and decided what information was relevant to share with the rest of the class; each student raised his or her own questions in literature responses; each student chose a different companion novel. Students wrote to different community organizations; and each family interview was, of course, a personal experience. Students often chose preferred genres to convey their learning.

Further, the social inquiry units did not take up the entire school year. The Growing into Me unit at the beginning of the year invited personal interests into the classroom, and the unit on mysteries led to flights of the imagination. In the poetry genre study, in the individual expert projects, in public speaking, and in other kinds of communication, students had free choice of topic. At these times, some students came back to social issues and others veered off into other interests such as sports, pop music, dreams of the future, and hobbies.

We saw an enormous energy in the classroom when the students were working on the same general topic, especially when several weeks of study had built up a common language and deep understanding of the period. "This year I always had something to write about," reflected Kirsten at the end of the year. The excitement of the leaders swept the laggards into action.

The shared background information made students a more appreciative audience for individual perspectives than if just one student had written about, for instance, the Depression. Shared informational background also made response groups more effective in responding to peer writing. Historical periods of social conflict seemed to be a magnet for a variety of themes of human life such as courage, endurance, faithfulness, hope, sacrifice, and survival, and students gravitated to personal choices of themes that had caught their imagination. It seemed important that each student take a different piece of the picture to share with the others, as if they were completing a complex puzzle with their individual pieces.

Each unit offered a variety of texts and writing assignments. Reluctant students were able to move relatively quickly from one assignment they could only tolerate to another that was more to their liking. Stanley, for instance, began his required review of the core novel *Roll of Thunder, Hear My Cry* by saying, "I really didn't like this book because it isn't the kind of book I'm into, but here goes, I'll write my review anyway." He was, however, proud of his extensive report on the 1930s banking collapse, and he ended his interview of his great uncle with this affirmative statement: "In conclusion, I really enjoyed getting to know my Great Uncle and what it was like to live during the Great Depression."

Writing from Richness

Immersion in a topic over several weeks promoted authority and conviction in student writing. By the end of a unit, using their research, interviews, photographs, and the background of their novels, the students could place their own characters in believable contexts. For the Depression era, they consulted their own disk encyclopedia to pull out details about factories blacklisting union sympathizers, fathers coming home empty-handed from the bank, families giving handouts to hoboes, and deaths of children from scarlet fever. In their World War II stories, students looked around the walls of the room for dates, events, and places with which to create realistic touches. Their European characters celebrated with dinners of salmon, walked on cobblestone streets, and rode bicycles. Their portrayals of struggling characters were influenced by factual information and by the stories of how people had handled adversity. At the end of the World War II unit, the students were no longer suggesting that the Jews should have fought back, and few students thought that "happy times" automatically returned to the United States after the Great Depression.

Becoming Strategic Inquirers

We enjoyed watching the ways in which students connected various pieces of their learning as they pursued a topic. It was evident that many of them had grown beyond merely following the research strategies Betty taught and were instead strategically thinking for themselves. Annalee explained that her I-Search report on Canada during World War II (a self-chosen topic) was enriched by her interview of her grandparents who are from Canada. She asked them how information in the encyclopedia fit with their life in Hamilton. At the end of the year, when Annalee was writing a reflection on herself as a writer, she emphasized the importance of her role as a researcher in her development as a writer. She had become comfortable with a curriculum in which she had to make a lot of choices. She wrote, "everything about school makes me curious! I have imagination, creativity, and will power!"

Mandy reflected on how her Holocaust poem came to be. She got the idea from "reading about the concentration camps, and the shaved heads, and how terrible it was. And I looked at a book of pictures. I got the barbed wire image there. At first it was hard, and then I had more to say." Referring to a minilesson Betty had given, she added, "Mrs. Slesinger told us about using questions and repetition and I used them." When Beverly responded that the poem made her feel how horrible the camp was, Mandy nodded with a satisfied smile on her face, and said, "It's pretty good, I think." How wonderful that a twelve-year-old student has this kind of confident satisfaction about her writing!

From a Voice to a Skillful Voice: Craft in a Socially Conscious Curriculum

We found that when students wanted to reach audiences and when they were invested in what they had to say, many of them were attentive to improving their writing. The social issues, the heartrending struggles of people, and the new purposes for reaching real audiences all stimulated an interest in being effective—in other words, learning the writer's craft.

In Betty's district, the 6-Trait Writing Assessment (Spandel, 2001) was used throughout the grades. This program was useful as a broadly applicable guide that promoted attention to the qualities of writing, organized in categories such as ideas and content (development), organization, voice, word choice, sentence fluency, and conventions. Most students came to Betty with some experience as writers and with the expectation that they would be held to standards of good writing, along with a mix of positive and negative feelings about writing. As described earlier in this chapter, Betty began the year with many discussions about the qualities of writing and gave students a copy of their own interpretation of criteria, to be placed in their writing folders. She continually monitored their growth in writing, and they periodically reflected on their progress in portfolio preparation. The qualities of good writing, however, came alive for the students through their experience with the variety of excellent authors in their readings and as they began to craft their own writing.

Reading Like Writers: Texts as Writing Mentors

One of the pleasures of teaching writing to these students was their interest in "trying on" the craft they saw other authors use. They were stimulated by learning "real tricks of the trade" used by real authors rather than a dreary set of guidelines in a language arts textbook. Discussions and minilessons that shared the wordcraft of a variety of authors was a foundational part of Betty's teaching. As students read, they took a few minutes to look at how the author wrote; sometimes they consciously studied a text. Every text was a potential source for lessons on writing craft. (See a list of professional texts on teaching the craft of writing in Additional Readings for Teachers at the end of the chapter.)

We ourselves have had the good fortune to be part of an active community of inquiring teacher-authors for many years. We and our colleagues such as Heidi Mills and Katie Wood Ray have enjoyed sharing our favorite authors and our writing discoveries with each other and with the teachers we work with.

At the beginning of the year, *Flowers for Algernon* (Keyes) provided a demonstration of how journal keepers can reveal their thinking in compelling ways, and *The Acorn People* (Jones) showed how a few telling details can bring a character to life. Gary Soto's *A Summer Life* was a rich repository of craft lessons, with many examples of striking words, sensory images, and symbols. When Soto's father carries his dead dog, "holding death in his arms," students saw how an author could express a hurt larger than descriptions can convey. Through the vivid descriptions of Cisneros's "Woman Hollering Creek," students felt the excruciating misery of the character Rachael crying in class.

The students who had chosen *Because of Winn-Dixie* (DiCamillo) to read for the family and autobiography unit shared the lead sentence:

> My name is India Opal Buloni, and last summer my daddy, the preacher, sent me to the store for a box of macaroni-and-cheese, some white rice, and two tomatoes and I came back with a dog.

Students liked the way this lead "sneaks up and grabs you." Christopher Paul Curtis's *Bud, Not Buddy,* a choice novel for the Depression-era unit, also contained a much-admired lead:

> Here we go again. We were all standing in line waiting for breakfast when one of the caseworkers came in and *tap-tap-tap*ped down the line. Uh-oh, this meant bad news, either they'd found a foster home for somebody or somebody was about to get paddled.

Starting with the basics of leads, supporting details, images, dialogue, and narrative sequence, students moved on to exaggeration, plays on words, and extended metaphor. They discussed passages, recorded some in their journals, and pursued assignments to examine how authors used grammatical elements. (See the Materials for Teachers section at the end of the chapter for other ideas for teaching writing through literature.) Always students thought about what the author was trying to do with words (Ray, 1999); they were not merely identifying parts of speech in a rote manner.

Trying on Writing Craft

Leads were one of the first elements of writing craft the students adapted in their own writing.

Colleen was feeling her oats as a writer when she wrote her report of bank failures in the 1930s. Most students wrote straight factual reports, but Colleen's lead was:

> Depression after depression after depression, then suddenly BOOM the Great Depression slams you into the ground with no money, no house, and no land. This change hit, and hit hard for most people on Black Thursday, the crash of the Stock Market, October 24, 1929.

Martin enjoyed playing with his lead for a report on Edgar Allen Poe:

> As I sat in class, weak and weary, thinking reading was so dreary, while being taught some ancient lore. Suddenly out of the blue, I'm hearing, a poem that the teacher is reading, written by a man who made my attention soar. Only this, but to me it was the key to a hidden door.

When Lydia was reading *The Westing Game* (Raskin, 1997) during the genre study of mystery stories, she was intrigued by the complex plot and elusive, impressionistic presentation of information. Later, during a short unit on poetry, she borrowed this style to translate a newspaper article into this dramatic poem with impressionistic flashes of images:

Dead on Stage, No Longer Acting

Bows
Screams

Shatters
Fainting bodies
Fainting shrieks
Run
Anxious people
Shooting cameras
As floors creak
On the stage
Crying
Loud sirens
No!
Please!
Blood flowing
Faces glowing
With scarlet rain
Darkness coming
Slipping
Leaving
No longer
Breathing.

Literary Devices

Betty did not know that Candy was interested in the minilesson on internal dialogue until Candy herself employed this literary device to show her deep empathy with the victims of the Holocaust; her poem was further strengthened by the use of repetition to add rhythm and emphasis. Betty asked Candy to share a draft of her poem on the overhead to give a further minilesson in how useful these devices can be in poetry. Shelley understood the device of using one "I" to stand for a group, so she chose a journal entry format instead of a more general description of hardship in the Depression (her journal entry is reprinted later in this chapter). Her sentence fragment, "Nothing of a salary," is a good example of a literary fragment that adds emphasis, and Betty also shared this with the class.

The flashbacks in Yolen's *The Devil's Arithmetic* were confusing to some students, but once they understood that authors often manipulate time to make a story more dramatic and interesting, they experimented with the technique in their own work. In one student's story, a Jewish girl, being herded into a concentration camp, slips a scrap of paper with her tattoo number on it into the pocket of the jacket she is forced to leave. The story then jumps to some months later when the clothes are being distributed to German civilians. A cold and grateful village girl accepts the jacket, and her attitude and life change when she discovers the tattoo number.

Irony and satire were also difficult to teach to this age group, but some students found that these literary strategies helped them express the horrific, conflicting experiences of the war. Byron created a touchingly ironic innocence on Anne Frank's part when he wrote a preconfinement diary entry in which she plants a small tree to beautify the yard. Clark's story about a young soldier, presented later in the chapter, had a strong ironic message, and his friend Edward wrote perhaps the strongest ironic message of all. He ended his story of neo-Nazis with a scene in which the young toughs destroy a store they think belongs to a Jewish family but which has just been sold to the uncle of one of the boys.

In a darkly forbidding poem written at the end of the year, talented Rina created her own subtle literary technique, saying what is true but not true, what happened but did not happen, to convey the confusing, destructive influence of war on relationships:

I Fell

I died when you died
Except I kept living.
You were younger
And you were stronger
And you always knew the answer
Except this time you didn't
And it scared me
because you were what I fell back on.
I trusted you
And when I leaned back
There was no one to catch me
And I fell
And I died.

Peer and Teacher Response

Like many devotees of Nancie Atwell (1998), Betty planned peer response to help students develop and revise their ideas. Groups were fluid, depending on the project. Betty encouraged students who were working on the same topic or the same genre to work together. When writing the results of their inquiry, the students spent less time in response groups discussing their drafts because they had already spent time discussing ideas and issues. When they did come together over drafts, Betty usually provided minilessons and forms to fill out. These rubric-based response forms highlighted critical dimensions of the genre and gave specific structure to the peer response meetings, a structure especially needed by the weaker students. Most of the forms grew out of class discussions, and Betty used student ideas or questions to amend or add onto a rubric.

With so much writing from so many students, Betty usually wrote responses at home rather than holding individual conferences. She would extend her brief suggestions on the papers in minilessons or comments made as she circulated in the room. Grades were usually split between content and writing conventions.

Many of Betty's comments addressed the content of the work rather than writing criteria. She wanted students to concentrate on conveying ideas effectively, not merely fulfilling requirements. Lewis's report on hoboes, for example, elicited two questions: "What would these people be called today?" and "Weren't they drafted during the war?" These questions show that Betty valued Lewis's research and positioned her as a fellow inquirer with a genuine interest in the subject. They also communicated to him an expectation that researchers care about providing sufficient information and pursue contradictions and holes in their information. (Betty also urged Lewis to be more careful with his sentences.)

As described in Chapter 3, parents and other adults also responded occasionally to student writing. Betty provided forms and guidelines to help parents respond positively and focus on what the students were learning at that time in the year.

When she began to see the assessment checklists as part of a whole context that she and the students were building together, Betty found herself continually wanting to alter a general checklist to fit more closely with a particular project. In the folders of saved work from several years are dozens of these adapted checklists. Looking back, Betty could see her evolution from evaluating a piece of writing to evaluating a writer's development over time. Writers were asked more searching questions, asked to look at themselves as much as at their writing, and continually asked to sum up where they stood in their writing growth. (See the section on portfolios in Chapter 3.)

Student Self-Reflection

Integral to students' growth in writing and control over their writing lives were frequent opportunities to reflect on their growing abilities, their processes, their weaknesses, their preferences, their risk taking, and their accomplishments. On informal exit slips and more formal forms, students repeatedly committed to paper their assessment of where they stood as writers. One of the most useful forms was this one that students attached to major papers before Betty graded them:

Why did you choose this topic?

What do you hope it gets across to the reader? (image, opinion, information, feeling, tone, etc.)

What do you hope a reader will notice?

What was difficult for you or needed work?

What do you like best in this piece?

Do you agree with what your reader had to say about your piece of writing?

What have you learned about writing that you can apply in the future?

What have you learned about yourself as a writer that you can apply in the future?

From time to time, students also sat down to list their accomplishments and specifics of learning. These lists were stapled inside their folders so that students could add new items. Here is Becca's list early in the year:

Things That I Can Do as an Inquiring Writer

I have a good imagination

Better organize writing

Have ideas

Indent

Combine sentences

Make papers longer

Ask good questions

From Empathy to a Committed and Critical Stance

Reading one story or even several stories would not have been enough to generate the thoughtful writing that students produced during the inquiry units. As the weeks went by and students learned more about what it meant to live in troubled times and came to care about characters as if they were family or friends faced with serious difficulties, their feelings poured out in their writing. The touching, emotional literature seemed to grant permission for them to voice their own meanings and beliefs and to explore their literary talents.

If the literature had not featured sympathetic characters caught in possible real life dilemmas, and if there had not been opportunities to test the stories against informational sources, we doubt we would have received deeply critical student stories such as this one by Clark, titled "Front Lines."

He provides a believable battleground context, but then goes beyond storytelling to impart a surprisingly insightful and ironical theme. His protagonist, a young American soldier from North Carolina, is reflecting on what the war has meant in this ending portion of a letter the young man is writing to his friend at home:

Front Lines

Today I moved into Germany. I am one of the hundreds of American troops. We are a special task force trained especially for ground combat. I spent two years in training for this. The first year I was training in Pennsylvania, the second in Vermont. I can pilot tanks, trucks, and I am a master in hand to hand combat. I shouldn't be in this war, I should be home farming with my folks. But a renegade sub killed them while they were in their boat off the coast of North Carolina. Since then I wanted to kill the Germans and everything they stood for. They destroyed my home, my family, my life.

I am traveling in a convoy of trucks, planes, and tanks. As we move into Germany I see many retreating and getting out of our way. We fire shots and wound or kill most of them. When we walk up to them I see that they are families trying to be free from this war.

Then the Chief barks out, "Just civilians lets get going!"

The thought of that day still clings in to mind. I remember the Chief's words "just civilians lets get going."

I wonder if that is what the Germans said when they shot down my parents not a general. I finally realize that we are too busy killing in this war to realize who we kill. We aren't killing troops, we are killing innocent people and animals. We have ruined the land. We have ruined ourselves.

Essays also had persuasive force. Tamara's essay "History," written at the end of the Depression-era unit, shows that she is working to construct a larger understanding that integrates her views of injustice in World War II with the different context of the Depression. She uses her new knowledge of economics to show how the war arose from the hard times of the Depression. Perhaps most impressive is the conviction she expresses at the end, as she calls for people to stand up against oppression:

History

I think that history does repeat itself and that we can learn a lot from it. Right now there are probably cases of Depression in the world and cases of horrible killings like the Nazi's did. I think we need to preserve every last piece of history so that our new generation will be able to see what has happened before them and decide what things were good and what things were bad.

From the Depression we can see that something that sounds good like the stock market can fall when you least expect it. In the

Depression study I learned how poor people were, and how there was a lot of racism. Which I think is ironic because usually when people go through a rough time together, they become closer.

A realization I have had about the depression and World War II is that they both are connected. I think that the Depression led to World War II. Everyone was poor including Germans, so that when Hitler came along and started telling everyone lies about how he was going to make everything better, the people believed him and were afraid to stand up against him. Hitler had the Gestapo and other cruel forms of punishment and killings to silence uprisings against him.

Sometime in the future, someplace in the world another Adolf Hitler will be born. This person will either rise and kill like Hitler, or this person will not be heard because people have stood up for what they know is right.

Next time a Hitler is running to be a leader, silence him by banding together and speaking what you feel is right in your heart.

Using a journal entry format, Shelley pulled together a wealth of information and combined it with a deep empathy for families caught in the economic hardships of the Depression. The wife writes:

Dear Journal,

I am tired and hungry and cold. But I feel lucky to be alive. I feel lucky to have a job. I feel lucky to have a beautiful son and a loving husband.

However, my husband is not here with us now. He has gone to Columbia to look for work.

I sit here at the kitchen table looking at our son, Michael, asleep on his wooden cot by the fireplace. The embers are burning brilliant colors of red and yellow. Michael used to have that same flame in his spirit but it has burned out.

Michael works ten straight hours every day at the textile mill alongside me. I feel so guilty for depriving him of an education and a happy childhood. A childhood which should not include back-breaking labor.

Our life used to be much better, though. Robert, my husband, had a job at the textile mill as well. But then he was blacklisted and fired for supporting a labor union.

That is why Michael must work.

True, our working conditions are quite horrible and we are paid very little. But a family cannot survive on an ego. We cannot live without shelter, money, and food. And so Robert left Marlboro County and headed north to Columbia, about seventy miles away.

We have received several letters from Robert, but none of them say whether he has found a job or not. I am becoming quite discouraged, for all he tells us of are the grand people and buildings. Nothing of a salary.

Imagining a Different Present, a Different Future

Henry Giroux (1992) says that a democracy needs citizens who are more than just active participants in society. For a democracy to endure and repair itself, it needs citizens who can imagine a different present and a different future. He hopes that if people can learn a language of social criticism that allows them to engage in the processes of "unveiling, negating, and problematizing" (p. 10), they will come to see that a different kind of future is possible. When citizens lack that kind of imagination, they may look at their community and not see anything wrong with the minimum wage being too low to pay the rent, or with parks in poor neighborhoods being bare and ill-kept, or with CEOs paying themselves extravagant salaries while they lay off workers. To sustain our democracy, we need citizens with a vision of a different present to call us to account and make us see that what we take for granted is wrong and should be changed.

Giroux's insights helped us see a greater significance in the students' writing. We could see in Shelley's scenario of poverty a strong critical stance regarding unfair conditions of life that might perhaps some day lead her to speak to her city council for more evenly distributed economic advantages. We could see in Clark's story and Tamara's essay visions of a future without war. We began to realize how important these final projects were in enabling students to express a social vision that was slowly emerging but not yet clearly defined or even fully conscious. Other opportunities to express large thoughts were provided later through an end-of-year essay on justice and a "lessons learned" final reflection.

Peer Pressure

Speaking out is not easy. We agree with Maureen Barbieri's (1995) observation that preadolescent girls are idealistic yet fearful of speaking out if it threatens their close relationships with other girls. Drawing on the work of Carol Gilligan, Barbieri points out that the strong "caring voice" of females makes it hard for the "justice voice" to be heard. There is a social cost to speaking out about injustices that occur among your own peer group. It is hard to say to a friend, "You are treating that girl badly." (It is difficult even for adults to say to friends, "That's wrong.") This kind of social pressure operated among our female students and also among the male students, and we came to appreciate the way in which the inquiry units allowed students to "try on" a voice of justice they were not yet ready to use in their peer groups. Kirsten, for example, chastises herself as she reflects on her earlier lack of understanding:

We were studying the depression and I did not understand how bad the white people were treating the colored. The Logans changed my view on the depression. I did not know the cruelty that went on and I did not have any compassion for the people that it happened to. Now I understand better and want to read more on the Depression to get my knowledge to where it should be. Kirsten

At this sensitive age, when students were in the process of forming their beliefs about the larger world and their adult stance toward it, they needed many opportunities to express their beliefs. Many of our students voiced strong opposition to racism in the world during classroom discussions, but only a few took any steps toward changing attitudes in our school. Perhaps reading and writing about society and its issues was a way to role-play into critical citizenship. Voices that were silenced by peer group pressures had opportunities to speak out. Literature discussions allowed students to discover the values they believed in even though they could not yet act on these beliefs.

Special Public Events for Authors

These energetic young authors needed opportunities to share their writing in special celebratory occasions. Holding special events for student presentations demonstrated that adults valued the products of student inquiry and thinking. Some of the festive occasions Betty planned included:

- Literary lunches. Monthly gatherings over lunch in the classroom for writers who wanted to share work informally with one another.

- Classroom presentations. Sending groups or one student to another class to present.

- Halloween mystery stories. Read with candles and sound effects.

- Family history coffee. Exhibits and presentations of autobiographies and family history projects at a late afternoon team open house with classmates and family members. Students proudly learned to make and serve coffee and donated treats.

- Writers Café. An evening to share writing and other performances with friends and family in a coffeehouse setting with an artistic printed program, candles in Coke bottles, MC, and microphone. Students performed vocal and instrumental music.

- Service learning puppet presentations. Performed in elementary schools.

The Genres of Democracy

As we understood better how citizens use writing to understand, collaborate, and communicate, certain genres and purposes grew in importance in the curriculum.

Informal Writing Useful to Peers

We had never thought of this as a category of writing, but the power of providing useful information for peers was soon evident as we watched the students at work. Betty restructured some of the writing-to-learn assignments so that research on historical eras was displayed on the wall or on the computer for all students to use in essays, fiction, poetry, and plays. Author-study bios were put on a disk for others to use. Exit slips that made suggestions about class procedures and assignments were used to make changes in the classroom. Students who had arguments or other conflicts sometimes wrote their positions out as a basis for negotiation. Questions were put on the board to be used in later work. This functional writing approached the kind of writing that citizens do—writing that has a specific purpose and a result.

Reports and Persuasive Writing

Reports had always been part of the curriculum but occurred as a separate event, and usually an artificial event, to show that students *could* write a report. When students were involved in inquiry, however, their information search was more personal and purposeful. Expert studies and family interviews brought the students' own lives into the classroom, and when they were shared, they helped other students understand how people live—how they live today or how they lived in an earlier period of history. Alternatively, students reported data they had gathered themselves in surveys about problems that needed to be corrected in the community. As they wrote, the voices of the real people they had surveyed influenced their writing.

Sometimes students were writing to pull together their personal points of view on matters of grave human importance—genocide, hatred, discrimination, poverty. Often these reports emerged from rich and lively, even heated, exchanges with their peers. What began as informational writing became opinion pieces and persuasive essays. Rather than being an isolated task, report writing was a part of the classroom life. As Donald Graves (1989) notes in his useful small book *Investigate Nonfiction,* once you have a real reason for communicating information, the processes of investigation become more important and more integral to the writing of the piece.

Poetry

The importance of poetry to inquiring students was an interesting discovery. Now we realize how difficult it is for young people to express their strong, emerging feelings about significant social issues. The ideas and emotions are larger than students can put into words. Certainly the ideas and emotions can be too diffuse and new to express in organized and connected discourse. Poetry is a medium that can give voice to a cry of protest or a hatred for what people have had to endure.

We learned that generalized phrases often stood for strong feelings, so Betty could not evaluate the poetry based on literary qualities alone. Nevertheless, a few students found striking images that had a strong impact on their audiences. Tess wrote a stunning symbol of hatred in her poem that used an extended metaphor of water: "In my time the pool was sometimes dirty / From what others left behind." Rina's poem, set as an epigraph at the beginning of this book, begins with a provocative couplet: "You can douse the fire, / Yet the flames still burn." Dan struggled to express his anger that injustice still continues and found an innovative format to end his ironic poem: "Never to happen again. / Sigh / What a lie."

Letters

As Lewis said when asked what was good about the year, "We wrote real letters that we mailed." Other students agreed. Students were eager to write letters, and often they wrote wonderful letters, full of detail and conviction. Surprising effort went into these letters to public figures, students returning to information they had gathered in surveys and consulting with peers to create a convincing argument. They felt empowered, almost equals, because they and the adults they wrote to shared knowledge and concern about the same issues.

The importance of letters was a surprise to Beverly. Writing letters had seemed like a trivial component of a middle school curriculum, but when students wanted to communicate a critical view, letter writing was crucial. Once the need for effective letter writing was obvious, we found that students did not know how to write letters. Betty had to teach every aspect; children no longer experience informal letter writing at home. They did not even know how to address an envelope. Teaching the formalities of business letters was not a tedious chore because students needed the information and therefore found it valuable. When they wanted the recipient to send a letter back, for example, they understood the need to provide a return address. Some of the many kinds of letters students wrote included:

- Letters to authors
- Letters to parents telling them what students were learning and doing
- Letters to parents about their portfolio selections
- Letters to organizations and businesses requesting information or materials
- Letters conveying the results of interviews and surveys to someone who needed to know
- Letters to community agencies and policymakers

Presenting Orally to Others: Growing into a Public Voice

When it was time for the schoolwide public speaking contest in the spring, students chose their own topics, and many of them drew on social issues explored in the inquiry units, sometimes because of a memorable personal connection. Here was evidence that students really cared about these issues. Jenna spoke on homelessness, Hope on racism, Clay on gun control, and Lakera on teen pregnancy. Lily, for example, spoke about supporting people with disabilities. Her younger brother struggled with multiple sclerosis, and for Lily the learning unit at the beginning of the year was a personal journey. Reading *The Acorn People* brought tears to her eyes, and during the year she read other personal stories of disability as her individual choice books. Her speech, full of background information, moved the adult audience of judges. After surveying different kinds of disabilities, she finished with the way disabled people are treated by others: "I don't think we have enough for people with disabilities. Sure, we have wheelchairs for people that can't walk, walkers, ramps, and braces. But what they don't have enough of is respect."

Presenting to the Class

Sharing work and projects publicly was essential in creating a community and establishing a sense of mutual classroom ownership. As Betty noted to a class one day, "Sharing like this lets us know what you are good at that we might never know." It was also important in achieving our democratic goals to develop a sense in the classroom of a public discourse. Citizenship often requires public performances, whether that means a telephone call or addressing a group. Sharing confidently in the classroom was a step toward embracing the risk taking and assertiveness necessary to participating in civic life. We found that students also learned to care about one another by sharing the strains and triumphs of public exposure. And as an audience, students were absorbing lifelong lessons about the issues it was important to talk about.

Solving Problems of Time and Peer Response

Experienced teachers know that listening to an entire class of student oral reports is not automatically a positive experience for the group. In fact, teachers tend to avoid "taking time out" for presentations. Betty recalled dreary presentation programs in the past. The students who were the best prepared and most confident volunteered to go first, and then the quality petered out. The last projects were minimal and repetitive, and the class became restless to the point of rudeness. The reports were something to endure, rather than a stimulating exchange of expertise. And the question of grading remained a nagging, unsolved problem.

Because they were a public demonstration of students' personality, oral presentations seemed to intensify the "pecking order" mentality in the classroom. Kids that confidently presented interesting, well-packaged information received high acclaim, while the shy, inept presenters were resentful about having to endure a negative reception. It was obvious that if Betty wanted to create a caring learning community, some rethinking was needed for the oral presentations.

She was assisted in this rethinking by the social issues subject matter. The combination of personal perspectives with extensive information, and the dramatic themes of injustice and oppression, contributed to improving the quality of the presentations. For expert project presentations, each student had interesting information not known to the rest of the class. In other presentations, students highlighted a good variety of well-crafted poems, stories, and interviews that caught the imagination of the audience.

Alternative Approaches to Oral Presentations

Once Betty realized that not all students had to present a project for each unit during the year, she was able to create alternatives that saved instructional time. On the day a major assignment was due, she checked off all projects completed and turned in on time. Then she used one of the following structures for oral presentations:

- Randomly she chose about one-third of the students to share a particular project with the whole class, yielding fewer than ten presentations per class. Others could present later on another project. Since there were two "large" project-type assignments almost every grading period, every student had an opportunity to present before the whole class several times a year.

- Students could present in small groups and then select one interesting project to be presented to the whole class.

- Once during the year, students could decline to present; thus, unprepared students could save face when they knew they would "bomb" in public. (They might present to Betty at recess or after school, if her time permitted.)

- Presentations were usually spread over a couple of days so they didn't take up an entire class period.

- During a presentation, two students per presenter assessed or commented using a rubric or sticky note. Or they might compare their classmate's presentation to their own work. Of course, applause and spontaneous response to the content of the student's work were offered.

With these modifications, presentations were more lively and productive. They had less of that round-robin mentality of not being involved when it's not your turn.

Last Thoughts

Throughout this book, we have presented examples of heartfelt writing that emerged from the study of society. Although some students never put their convictions down on paper, an atmosphere that encouraged speaking out emerged. Poetry like Brenda's lingers in her listeners' minds, especially lines such as this poignant, critical plea that ends her World War II poem:

> But when I do die I want you to remember me.
> You think I'm different since I'm a Jew.
> But I have a heart and mind just like you.
> And, I don't want this to happen again.

Lydia, vivacious and outgoing, came to seventh grade a popular student with a love of dramatic images such as, for instance, those quoted earlier in the chapter ("Faces glowing / With scarlet rain"). During the year, she grew into deeper thoughts about life. Here is her insightful poem written in May using the silenced voice of a street person:

On the Streets

> I walk through your streets everyday,
> But you seem to pass me by.
> I turn every corner you do, but you don't
> even notice I'm there.
> I speak the same language you do,

But you treat me like a foreigner.
I look and act just like you,
but you don't even care.

I'm no different from the rest,
Just I have no place to go.
All I want is a friend,
But you treat me so low.
We're supposed to be brother and sister
But you treat me like a stranger.
The same guy died for all our sins,
And he was born in a manger

Why am I called different?
Is it the clothes that I wear?
You seem to always ignore me.
Like I am never there.
Even if you're cold and hungry,
You have a place to go.
When I get cold and hungry,
I have to sleep in the snow.

You think you have nothing.
But take a look at me.
Your world is like a paradise.
You even have a T.V.
Maybe when we realize
how much there is to share,
We'll find too much in common,
To pretend it isn't there.

Additional Literature for Students

Books about Writing and Writers

Christelow, E. (1997). *What do authors do?* New York: Clarion.

Creech, S. (2001). *Love that dog.* New York: HarperCollins.

Fletcher, R. (1999). *Live writing: Breathing life into your words.* New York: Avon.

Fletcher, R. (2000). *How writers work: Finding a process that works for you.* New York: HarperCollins.

Krull, K. (1994). *Lives of the writers: Comedies, tragedies (and what their neighbors thought)*. San Diego: Harcourt Brace.

Livingston, M. C. (1997). *I am writing a poem about . . . : A game of poetry.* New York: McElderry.

Paulsen, G. (2001). *Guts: The true stories behind Hatchet and the Brian books.* New York: Scholastic.

Publisher That Prints Student Books

Willowisp Press (1-800-877-8090)
For example, see *How the Eagle Got His Good Eyes* (1995). Written by fifth-grade students and illustrated by seventh-grade students at Oscar Blackburn School, South Indian Lake, Manitoba, Canada.

Magazine on Writing for Students

Writing! The Continuing Guide to Written Communication. Curriculum Innovation Group. This interesting magazine features provocative examples of a different genre each month, with a multitude of writing tips and grammar practice.

Additional Readings for Teachers

Fletcher, R. (1992). *What a writer needs*. Portsmouth, NH: Heinemann.

Fletcher, R., & Portalupi, J. (1998). *Craft lessons: Teaching writing K–8*. York, ME: Stenhouse.

Fletcher, R., & Portalupi, J. (2001). *Writing workshop: The essential guide.* Portsmouth, NH: Heinemann.

Graves, D. (1989). *Investigate nonfiction*. Portsmouth, NH: Heinemann.

Lane, B. (1993). *After the end*. Portsmouth, NH: Heinemann.

O'Keefe, V. (1995). *Speaking to think, thinking to speak: The importance of talk in the learning process*. Portsmouth, NH: Boynton/Cook.

Portalupi, J., & Fletcher, R. (2001). *Nonfiction craft lessons: Teaching information writing K–8*. Portland, ME: Stenhouse.

Materials for Teachers

Using Trade Books as Writing Models

Following are samples of activities that students can engage in during or after reading. Think of your own variations.

Vivid Words

List the five best description words or five strong verbs in a chapter or story the class is reading. Explain what these words show. Ask students to describe how these words affected them and improved the writing of the story.

Ask students to copy adjectives an author used in the story instead of the general, overused adjectives such as *nice, good, bad, interesting, boring, fun.*

Ask students to copy strong verbs an author used in the story instead of general, overused verbs such as *walk, get, did, go, eat, run, see.*

Ask students to find at least three examples of comparisons the author made that were fresh and specific, *not* overused and old. These could be similes *(as small as an ant),* metaphors *(the baby was an angel),* or longer, descriptive comparisons.

Create basic, "empty" skeleton sentences about a story and put them on the overhead/handout/screen. Have students recall or find specific words and details from the story and embed them in the sentences to liven up this dull writing. Compare to the author's original.

Conventions

Ask students to find a dialogue passage in their story. Have them copy out from the text at least two exchanges between characters, and then ask them to write down the "rules" about punctuation they can learn by studying this passage. Follow up with a class discussion of their rules compared to those of their grammar text. (Can be used for other language conventions.)

On a handout or the overhead, present a dialogue passage from an article or book with punctuation deleted. Ask students in pairs to punctuate the conversation correctly. Compare to text original.

Find or alter a passage so it is all in the past tense. Have students rewrite it in third-person singular present tense. For problems with irregular verbs, find and copy sentences with these problem verbs and require students to change tenses to alternate times and forms.

Ask students who are misusing apostrophes to find three sentences with contractions and possessives. Have them examine and compare the situations and uses and then decide on some generalizations about using apostrophes correctly.

Sentences

Have students copy several sentences with subordinate clauses. (You can simply ask kids to find the part of the sentence beginning with *while, if, although, since,* etc.) Do the same thing with sentences having participles (*-ing, -en* verbs) in them. Have students compare these complete text examples with fragments you have taken from student papers (not from the current class) and put on an overhead.

Using simple kernel, repetitive sentences, prepare a rewrite of a passage (or chapter summary) of a novel the students are reading. Ask students to combine sentences using transition words and conjunctions to make an interesting and clear paragraph. Compare student combinations to the original and discuss what makes the difference and which they would rather read.

Style

Beginnings and Endings: Pass around transparencies and pens and have students copy down several chapter beginnings they like from a book they are reading. With the beginnings on the overhead, ask students to discuss what makes them intriguing and helpful to readers. On a chart, list students' general ideas about good beginnings, such as it describes the scene, it starts with action. Do the same activity with endings. Post the chart to be available for help during student writing.

Images: Ask students to find descriptive passages in a text and make a list of the types of things the author describes and how it's done—vivid words, figurative language, contrast. Sketch the mind picture that a passage creates either symbolically or realistically.

Point of View: Using a piece of literature familiar to the students, brainstorm a list of (1) feelings/attitudes and (2) information the reader learns from (a) the real author and (b) the protagonist. Using the resulting chart, talk about how an author creates a point of view.

Point of View: Ask students to rewrite a short passage from a different point of view.

Tension/Suspense: What makes students want to keep reading or listening to a story? Find and read aloud examples of how the author created this interest, and describe how the author made it work.

Guide for Planning an "Issues" Speech

Select your topic. Think about the interest and age of your audience.

State your purpose. Example:

To explain what it is like to live in _____.

To provide instructions for learning to ski, make bread, etc.

To increase awareness of a problem such as the need for more after-school buses.

To explain how an organization such as the Red Cross helps a community.

Determine a focus and message for your audience. (Remember to work key phrases about your topic and message into your speech several times.) Consider the following questions:

What is your connection to your topic?

Why is your topic of interest to your audience?

Why should people care about this topic?

Gather research information.

Make phone calls to experts, use the Web, examine library resources, check newspapers and TV news and informational shows.

Choose main points, facts, ideas, events, skills, or steps in a process related to your project, making sure to jot down notes and the sources where you found information.

Plan an opening.

Include your topic and purpose.

Get the listener's attention through:

A narrative (little story related to your topic)

A "shocker"/surprise

A question

Common ground (something you and the audience might share)

Plan the body of the speech. (This is the informative section of your talk.) ▶

Have a list of your key ideas or steps in a process.

Fill in with examples, experiences, descriptions, feelings, explanations, and quotes from experts and references.

Decide on transitions to get you from one point to the next.

Create a persuasive conclusion. Many endings come full circle to something mentioned in the beginning of the talk. Try one of these:

Summarize or restate the importance/meaning of the topic.

Answer a question if you began with one.

Use an analogy or small story to highlight a key point.

Use a related quote.

Create a related visual aid. Plan how and when you will refer to your visual aid. Consider these:

A prop (object connected to your topic)

A graph, chart, or diagram

A map, large photo, or overhead transparency

Wearing a costume

8 Contributors and Critics: Students in the World

It's important not only to study . . . social problems, but to encourage students to take thoughtful action. By doing this they see themselves as actors in the world, not just things to be acted upon.

Bob Peterson, *Rethinking Our Classrooms: Teaching for Equity and Justice* (Bigelow et al.)

CHAPTER OVERVIEW

In this chapter, readers will find a variety of perspectives on student activism. First we discuss the conditions that promote the urge to take action—how the desire to be an activist emerges from a combination of awareness and empathy, and how schools can create these conditions. Next is a description of the activities in a media watch project that raised student awareness about the manipulation of social attitudes by the media. A spontaneously emerging mini-unit on child slavery describes how students' compassionate concerns can create curriculum.

The rest of the chapter compares two different avenues to social action: teacher-assigned and student-initiated projects. The final pages describe Betty's students as they took their critical voices into high school and beyond.

A Story of Contagious Student Initiative

Betty expected a quiet, routine week after a four-day February break. To ease back into school, her seventh graders shared their latest writer's notebook entries on issues in the news. Amelia and Rina read their particularly strong entries about school prayer, each with a different and definite point of view. Immediately, Lydia's hand began to wave. Betty expected her to take one side or add her own opinion, but Lydia was already thinking beyond the entries, caught by a larger vision: "Why couldn't we have a debate about some of these things, Mrs. Slesinger?" There was a buzz of interest in the room and students started adding ideas. "Let's have a debate club—not everyone would have to do it, not everyone would have to listen, it could happen during homeroom time or after school." They were getting excited. Other classmates agreed enthusiastically: "You know we love to argue. Now you wouldn't have to try to shut us up!"

The idea of having new clubs at school got several girls going in other directions. Therese and a friend had been reading to children in their own neighborhood on Saturdays, and they asked, "Could we have a club to read to kids at the homeless kindergarten?" Jill was upset about the condition of the school's nature trail, and she wanted to start a recycling club. Addy told about having been worried since she had done her survey on animal abuse and how she had been thinking about a plan to create a school service that would connect kids and families who wanted to give up animals with those who would like to adopt.

It certainly wasn't a ho-hum week! An activist atmosphere was surfacing in the seventh-grade team. Throughout the year, Betty had been inviting the students to have a more powerful voice in decisions about their learning. They had expressed greater satisfaction in their choices and work but stayed for the most part within the bounds Betty had established. She had also encouraged them to make connections between schoolwork and society and to act on their beliefs, but only a few students had followed this route. Now the enthusiasm of a group of students had begun to create a swell of interest through all her classes.

The students had gotten hold of something important and they wouldn't let go. Other students began to join in. Kirsten, who worked as an aide in the library, told Betty that she could help by going on the Internet to find out what other kids were doing. The next day Lydia (one of two students selected to be on the School Improvement Council) reported that she had asked the council at the previous night's meeting for books on debating to help start the debate club. A few days later Lydia followed up her interest by bringing in an article on letters that don't get published in school newspapers that are about issues she thought students would like to debate. The following week Addy arrived in homeroom with posters and a flier to start a school Adopt-a-Pet service (see Figure 8.1). The posters were complete with graphics and a tear-off response section that she had composed on her home computer.

Another project got started when Kirsten and Erin, watching *The Oprah Winfrey Show,* learned about some students in Michigan who did

Figure 8.1. The text of Addy's flier announcing a schoolwide Adopt-a-Pet program.

not have winter coats. They worked out a plan with the team's teachers to collect coats in homerooms. The girls made persuasive announcements, raided lost-and-found boxes, and got enough contributions to create a pile of jackets. They went to the home arts teacher to use the washer and dryer, and convinced the dry cleaner in the neighboring mini-mall not to charge to clean the woolen coats. They pulled Erin's mom into the packing and shipping. What a thrill for them later to find their names in the congratulation credits of an Oprah show.

What had galvanized these students? Not any one event or even any one unit of study. In the day-to-day work of the classroom, changes in student attitudes seem to move glacially. Apparently, the urge to act had been simmering beneath the surface of ordinary schoolwork and school days. Once Betty's students understood that the school would support their projects, it was as if their energy was released. Betty's own evolving priorities about what was important in the curriculum, and her growing ability to notice new movement in the classroom, may have drawn student initiative out into the open. It seemed she and the students had come to mutual interests that went beyond the habitual routine of school. Now Betty's problem was finding the energy and time to support all of this student enthusiasm.

Value of Student Contributions

Contributions to the Community

As part of her effort to create a more democratic atmosphere in the class-room, Betty offered students many opportunities to make suggestions, undertake roles in the daily life of the class, and participate in decisions and new directions for the class. She found some of the students quite eager to extend these contributions beyond the classroom. Making a positive contribution to the world of adults seemed to be a developmental need at this transitional age, but too few students had experienced the satisfaction of working in their community. When they worked on their community projects, their increased energy was noticeable in the classroom. With adult support, they carried out innovative projects with a responsibility that sur-prised some adults in the school. As Jon Graves, a principal who initiated community work for students in Oregon, says:

> These kids are ready and capable of making meaningful contribu-tions NOW, not ten years from now when they are "income produc-ing" adults. . . . [Y]ou don't have to have a high school diploma to be a citizen or you don't have to be a certain age or have a certain level of education to have an opinion that matters. (Perrone, 1999)

When students begin to recognize social problems and injustices, they may become cynical or depressed if they have no outlets for action. It is damaging to middle school students' development to become aware of world issues and yet not have responsible roles to play in them. Abdi-cating responsibility with the excuse that "nothing can be done" when adults do not provide avenues for their active contribution may be a natu-ral response. In our society, we see teens putting their energy into form-ing their own antisocial cultures, causing adults to criticize or dismiss them as irrelevant. Adults may be unwitting contributors to these antisocial be-haviors. When Betty's students learned about suffering, they wanted to respond to it. Feelings of caring and a belief in fairness were strong, and Betty had to find ways for the school to support these impulses.

What Promotes Activism?

Awareness

Knowledge about the world is a necessary component of activism, both knowledge about the problems that exist and knowledge of how these problems might be solved. Throughout the year, the students absorbed layer after layer of information about life problems and human nature. Most of this knowledge came from vicarious experiences, literature, Web sites, newspapers, and interviews. Remarks like Matt's and Leigh's were reiterated time and again in students' reflections at the end of the school year: "I understand that some people have to go through harder times than others," and "A lot of people need help; they don't live as happy as others." Slowly, students became more aware of the problems and inequities in society. And like healthy citizens, as middle school students become aware of the world, they want a role in it.

Most students in Betty's classes did not know what organizations existed in their community or how to be part of them. Not knowing what these organizations did, of course they had no impulse to contribute to their work. And when they did begin to be interested, many did not know whom to contact for information, how to make a purposeful phone call to an involved adult, how to write a request or protest letter, or how organizations and governmental bureaus work.

They gained knowledge by going out into the world on field trips, interviews, and service learning projects. They broke out of their isolated, specialized environment to watch citizens at work and to become part of the working community in small ways. Although it was limited, their access to the world around them provided a beginning of the knowledge that critical citizens need.

The students' impulse to act was geared primarily toward the direct alleviation of hurt and suffering, and they had as much empathy for animals as for people. Although they gained a certain amount of knowledge about the underlying systems of inequity, only rarely did they see themselves as individuals who could address those systems. Students spoke out against racism in the school, but only a few followed up with more concrete action. Students gathered coats for children in need but did not think to write Congress about the minimum wage. Their impulse to help reflected the adult community around them. We too find it easier to help someone than to attack the cause of problems. It might be too much to expect these young people, in the first blooming of awareness of social issues, to take giant steps for social change.

Empathy and Compassion

What made students want to act on their awareness? When they cared about other individuals who suffered, students wanted to relieve that suffering. Concern for others occurred when, through stories and articles, students understood the conditions that made people's lives a struggle. They needed to feel the difficulties people faced in trying to make a good life for themselves and their families.

As the year progressed, students lived with dynamic characters who were caught in unfair situations, such as the Logan family in *Roll of Thunder, Hear My Cry,* the Whites in *When the Stars Begin to Fall,* and the Franks in the various stories and articles surrounding Anne's diary and death. Shana said in her end-of-the-year reflection, "It's not just what I learned about history from the books I read this year, it's what I now understand about human nature." The students' family interviews seemed to provide an important bridge between faraway life problems and their own lives today. They saw that their own families could be, and sometimes were, caught in difficult situations—domestic struggles, such as divorce; medical crises; and job losses.

Supportive School Environment

We now realize that school has been standing in the way of children's natural urge to respond to the needs of others. A fundamental question educators should be asking is why schools prevent kids from operating in the world. A simple step toward activism would be to remove school barriers when students want to take action, but schedules, assignments, and legal issues seem to be almost insurmountable obstacles, requiring collaboration among many parties, from the central office down to teachers and parents who may have differing views on the subject. Apparently it is easier for teachers to organize a planned service learning program than to let service grow out of student awareness.

Activist Classroom Atmosphere

The student activism that began to percolate in Betty's classroom had been fostered in a number of ways during students' daily lives together in the classroom. Betty encouraged student decision making about learning, empowered students to ask questions and give suggestions, and used their suggestions in her teaching. Students' belief in the value of their concerns grew as they became more confident with an inquiry approach to learning.

Some of the classroom practices that encouraged students to take an activist stance (described in more detail in Chapters 3 and 4) are as follows:

- Establishing a community with an inclusive and supportive tone to empower individual voices.
- Asking questions, making suggestions, and contributing new ideas, which become a way of life in the classroom.
- Providing sensitive scaffolding for student work; letting students grow into independence and responsibility.

- Using the writing process for diverse real life purposes.
- Connecting literature with issues of society, the community, and school life.
- Working on projects collaboratively.
- Providing many opportunities to present publicly.
- Providing choice and opportunities to modify assignments and curriculum.
- Encouraging reflection and self- and peer assessment.
- Providing models of activist people and organizations.

Social Issues: Informed Opinion to Public Voice

Guided Exploration through Journals on Media Stories

In early spring one year as they were reading the novel *When the Stars Begin to Fall,* students refocused their journal entries away from their literature toward the social issues discussed in newspapers and magazines. During this time, students collected articles about people who made a positive contribution to society and those whose activities affected society negatively (People Who Care and People Who Harm). Another year, Betty asked students to pick out news stories that implicitly dealt with citizens' rights and responsibilities as derived from the Bill of Rights and later amendments. (She provided a list of these rights on a handout.) Students wrote about the connections to the Constitution and explained how and why these stories or cases were important to our society.

As students were pushed to notice topics of and in society, some journal entries became more probing. Matt, in regular language arts classes for the first time, still struggled with writing but had things to say on a variety of significant social issues. He wrote about the error of thinking that prisons are a solution to social violence, and he agonized about church burnings. But most moving was a reflection in which he recognized his complicity in the cruelty of the world. This gentle boy bemoaned the violence that pervaded what should be a powerful and peaceful country: "We have people running for President that we can tell wouldn't do half the stuff they say they would. How are we going to change our cruel people including myself also?"

A few students went beyond witnessing the hurt in the world to suggest remedies. Teria, for example, wrote of the need for programs and counseling to help victims of domestic violence and child abuse, and offered to support outcast children by bringing them into her own suburban neighborhood. Some students were highly critical of the violence in society. Rhiannon wrote: "Our society is pathetic and doesn't care about what happens to others. We are selfish and there is no way to make people realize how bad our generation really has become."

An unsolved problem with this assignment was that some students continued to focus on criminal stories because they dominated the news, and these students' journals turned into extended accounts of violence. (It was difficult to get across to students the idea that violence might be featured because the exciting story attracts an audience—and a positive balance sheet for the news corporation.) It seemed time to refocus students' attention on more positive community activity.

Scarcity of Social Activist Models

While students found many examples of incidents that constituted attacks on democratic values, they overlooked local citizens who were acting to safeguard democracy and were standing up for the rights of others. Although there were ongoing campaigns in the surrounding community to take down the Confederate flag from the statehouse, to arrest drunk drivers (including sitting judges), and to equalize school district financing, by and large students were unaware of the dedicated people in these and other local causes. The students noticed articles about entertainers such as Willie Nelson and Hootie and the Blowfish who donated concert proceeds to charity, rather than those about ordinary citizens who were actively working to improve our community. They chose stories of heroic rescue workers such as the police officer who nabbed a thief running from a convenience store, or of public figures such as Colin Powell, who could be models for youth. They had not grasped that anyone with conviction could work with others for a cause.

One student did feature the director of a local shelter for homeless families, and another was attracted to the issues surrounding Dr. Kevorkian, but the only activist group the students noticed were protesters at Chernobyl who chained themselves to a railroad track over issues about cleanup of village lands. The school had few resources on contemporary activists. One book, *Everyday Heroes* by Beth Johnson, purchased through a request Betty made to the Service Learning Committee, featured personal triumphs over disease and natural disasters. Although Betty later found better examples (see Additional Literature for Students at the end of the chapter), it is evident that schools need more readily available sources on contemporary activism.

Political Cartoons

One year, when students were practiced in reading below the surface message of visual images, they collected political cartoons, the epitome of critical opinion in our culture. At first students worked together dissecting the difficult images, symbols, labels, figurative language, and puns that were layered onto a news event or personality. Using an instructional strategy familiar to the students, for a few days Betty began each class with discussion of a cartoon she displayed on a transparency, and students wrote a paragraph on its meaning. Then students created political cartoons of their own on a wide variety of topics (see Figure 8.2). They exposed school problems, such as crowded lockers and long, slow-moving lunch lines, and featured local issues such as the Humane Society's three-week limit on housing stray animals and the unused and expensive sidewalks that were installed to prettify a neighborhood. National and world topics included Mrs. Clinton's focus on her political career rather than on her family and the continued bombing of areas of Iraq while the United States calls itself a peace-loving country.

As might be expected, the cartoons varied widely in their ability to fulfill the potential of social critique. Some were astute and clever criticisms of society, and others were more like posters for a worthy cause such as saving the manatee. Nevertheless, students got a valuable experience in speaking out, even if not everyone was able to grasp the double layer of meaning that political satire requires.

Surveys on Social Issues

To continue the students' inquiry into social issues, Betty planned a series of loosely connected activities to gather information, develop opinions, and communicate opinions in a public forum. Each year she integrated these activities into other work—sometimes a nonfiction genre study, sometimes a novel study, sometimes a service learning activity. Surveying was one of the priority modes of research Betty had identified as an important competency of informed citizenship, and it was also a requirement of seventh-grade standards. One year she was lucky enough to have a parent who worked as a poll designer for the University of Michigan who gave a wonderful lesson to her son's class on the uses and types of surveys. She, like other experts brought into the classroom, provided a connection beyond school and served as a useful resource for the students and Betty.

Students began their survey projects by trying to identify interesting topics representing unsolved problems in their community. One year

Figure 8.2. One student's political cartoon highlights the issue of privilege in the United States.

they followed through on issues they had discovered through their media journals. Another year they looked through folders of past issues of *Current Events,* a simplified news publication for middle schools. The format, writing level, and subject matter made them accessible and interesting. Although Betty intended *Current Events* to be a stimulus for coming up with personally compelling topics, some students ended up picking one of the published topics. Less interested students needed support so that they wouldn't give up, and Betty thought that providing assistance was preferable to assigning topic choices.

After students jotted down several topics and possible questions for a survey, they talked with partners to finalize which issues they would like to pursue. Choices included connections between rap music and violence, changing rules for sports league teams, and overdevelopment of the town's mall. Creating a survey was a challenging project. Betty gave considerable attention to helping students match their sample of survey respondents with the questions. She showed examples from the previous year and provided guidelines that included requirements for the phases of the survey project: (1) questions with "why" probes, (2) choice of respondents, (3) brief field notes, (4) a summary report, (5) a graphic visual of the data, and (6) someone who needs to know this information.

Allen's survey question was "How can we help the homeless?" and he interviewed his family, neighbors, and peers at school. He summarized the ideas of his respondents in the following list:

Responses to Allen's Survey: Ways You Can Help the Homeless

1. Respond to them with respect and kindness—it raises their self-esteem.
2. Carry fast food gift certificates to give them.
3. Give them spare change or dollar bills.
4. Bring them canned goods, a bag of groceries, or a meal.
5. Give them spare clothing.
6. Give them toys you don't need.
7. Give recyclables to shelters.
8. Help at a shelter or soup kitchen.
9. Volunteer your professional talents to help organizations that help the homeless.
10. Volunteer your hobbies.
11. Tutor homeless children or take them on trips.

Allen's survey responses revealed a general willingness to help homeless people. But it is also evident that none of his respondents took a critical stance toward the economic policies and power in the United States that create homelessness. Responses such as these are a bittersweet victory for teachers. On the one hand, it is a step forward for students to be researching and talking about these issues in school. Some of the students had not even realized there were homeless families here in our own community. The survey suggestions are not only quite positive about citizens that many people view as "undesirable," but also some of them involve taking beneficial action. On the other hand, although we believe that the inquiry approach is valid and that it is more important to activate student questioning than to "teach" certain bits of information, we also wish for a society in which students doing such a survey would uncover at least one neighbor who suggests changes in economic policies.

Students then used their persuasive writing techniques to write editorials on the issues they had investigated in their surveys. Thanks to the cooperation of the communications teacher, many of these editorials were published in the school newspaper.

Connecting to Community Organizations

Betty wanted students to know about organizations that work to improve the lives of citizens. Students knew only a few such groups through their churches, television news, or parents' volunteer work. A representative of the Salvation Army had given a presentation at school, vividly demonstrating the burdens of poverty by explaining that each homeless family member could bring to the shelter only what could fit into a plastic garbage bag. But students had no idea of the large number of groups in their community that daily provided services to citizens in need and worked to improve conditions. So Betty began to alert them to these groups in a variety of ways—inviting other teachers to share, showing newspaper ads and promotional material, having them search through telephone books.

To take student awareness beyond the surface level, Betty asked each student to select an organization that he or she believed was doing valuable work and then to create a brochure that publicized the organization's services. The text would need to explain the organization's purpose, describe services, list staff members, give "information a citizen would need to know," and so forth, as well as be appealing to the eye so that people would both want to read it and find it easy to read.

Rina and Kara decided to make a personal visit to the Ronald McDonald House to find out more about its purpose for their brochure, which prompted other students to extend their brochure writing assignment with actual visits. Students gathered firsthand information from managers of programs such as a sheltered workshop for people with disabilities and a state fish hatchery sponsoring a catch and release campaign.

Most of the students chose organizations that offered supportive services but did not take an activist stance. On the spur of the moment, Betty decided to show a video that chronicled the history and goals of the Southern Poverty Law Center, an organization that fights discrimination and violence against minority groups. The students followed the growth and struggles of the organization and how it survived bombings, threats, and lawsuits. The film chronicled both the injustice in our society and the opposition to the center's work. The Southern Poverty Law Center continues to fight for the rights of the disenfranchised—Vietnamese fishermen trying to break into the shrimp industry, the poor living in areas where big corporations dump dangerous waste, and small farmers being forced out of production by agribusiness. (The center's magazine *Teaching Tolerance* is a wonderful teacher resource, and the organization also has videos and written materials for students that fit many topics of injustice.)

When this documentary video ended, Betty was surprised and delighted that the students applauded. And when Teria blurted out, "I didn't know *organizations* fought for justice!" Betty realized that the fight for justice had mostly been shown to students through the efforts of a few exceptional heroes and heroines, such as Martin Luther King Jr. and Rosa Parks in the civil rights movement. Unfortunately, most of the literature on social action featured a solitary and heroic person who worked for good or who stood up against injustice. Rosa Parks is often portrayed as a tired woman who was suddenly inspired to take action that resulted in a major change in racial laws, while the long-term collaborative work of the local NAACP, of which Parks was a longtime member, is ignored (Kohl, 1995, pp. 30–56).

We now understand better how schools have prevented students from understanding the work of groups that build, maintain, and renew our democracy. More than individuals, persistent groups create social change. In real life, it takes people working together to solve problems.

Sending Information to Someone Who Needs to Know

After completing their surveys and brochures, students began the process of deciding where to send the information they had gathered in their surveys, or (in other years) where to send the editorial they had written. At first some students didn't believe they were actually going to mail their letters to real adults. When the stamps, stationery, and envelopes were laid out, however, the skeptics realized this was not a pretend communication and began to give more serious thought to the assignment.

In an effort to attract attention to issues of child labor, Bruce faxed his opinion letter on that topic to a local radio station and asked them to speak out. Allen sent a copy of his report of help for the homeless to both a local mission and to the Salvation Army. He encouraged them to make a list of the shelters available for the homeless around the city and also a list of the kinds of help they would like from teens and adults. Allen commented on his personal satisfaction with this project: "This was a wonderful project and I really enjoyed it. It has taught me future reference skills, social skills and enjoyment, it helped me with my everyday shyness problems and now I'm a lot better at surveying that I was before! I enjoyed this a bunch."

Public Responses

When they saw the students' survey visuals displayed in the halls, teachers and classmates beyond the classroom praised the work and even questioned the surveyors about their topics. Editorials got attention when they were printed in the school and the local weekly newspaper. Response letters from organizations began to appear in the school mailbox. Students were elated to receive promotional information, pencils, and the like from their organizations. Receiving a letter was unusual enough, and to be treated like an adult, even through a form letter, was an exciting event. Two girls were allowed to leave class to receive a phone call, with praise for their interest in important issues. The class was buzzing when Addy received a letter from President Clinton in response to her long and impassioned explanation about the United States' role in rain forest destruction. Each of these small incidents was a vivid and welcome intrusion of social reality into the artificial world of school.

The most exciting responses were letters detailing actions that would be taken as a result of the students' research and suggestions. Amelia's letter about the lack of cleanliness at a local fast food shop prompted a long, detailed response (addressed "Dear Ms. . . .") promising to rectify the problem. Edward could hardly contain himself when he received a letter from the town council. He had written to state the need for a skating park for street hockey and skateboarding and how it would keep kids out of trouble. The reply said the council had agreed with his findings and opinions, and a skate park would soon be constructed. Cheers erupted and Edward went around the classroom high-fiving other skaters. Not knowing the background of the decision on this issue, Edward thought he had accomplished this feat single-handedly. He was a team hero that day.

Teria, concerned about the increasing number of gangs in our area, sent her survey information about why kids join gangs and how these gangs affect our community to the Columbia Crime Stoppers division. She not only received an appreciative letter (addressed "Dear Ms. . . ."), but even more exciting, Crime Stoppers also sent her report to local police and sheriff departments. What an incentive for Teria to continue to speak out!

Some projects stimulated an extended interest in the issue. Rick and Kara were awed to question Rosa Parks online, and they followed news and special programs featuring black history for several weeks afterward. Once Lance wrote his letter of support to Jack Kevorkian, he was mindful of the current trial and continued to report to the class about its progress. Students questioned the popular media's antagonism toward Dr. Kevorkian.

Discovering Contemporary Child Slavery

When some of the students discovered the slavelike conditions in which millions of children in emerging nations are forced to work, their shock pushed the class into more research. Iqbal, a Pakistani boy from a destitute family, had become a bonded rug worker at the age of four. He had been chained to a carpet loom for six years until he was rescued by an international organization. Iqbal then began a crusade to ban the exploitation of child workers around the world, and he traveled to many countries speaking on this issue. But on returning to his homeland in his early teens, he was murdered. Students were stunned by Iqbal's plight, and Betty helped them pursue their outrage with additional investigation.

Betty started with Freedman's *Kids at Work,* which documents child labor here in the United States in the early 1900s with photos and narratives of kids working in cotton fields, shellfish beds, canning factories, and textile mills, with many examples from our own state. Once the topic of child labor was a focus, Betty began to be aware of related resources, such as old *Read* magazine Skillmasters that focused on labor issues. (Each Skillmaster page features a language skill or literary element in the context of compelling fiction or nonfiction.) Students were moved by the work conditions they saw, and their concern grew as they read about dangerous, health-threatening conditions of children who had worked in a Pennsylvania coal mine and in a South Carolina textile mill. Adrian wrote in her journal, "I looked at the picture of that little girl picking cotton barefoot and in the heat of summer and I thought about my summer vacation and felt grateful for my life and family."

When they learned that students near Boston were raising funds to build a school in Iqbal's hometown as a memorial, Betty's students suggested a team collection. Giving a brief spiel on Iqbal and child labor in each of the team's five homerooms, the concerned students collected donations daily before noon team time. By the end of the week, they were able to send a check that would buy a bundle of bricks for the school.

The following year, when child labor issues surfaced again, Betty had a larger collection of texts. She had seen the connection to novels such as *Lyddie* (Paterson), *Where the Lilies Bloom* (Cleaver & Cleaver), *No Promises in the Wind* (Hunt), and Joan Lowery Nixon's Orphan Train books. Web sites that track slavery worldwide revealed that many children are still held in bondage today. Students read about the positive and negative effects of banning imports made by child labor and wrote responses to support a position on the issue. They had to consider the bigger picture—not just the cruelty of child labor to the individual child, but also the plight of destitute families who depend on their children's work for survival.

Then a new twist on the topic emerged. When students thought about what might constitute child labor in contemporary U.S. society, they struggled to come to agreement about what was legitimate work for young people and what was unfair. Was a regular babysitting job on Saturday evening different from having to babysit every day right after school until a parent returned from a second-shift job? What about working after school, such as a six-hour evening shift at a Quick Stop to pay for clothes? Is the issue a matter of being compelled to do such work, or of being prevented from working? Is the work a hardship or a privilege? What economic obligations do parents and children have to one another? These were complicated questions with no clear-cut, definitive answers.

This mini-unit on child slavery provided the opportunity to unite requirements of the language arts curriculum (technology use, nonfiction reading and writing, persuasion, descriptive imagery) with exposure to issues of economics and social customs. Betty's role was to provide materials and activities for students to explore a topic that had caught their attention and to help them build habits of democratic discourse: gathering data, listening to diverse points of view, looking at connections between data and opinion, critiquing sources of data, coming to (somewhat) informed opinions, and, sometimes, acting on their convictions.

Student-Initiated Projects

This chapter opened with scenes of lively student-initiated activism. The accumulation of connections between literature and life during the year had helped students become more mindful of needs in society, and the critical stance had activated an impulse to do good. They came to believe that life was unfair for some people (and animals), and when they saw that school could be a place to act on their new understandings, some of them did. They did not yet see that they could walk up to the door of a chemical plant and question its environmental policies; they *did* see that they could save pets and contribute material possessions to those in need. They thought about underlying causes, but they acted to relieve immediate suffering. Their initiative was a new phenomenon at the school.

The debate club Lydia proposed in the opening story of this chapter survived only two meetings, but Addy did not give up on her Adopt-a-Pet project. On her own, she made posters and mounted them throughout the school. To Betty's surprise, four pets were placed! Addy even brought a rescued animal, a greyhound she found at the side of the road, to school to raise money for his vet bills. School administrators were unenthusiastic about this intrusion, but her determination—and the weight of student opinion—was hard to oppose.

Jessie, Therese, and Tamara were inspired to use service learning funds to shop after school to fill individual surprise boxes for youngsters at the Children's Hospital. Once the fifteen boxes were stuffed and wrapped, the girls and other classmates visited the hospital, not only to distribute the gifts, but also to play and read with the children. In a journal entry, Tamara reveals that her experience had led her to some deep, long-lasting understandings about what illness does to one's humanity:

> I think this kind of attention [special visit and gifts] is crucial to kids who have been probed and prodded with needles and dosed with medicine. I think they need human, personal contact, other than the medical, high tech surroundings they are living in. Most of the time people who are taken to the hospital are treated as invalids and different. Reading stories to them and playing games like regular, healthy kids will make them feel as they had before they were in the hospital, if there was a before [i.e., they might have been ill their entire lives], and like a normal kid again.

Widening Circles of Activism

A few empowered students inspired confidence and ideas in others, who then felt they were part of a group who could make a difference. As a service learning project for our team, student volunteers went to the school's special education unit to tutor and play games. Earlier in the year, Betty's students had been touched by the plight of "special" students as portrayed in *Flowers for Algernon* (Keyes) and *The Acorn People* (Jones) and were incensed at their harsh treatment. Literature engagement had inspired them to act with more respect in their own school. They thought it was wrong that the special education students did not have the same opportunities as other students. Lois, Nikki, Rachel, and Omkar, all in the school orchestra, decided that the special education students deserved more. They decided to perform some serious music for these students. Taking lunch breaks and after-school time, they formed a string quartet and gave a performance in the special education room. They explained the instruments and their own problems in learning to play them. They were serious and gentle about answering questions and allowed close, hands-on inspection of their instruments from these physically awkward and emotionally volatile students of their own age.

Other students also initiated projects. Sam, our own "techie," researched at home interesting Web sites for classmates to use for various topics that were studied during the year. One class asked to write a "Guide to Middle School" to hand out to the rising fifth graders who visited our school for an orientation in the spring. The counselor said the guide was comforting to these nervous students, and they left clutching their pamphlets like life jackets for the rough seas to come.

The majority of the students, of course, never did initiate projects on their own. Many were happy to assemble gift boxes, color in lettering on a poster, or contribute baked goods to another classmate's project. These activities were inclusive opportunities that required skills different from those in academic work. Activism spread in a widening arc. For example, Erin and Kara's second joint project, a series of recess bake sales to raise money for a child's cancer treatment, provided opportunities for other kids to help or, at least, to buy goodies. Belinda, a passive, low-achieving student, was very popular when she brought in a beautiful chocolate layer cake for a raffle at one of the sales. But even the indifferent students who never participated unless it was required for a grade did not interfere with individual student activism. They seemed to accept that this was what we did in school, or at least this was what we did in this class.

It was gratifying to see the students appreciate the leadership of their peers. Comments were heard like "We could do like Hope did when she . . . ." Jill, on the nominating committee for a school service award, asked Betty at the beginning of class, "Don't you think that with all she's done, Kirsten should get the award, Mrs. Slesinger?" and classmates chimed in, "Yeah. Of course!"

Addressing Conditions That Create Inequity

A few students dared to try to change the status quo. Kelsey, a gentle, good-natured, and well-liked girl, ran for a student council office in a late spring election. Each candidate presented a platform at a school assembly. The three opponents who spoke before Kelsey predictably proposed better cafeteria food, more dances, and a revised dress code to allow hats. Kelsey, however, promised that, if elected, she would have student committees try to find ways to reduce the violence, disrespect, and hurtful graffiti she had seen around school: "These acts contribute to the hate and racism in our school," she said, "and they keep students from doing what they should in classes. I have learned that these feelings and acts are the same things that cause problems like riots and wars out in the world."

Betty was amazed at Kelsey's courage and confidence. Walking back to the classroom, she caught up with Kelsey to congratulate her on a daring speech. When asked how she decided to focus on such serious and controversial topics in her speech, Kelsey replied that she had thought back to our study of the Holocaust and World War II and realized that bringing up hatred and violence here at school was important. Someone should do it, so she did.

Later, when reviewing student end-of-the-year portfolios, Betty read a reflection Kelsey had written for the unit:

> I have learned so much. I don't know what I would do if I was a Jew living during WWII and the Holocaust. They treated the Jews so badly. I hardly know where to begin to talk about it. It makes me realize how lucky I am and I know that I can't live like that. I can't hate and I can't raise my children to hate each other or anyone. (Slesinger & Busching, 1995, p. 50)

Kim wanted more minority literature and history worked into the regular curriculum instead of honoring the same African American leaders in an annual Black History month, a practice she considered artificial. She wrote a letter requesting these changes to the assistant superintendent, not once, but twice, when her concerns were not answered in a timely manner. Finally, she received word that a social studies curriculum committee would address her suggestions.

Leanne deliberately set out to make a change in children's perceptions when she wrote and illustrated a little book to send to the Salvation Army. She thought beyond merely "helping" these children. She wanted her story, "What Is Racism?," to mold these young homeless children into workers for justice. She showed the bad effects of racism and offered ways to change attitudes, lavishly illustrating the book with clippings from magazines. The book ended powerfully with the statement, "If we're not careful, racism will follow us into tomorrow. We must learn how to live together, because our future depends on today." Leanne had a view of how she would remake the world and the confidence to carry out her ideas.

Teacher-Initiated Service Projects

Not all of the activist projects were student initiated. Betty's school required each team to plan service learning projects. Already swamped with work, Betty looked for ways to connect the service projects to her curriculum and provide opportunities for student leadership and participation. Because of the students' awareness of society, she discovered many natural connections in applying content knowledge. National guidelines (Totten & Pedersen, 1997) for effective service learning were easy to implement.

Mandy's and Teria's strong organizing, writing, and computer skills, as well as their easy ways of relating to others, made them natural candidates to lead a service learning project, and they took on the responsibility eagerly. After a survey of project preferences, the students in the team chose tutoring in an elementary school. Mandy and Teria then took over leadership of the project. They wrote letters to elementary principals to make the initial contact, and once a school agreed to participate, they wrote to the teachers to organize schedules and activities. Drawing on their class experience with rubrics and learning reflections, Mandy and Teria created reflective response sheets for returning tutors. They assigned and reminded thirty or more tutors of dates and obligations and kept an ongoing check-off list of who had gone, what job they did, and if they had turned in a reflection. All these obligations were kept on a wall chart through the second half of the school year. Several fellow students remarked that these girls were doing a great job, and they were.

As experienced teachers, we had to smile at the comments of the students who tutored in the elementary school. We could imagine the problems that had led them to these insights: "They need to be kept under control"; "Kids can't always do what they want if you need to keep the classroom going"; "Kids get bored quickly"; "It gets easier when there is a routine." They began to better understand some specifics of learning: "It's hard to learn the difference between q/g, b/d, p/g"; "They need work on their numbers"; "They have trouble counting money." Students had the opportunity to take knowledge out into the world and meet real problems, and they were full of good solutions to those problems.

We agreed with Washington, D.C. middle school teacher Patricia Bradley who remarked in a May 1998 workshop, "I ask students to tell me what you can do with what you know. Don't tell me what you know. Tell me what you can do because you know something." When Betty asked her tutors, "How do you think what you did today mattered?" here were some of the proud answers:

I helped Keasha feel better about mistakes.

I comforted a child who missed her mom.

I helped them learn to put things in order, and write letters.

I helped someone read.

I taught a child not to be rough with the playthings.

One limitation of the service learning projects was that few of the boys were active. Except for the day the students created a small bird environment by planting and putting up feeders in the team area as a follow up to ecology studies, the boys held back. Better opportunities for boys to serve were needed.

Conflict Resolution Puppet Shows

Betty wanted students to take the school conflict resolution program more seriously and saw an opportunity to tie the elementary school tutoring project to conflict resolution puppet shows. Having a cardboard stage in the corner of the room was a good stimulus to getting student partners started on scripts. Each pair came up with a real life situation in which two or more people have a conflict and must find a way to settle it without resorting to violence.

A few students, such as Leanne who based her script on students' rights in locker searches, perused the classroom collection of articles for story line prompts. Shoplifting, choosing between friends, sharing a bedroom with a sister, or helping a working parent were more usual topics. A play from Scholastic's *Scope* magazine served as a model of the genre of theatrical scripts. The class studied the essential elements of a play—narrator, setting, stage directions, and so forth. After writing the script and presenting it, each pair turned in one clean, correct copy. Betty demonstrated simple puppet choices—stuffed animals and dolls students already had; magazine cutouts mounted on heavy cardboard strips; or figures made from plastic spoons, paper plates, or socks. The classroom community was strengthened as classmates read parts in their friends' vignettes. The lively performances, with the help of our traveling stage, were enjoyed by other classes and by the third graders the students had been tutoring.

A Small Democratic Community on the Road

In May, Dixie Goswami, a professor at Clemson University, organized a weekend meeting for South Carolina teachers who had attended the Breadloaf School of English. The sessions featured authentic learning experiences with community connections. Teachers were encouraged to bring students who could share ideas and enthusiasm, so Betty invited several girls who had been actively involved in service learning projects or who had taken personal action on an issue.

On a Friday afternoon, Betty and a quartet of girls loaded the car and headed toward the coast. It was a multicultural group—Kara and Teria were African American, Tamara was European American, and Shira was from India and had recently visited her extended family there. The other girls were fascinated by Shira's stories of the confined lives led by her female relatives in India. Shira vowed that she would never be caught in such a life and would certainly refuse an arranged marriage. The girls chatted nonstop, creating bonds through their mutual disgust with "what a pain little brothers and sisters are" and their pleasure in the return of "cool, hippy" clothes.

Before heading to the cottage, the group shopped for groceries. It was interesting to watch the girls, left to themselves, skillfully negotiate the choices of food for the weekend. These decisions were potential cultural landmines, taste preferences and preparation included. Tacitly recognizing their cultural differences, the girls approached food choices as open questions. Shira helped the process along with her cheerful acknowledgment that she was a vegetarian, which encouraged Tamara to admit this was her preference also. The girls kept the chatter going until they had negotiated fair choices for all, even remembering to ask Betty for her preferences. Perhaps a release of tension when they saw that these shared agreements were successful created a sense of closeness that evening. Sitting on the porch after dinner and showers, the girls took up the next issue that required decision making: who would sleep where. This question solved, they moved on to hair, music, and scary stories when an owl hooted in an adjacent wooded lot.

Most of Saturday was spent in meetings with other students at historic Penn Center, established in the 1870s by Quakers and Unitarians. The earliest school in the South to educate African Americans, it was also a meeting place for civil rights leaders of the sixties. At the gathering, students shared service projects and discussed ways to equalize schools and empower minorities. Then the group headed out to the beach to walk, swim, and play Frisbee.

For Betty this weekend was a fitting culmination of a year of work revolving around issues of equality and fairness, for here was living proof. The girls were especially sensitive in their openness to and tolerance of others, and had, in Bill Ayers's words quoted earlier in this book, created democracy "in their small corner of the world."

These four girls were eager for opportunities to stretch their social boundaries. When they talked to Betty afterwards, it wasn't the planned group meetings that seemed to resonate with them, but the steps they had taken to create new bonds with each other—cross-racial bonds, though they did not use those words. Their closeness could be felt in the car during the return trip and in their interactions during the last couple of weeks of school.

Still Active in High School

We wish we had more evidence of long-term effects of the social issues curriculum on the students, but we have to be content with a few hints. Cynthia was outspoken about her new commitments in seventh grade: "Even I can make a small difference in 'ethnic cleansing' if I try to stay away from it myself. . . . I will do my part to help our world stay prejudice free." In high school, Cynthia continued her interest in speaking out on serious issues as a staff member of the school newspaper, *The Stinger.* One compelling piece described what she had learned about cultural conflict in her student exchange experience in Ireland. Recently, Cynthia's mother told Betty that Cynthia was planning to major in journalism when she goes to college "so she can continue to speak out."

When Betty opened a spring edition of *The Stinger* last year, she was excited to find that other students were still active. The school administration's cancellation of a concert by The Indigo Girls, a lesbian musical group, in the school stadium had stirred up a controversy, and eight of the eleven letters to the editor were written by her former students. The editor of the paper had been in Betty's class as well. Students felt that the administration had betrayed its professed beliefs about diversity. Mitch, who had spoken out so strongly about racism in World War II, wrote (in part):

> Allowing a small number of parents to influence a major administrative decision is ludicrous. Overt discrimination is morally wrong and simply disgusting.
>
> Public schools are supposed to teach students tolerance and acceptance of diverse cultures and life-style in our community. Instead, [our] high school symbolizes prejudice, oppression and intolerance. Our administration has discounted the life-styles of many of its students.

Concluding Thoughts and Questions

Students need to be *in the world* before they are motivated to work *on the world,* but in most schools engagement of any kind with the world outside the school is sadly lacking. Although Betty wished to do more, at least her students were encouraged to act on their convictions and take action that made a difference in their small part of the world. When Betty asked students "What changes in yourself as a community member have you noticed?" on their year-end reflection, it was interesting to see that some of them envisioned themselves not just as a classroom community member, but also as a member of the adult—even world—community. Here are some of their responses:

> Therese: I know about the way things are done, for example, we're governed by the law and the judicial system.
>
> Les: I started helping with recycling and know more community projects.
>
> Lisa: I understand more problems in the world and I'm reading the newspaper.
>
> Tess: Our society hides the truth [about] things we try not to admit ever happened or will happen.
>
> Lucy: I accept the hurt in the world and the harshness in people. I accept helping other people and getting hurt.
>
> Kirsten: Going out in the community and speaking as an expert. I know I am somebody.

Many teachers everywhere are finding ways to help their students live more like citizens should live, but we have only begun to know what students can do in the world. Some day, perhaps, schools, families, and community organizations will join to bring children out of the school into the working community. When that happens, they will be different children, and our communities will likewise change when energetic and questioning children become an active part of civic life.

Additional Literature for Students

Nonfiction: Social Issues and Activism

Ash, R. (1997). *The world in one day*. New York: DK Publications.

Buscher, S., & Ling, B. (1999). *Mairead Corrigan and Betty Williams: Making peace in Northern Ireland*. (Women Changing the World Series). New York: Feminist Press at CUNY.

Chambers, V. (1998). *Amistad rising: A story of freedom*. San Diego: Harcourt Brace.

Cooper, M. (1999). *Indian school: Teaching the white man's way*. New York: Clarion.

Gaskins, P. F. (1999). *What are you? Voices of mixed-race young people*. New York: Henry Holt.

Kilborne, S. (1999). *Leaving Vietnam: The true story of Tuan Ngo, a boat boy*. New York: Simon & Schuster.

Kuklin, S. (1998). *Iqbal Masih and the crusaders against child slavery*. New York: Henry Holt.

Lester, J., & Brown, R. (1998). *From slave ship to freedom road*. New York: Dial.

McKee, T. (1998). *No more strangers now: Young voices from a new South Africa*. New York: DK Publications.

Parks, R. (1996). *Dear Mrs. Parks: A dialogue with today's youth*. New York: Lee & Low.

Patent, D. H. (1997). *Back to the wild*. San Diego: Harcourt Brace.

Robinet, H. G. (1998). *Forty acres and maybe a mule*. New York: Aladdin.

Fiction and Nonfiction: Collective Social Action

Arnold, C. (1998). *Children of the settlement houses*. Minneapolis, MN: Carolrhoda Books.

Fleischman, P. (1999). *Seedfolks*. New York: HarperTrophy.

Lewis, B. (1998). *The kid's guide to social action*. Minneapolis, MN: Free Spirit.

Myers, W. D. (1979). *The young landlords*. New York: Scholastic.

Schraff, A. (1999). *Ralph Bunche: Winner of the Nobel Peace Prize*. Springfield, NJ: Enslow.

Additional Readings for Teachers

Bigelow, B., Christensen, L., Karp, S., Miner, B., & Peterson, B. (1994). *Rethinking our classrooms: Teaching for equity and justice*. Milwaukee, WI: Rethinking Schools.

Danks, C., & Rabinsky, L. B. (Eds.). (1999). *Teaching for a tolerant world:*

Grades 9–12. Urbana, IL: National Council of Teachers of English.

Eyler, J., & Giles, De. E. Jr. (1999). *Where's the learning in service learning?* San Francisco: Jossey-Bass.

Robertson, J. (Ed.). (1999). *Teaching for a tolerant world, grades K–6: Essays and resources*. Urbana, IL: National Council of Teachers of English.

Materials for Teachers

Guide for Cause or Service Organization Brochure

Purpose—Brochure is about a worthwhile cause or effort in our community.

Resarch/Comprehension—States and explains the purpose of the organization and how it contributes to the community. Shows understanding of a situation, a problem, or a need. It also shows that research was done to gather important, necessary, and accurate information.

Writing Style—Is clear, specific, and persuasive. Words capture the reader's interest and encourage involvement. Details are used to convince the reader of the worthiness of the organization.

Think about:

a slogan	a message	a testimonial
statistics	personal quotes	a comparison
a recommendation	figurative language	

Writing Conventions and Neatness—The writing is edited carefully for correctness. Hand lettering, graphics, etc., are neat and clear.

Presentation—Has clear organization of material and a pleasing or dramatic layout and design. The presentation is appropriate for both the purpose of the organization and the audience who will be looking at the brochure. There is something unique or special to catch the reader's eye and attention. Includes titles, subheads, text, and illustrations.

Think about:

shape	color	arrangement
folding	highlighting	lettering
print	photos	graphics
stickers	tear-offs	symbols
textures	cutouts	drawings

References

Children's Literature

Agee, J., & Evans, W. (1988). *Let us now praise famous men: Three tenant families*. Boston: Houghton Mifflin.

Agosin, M. (1994). *Dear Anne Frank: Poems* (R. Schaaf, Trans.). Washington, DC: Azul.

Baker, R. (1982). *Growing up*. New York: St. Martin's Press.

Bloor, E. (1997). *Tangerine*. New York: Scholastic.

Brooks, B. (1998). *The moves make the man*. New York: HarperCollins.

Burch, R. (1966). *Queenie Peavy*. New York: Scholastic.

Cisnero, S. (1991). *Woman hollering creek and other stories*. New York: Random House.

Cleaver, V., & Cleaver, B. (1989). *Where the lilies bloom*. New York: Harper Trophy.

Collier, J. (1986). *When the stars begin to fall*. New York: Dell.

Crew, L. (1995). *Fire on the wind*. New York: Dell.

Cummings, P., & Cummings, L. (Eds.). (1998). *Talking with adventurers*. Washington, DC: National Geographic.

Curtis, C. P. (1999). *Bud, not Buddy*. New York: Delacorte.

DiCamillo, K. (2001). *Because of Winn-Dixie*. Cambridge, MA: Candlewick.

Dickens, C. (1992). *A Christmas carol*. Excerpt in *Junior Great Books: Series 7*. Chicago: Great Books Foundation.

Fleischman, P. (1999). *Seedfolks*. New York: HarperTrophy.

Freedman, R. (1990). *Franklin Delano Roosevelt*. New York: Scholastic.

Freedman, R. (1993). *Eleanor Roosevelt: A life of discovery*. New York: Scholastic.

Freedman, R. (1994). *Kids at work: Lewis Hine and the crusade against child labor*. New York: Scholastic.

Freedman, R. (1995). *Immigrant kids*. New York: Puffin.

George, J. (1992). *Who really killed cock robin? An eco mystery*. New York: HarperTrophy.

Greene, B. (1973). *Summer of my German soldier*. New York: Bantam.

Hampton, W. (1997). *Kennedy assassinated! The world mourns: A reporter's story*. New York: Scholastic.

Hesse, K. (1996). *Music of the dolphins*. New York: Scholastic.

Hesse, K. (1997). *Out of the dust*. New York: Scholastic.

Hunt, I. (1985). *No promises in the wind.* Littleton, MA: Sundance.

Innocenti, R. (1990). *Rose Blanche.* New York: Stewart, Tabori, & Chang.

Johnson, B. (1996). *Everyday heroes.* Marlton, NJ: Townsend.

Jones, R. (1999). *The acorn people.* Littleton, MA: Sundance.

Keyes, D. (1995). *Flowers for Algernon.* New York: Harcourt Brace.

King, C., & Osborne, L. (1997). *Oh freedom: Kids talk about the civil rights movement with the people who made it happen.* New York: Knopf.

Klass, D. (1994). *California blue.* New York: Scholastic.

Laird, C. (1997). *Shadow of the wall.* Fairfield, NJ: William Morrow.

Levine, E. (2000). *Freedom's children: Young civil rights activists tell their own stories.* New York: Puffin.

Lowry, L. (1989). *Number the stars.* Boston: Houghton Mifflin.

Lowry, L. (1993). *The giver.* Boston: Houghton Mifflin.

Mazer, H. (1979). *The last mission.* New York: Dell.

Meltzer, M. (1991). *Brother, can you spare a dime? The great depression, 1929– 1933.* New York: Facts on File.

Meltzer, M. (2000). *Driven from the land: The story of the dust bowl.* New York: Benchmark.

Meyer, C. (1994). *Rio Grande stories.* San Diego, CA: Harcourt Brace.

Meyer, C. (1997). *Jubilee journey.* New York: Harcourt Brace.

Murphy, J. (1993). *The boys' war: Confederate and Union soldiers talk about the Civil War.* New York: Clarion.

Myers, W. D. (1992). *Somewhere in the darkness.* New York: Scholastic.

Naidoo, B. (1988). *Journey to Jo'burg: A South African story.* New York: HarperCollins.

Paterson, K. (1988). *The sign of the chrysanthemum.* New York: HarperTrophy.

Paterson, K. (1990). *Park's quest.* New York: Puffin.

Paterson, K. (1991). *Lyddie.* New York: Scholastic.

Peck, R. (2000). *A year down yonder.* New York: Dial.

Peterson, P. J. (1981). *Would you settle for improbable?* New York: Dell.

Raskin, E. (1997). *The Westing game.* New York: Puffin.

Raven, M. T. (1999). *Angels in the dust.* Mahwah, NJ: Troll.

Reiss, J. (1972). *The upstairs room.* New York: HarperTrophy.

Robb, L. (1997). *Music and drum: Voices of war and peace, hope and dreams.* New York: Philomel.

Rogasky, B. (2001). *Smoke and ashes: The story of the Holocaust* (2nd ed.). New York: Holiday House.

Ryan, P. (2000). *Esperanza rising.* New York: Scholastic.

Rylant, C. (1992). *Missing May*. Danbury, CT: Orchard.

Sis, P. (1996). *Starry messenger*. New York: Farrar, Straus & Giroux.

Snyder, Z. K. (1996). *Cat running*. New York: Dell.

Soto, G. (1990). *A summer life*. New York: Dell.

Spedden, D. C. S. (1994). *Polar, the titanic bear*. Boston: Little, Brown.

Spiegelman, A. (1991). *Maus I: A survivor's story*. New York: Pantheon.

Stanley, J. (1992). *Children of the dust bowl: The true story of the school at Weedpatch Camp*. New York: Crown.

Stevenson, R. L. (1988). *Treasure Island*. New York: Scholastic.

Tate, E. (1997). *The secret of Gumbo Grove*. New York: Dell.

Taylor, M. (1976). *Roll of thunder, hear my cry*. New York: Penguin.

Taylor, M. (1990). *The road to Memphis*. New York: Scholastic.

Taylor, M. (1998). *The friendship*. New York: Scholastic.

Vonnegut, K. (1992). "Harrison Bergeron." In *Junior Great Books: Series 7*. Chicago: Great Books Foundation.

Yolen, J. (1990). *The devil's arithmetic*. New York: Puffin.

Professional Sources

Apol, L. (1998). But what does this have to do with kids? Literary theory and children's literature in the teacher education classroom. *Journal of Children's Literature, 24*(2), 32–46.

Applebee, A. N. (1993). *Literature in the secondary school: Studies of curriculum and instruction in the United States*. NCTE Research Report No. 25. Urbana, IL: National Council of Teachers of English.

Atwell, N. (1990). *Coming to know: Writing to learn in the intermediate grades*. Portsmouth, NH: Heinemann.

Atwell, N. (1998). *In the middle: New understandings about writing, reading, and learning* (2nd ed.). Portsmouth, NH: Boynton/Cook.

Ayers, W., Hunt, J., & Quinn, T. (1998). *Teaching for social justice: A democracy and education reader*. New York: Teachers College Press.

Barbieri, M. (1995). *Sounds from the heart: Learning to listen to girls*. Portsmouth, NH: Heinemann.

Bernabei, G. (1996). Baby steps: The story of a peace movement. *Voices from the Middle, 3*(2), 19–24.

Bigelow, B., Christensen, L., Karp, S., Miner, B., & Peterson, B. (1994). *Rethinking our classrooms: Teaching for equity and justice*. Milwaukee, WI: Rethinking Schools.

Bloome, D. (1993). Literacy, democracy, and the pledge of allegiance. *Language Arts, 70,* 655–58.

Busching, B., & Slesinger, B. (1995). Authentic questions: What do they look like? Where do they lead? *Language Arts, 72*(5), 341–51.

Busching, B., & Slesinger, B. (1999). Third class is more than a cruise-ship ticket. In C. Edelsky (Ed.), *Making justice our project: Teachers working toward critical whole language practice* (pp. 191–208). Urbana, IL: National Council of Teachers of English.

Christenbury, L. (1994). *Making the journey: Being and becoming a teacher of English language arts.* Portsmouth, NH: Boynton/Cook.

Cochran-Smith, M., & Lytle, S. (Eds.) (1993). *Inside/outside: Teacher research and knowledge.* New York: Teachers College Press.

Danks, C., & Rabinsky, L. B. (Eds.). (1999). *Teaching for a tolerant world: Grades 9–12.* Urbana, IL: National Council of Teachers of English.

Edelsky, C. (1994). Education for democracy. *Language Arts, 71*(4), 252–57.

Edelsky, C. (1996). *With literacy and justice for all: Rethinking the social in language and education* (2nd ed.). London: Taylor & Francis.

Edelsky, C., Ed., (1999). *Making justice our project: Teachers working toward critical whole language practice.* Urbana, IL: National Council of Teachers of English.

Fishman, S., & McCarthy, L. (1998). *John Dewey and the Challenge of Classroom Practice.* New York: Teachers College Press, & Urbana IL: National Council of Teachers of English.

Fletcher, R. (1996). *Breathing in, breathing out: Keeping a writer's notebook.* Portsmouth, NH: Heinemann.

Freedom Writers, The, with Gruwell, E. (1999). *The freedom writers diary.* New York: Doubleday.

Giroux, H. (1992). Educational leadership and the crisis of democratic government. *Educational Researcher, 21*(4), 4–11.

Graves, D. (1989). *Investigate nonfiction.* Portsmouth, NH: Heinemann.

Greene, Maxine. (1995). *Releasing the imagination: Essays on education, the arts, and social change.* San Francisco: Jossey-Bass.

Harvey, S. (1998). *Nonfiction matters: Reading, writing, and research in grades 3–8.* York, ME: Stenhouse.

Harvey, S., & Goudvis, A. (2000). *Strategies that work: Teaching comprehension to enhance understanding.* Portland, ME: Stenhouse.

Jennings, L., O'Keefe, T., & Shamlin, M. (1999). Creating spaces for classroom dialogue: Co-constructing democratic classroom practices in first and second grade. *Journal of Classroom Interaction, 34*(2), 1–16.

Keene, E. O., & Zimmerman, S. (1997). *Mosaic of thought: Teaching comprehension in a reader's workshop.* Portsmouth, NH: Heinemann.

Kohl, H. (1995). *Should we burn Babar? Essays on children's literature and the power of stories.* New York: New Press.

Macrorie, K. (1988). *The I-search paper.* Portsmouth, NH: Boynton/Cook.

McKeown, M., & Beck, I. (1994). Making sense of accounts of history: Why young students don't and how they might. In G. Leinhard, I. Beck, & C. Stainton (Eds.), *Teaching and learning in history* (pp. 1–26). Hillsdale, NJ: Lawrence Erlbaum.

Meier, D. (1995). *The power of their ideas: Lessons for America from a small school in Harlem.* Boston: Beacon Press.

Nye, N. (1989). *Elements of literature: First Course.* Austin, TX: Holt, Rinehart and Winston.

Owens, Caroline. (1996). Inquiry is . . . what? *PDS Proceedings.* Vol. 14. Columbia, SC: University of South Carolina College of Education.

Paterson, K. (1981). *Gates of excellence: On reading and writing books for children.* New York: Elsevier/Nelson.

Perrone, V. (1999). *Living and learning in rural schools and communities.* Cambridge, MA: Harvard Graduate School of Education.

Peterson, R. (1992). *Life in a crowded place.* Portsmouth, NH: Heinemann.

Peterson, R., & Eeds, M. (1990). *Grand conversations: Literature groups in action.* New York: Scholastic.

Ray, K. W. (1999). *Wondrous words: Writers and writing in the elementary classroom.* Urbana, IL: National Council of Teachers of English.

Rief, L. (1999). *Vision and voice: Extending the literacy spectrum.* Portsmouth, NH: Heinemann.

Robertson, J. (Ed.). (1999). *Teaching for a tolerant world, grades K–6: Essays and resources.* Urbana, IL: National Council of Teachers of English.

Rosenblatt, L. (1995). *Literature as exploration* (5th ed.). New York: Modern Language Association.

Short, K., & Burke, C. (1991). *Creating curriculum: Teachers and students as a community of learners.* Portsmouth, NH: Heinemann.

Short, K., Harste, J., with Burke, C. (1996). *Creating classrooms for authors and inquirers.* Portsmouth, NH: Heinemann.

Slesinger, B., & Busching, B. (1995). Practicing democracy through student-centered inquiry. *Middle School Journal, 26*(5), 50–56.

Spandel, V. (2001). *Creating writers through 6-trait writing assessment and instruction.* New York: Longman.

Totten, S., & Pedersen, J. (1997). *Social issues and service at the middle level.* Boston: Allyn and Bacon.

Whitin, P. (1996). *Sketching stories, stretching minds: Responding visually to literature.* Portsmouth, NH: Heinemann.

Yevtushenko, Yevgeny. (1991). *The collected poems, 1952–1990.* New York: Henry Holt.

Authors

Beverly Busching, professor of education at the University of South Carolina, teaches courses in language arts education at the graduate and undergraduate levels. As director of the Midlands Writing Project and as an active leader of the USC Professional Development Site Network, she has collaborated with teachers in elementary and middle schools on research and instructional development. She is coeditor of *Integrating the Language Arts in the Elementary School* (1983) and author of articles about teaching and learning in a variety of professional journals. Busching's first two public school teaching positions—in the Lower East Side of Manhattan and on a small reservation in California—stimulated her interest in people who struggle to find a place for themselves in U.S. society, and she has enjoyed writing this book about a curriculum that puts students in touch with the realities of a democratic society and its issues. She has recently relocated to New Mexico.

Betty Ann Slesinger has spent over twenty years teaching middle school language arts in urban, suburban, and rural communities across the country. She has taught middle school reading and language arts in South Carolina for twelve of the last fifteen years and now teaches sixth grade at Lady's Island Middle School in Beaufort. Slesinger has received various state and REACH (Rural Education and Collaboration for the Humanities) grants, and has been a member of an Eisenhower professional development program, a Dewitt Wallace teacher-scholar at Middlebury College's Bread Loaf School of English, and a participant in a three-year NEH teacher seminar featuring state history, culture, and literature. She also has been an active member of the South Carolina Writing Improvement Network and of the West Chester (PA) and Midlands (SC) Writing Projects, and has received a reading teacher award from the Columbia (SC) Area Reading Council. Currently she is training to become a mentor in a Milken-sponsored school initiative. Slesinger and Beverly Busching have frequently presented topics from their classroom inquiries at state and national conventions. Their joint articles and chapters about middle school curriculum and practices appear in *Middle School Journal, Language Arts,* and *Making Justice Our Project: Teachers Working toward Critical Whole Language Practice* (1999), edited by Carole Edelsky. Slesinger also has a chapter in *Portraits of Whole Language Classrooms: Learning for All Ages* (1990) coedited by Heidi Mills and Jean Anne Clyde.

This book was typeset in Garamond and Avant Garde by Electronic Imaging.
Typefaces used on the cover were Bodega Serif and Adobe Palatino.
The book was printed on 50-lb. Husky Offset by IPC Communications.